AUTOBIOGRAPHY
of an
AVADHOOTA
Part II

Author
Avadhoota Nadananda

©Avadhoota Nadananda, 2016
All rights reserved.

No part of this publication may be reproduced, stored in a retrieval system or transmitted by any means, electronic, photocopying, recording or otherwise, without the prior written permission of the author

Cover design:
Mohana Hanumatananda

1st completely revised edition published in 2016 by Gurulight

Email: info@gurulight.com

Web: www.gurulight.com

ISBN 9788193309124

Bhagavan Sri Dattatreya

Paramaguru Nityananda Bhagavan

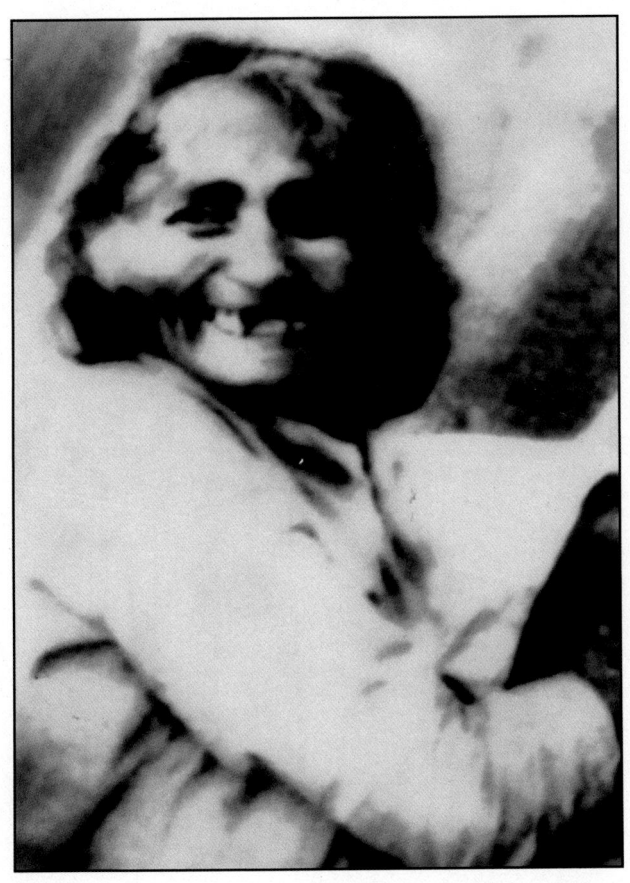

Sadhguru Avadhoota Tara Mayee

Avadhoota Nadananda

The Path of Thorns

Gratitude of Earth to The Glorious Feet

Alphabet to Awareness

From my Heart with Gratitude

LOOKING AT THE past, I cannot begin to imagine the amount of grace that has flowed between my first meeting with Avadhoota[1] Nadananda in mid December 2015 and this day in mid November 2016 as I am writing this article for the second volume of Autobiography of an Avadhoota. Gratitude overwhelms my being. How powerful is our tradition! How unfathomable is the love of the masters of Gyanganj[2]! How they orchestrated the process of making a raw piece of rock into a substantial idol! How amazing are the invisible hands of the divine mother who nurtures, protects and guides unseen in the most unexpected ways! It is just awe! Sheer Awe! It is only awe. The creation, the consciousness, the

---

1 Avadhoota' is a Sanskrit term referring to a particular type of mystic or saint who is beyond egoic-consciousness, duality and common worldly concerns and acts without consideration for standard social etiquette. He/she is a spiritual guide to many souls and enlightens the path of those on a psychic journey.

2 Gyanganj is the legendary city-kingdom of mysterious immortal beings, from ancient Indian and Tibetan mythology. It is said to be inhabited by yogis and saints of high order, and is also a place of spiritual training. Situated in a valley somewhere deep in the Himalayas, and though hidden from the world, still influencing it in various subtle ways when necessary. It is said that Gyanganj is cunningly camouflaged or may even be existing in a completely different plane of reality.

Guru Mandala[3], the family-ship and above all the law of karma! How can we ever stop admiring the creation in its full glory!

When the task of writing this article fell on my lap, I spontaneously revisited the days past. I had written two major blogs about my experiences with Avadhoota Nadananda which can be read from pkmohan.wordpress.com. Enchanting remembrances of the things past! I shall not drag your attention to unnecessary details. My memories are not scattered. Yet, I shall write this as it flows, allowing the divine to handle my brain, hands and the flow. Mohanji does not write this. Mohanji does not exist here and hence sequentially it flows . . .

Invitation for breakfast at Sri. Nagarajan's house in Banaras in 2015 January. His gift of Avadhoota Nadananda's autographed book. My becoming enchanted by his picture and asking Sri. Nagarajan for his contact details. Trying to reach him in vain numerous times not knowing why Sri. Nagarajan helped again to reach Avadhoota Nadananda. First meeting at Dhar in Madhya Pradesh a day before Datta Jayanthi (Birthday of Lord Dattatreya) in mid December 2015. His question "Why have you come to see me? What do you want from me?" I replied "Nothing". I felt like seeing you. A deep urge without any apparent reason! My heart is already filled." He replies "Mother will tell me the purpose of your visit in due course". He asks us to stay for another day and participate in Datta Jayanthi celebrations. On Datta Jayanthi day, by mid-day, as the celebrations were taking place, he suddenly comes out of his room, declares his intention to honour me despite my best efforts to avoid any such things, as I was quite satisfied with his love, kindness and over all his darshan (sight). He insists, decorates me with a shawl and a Shree Yantra. Months later he

---

3 Guru Mandala is the fraternity of sages, rishis and gurus who had themselves acquired a very high position in the hierarchy of spiritual evolution. All these sages were an 'Awakened' lot and formed a spiritual league to help humanity enjoy the divine bliss which they had themselves experienced.

writes in a communication to his devotees that while he was sitting in his room, he heard the voice of Mahatapa Babaji, of Gyanganj asking him to "take care of Mohanji". After that visit, we became closer by phone and we spoke frequently. I was not aware of his communications with the masters of Gyanganj and their guidance and plans. Guruji asks me to celebrate my Indian calendar birthday in Dhar. I agreed. I told him that there should not be any celebration; instead I would be more than happy to spend some time near him. Just some quiet time. Birthday fell on March 2nd 2016 and he had organized *annadaan* (Serving food) as well as music as well as celebrations. He told me "there is a reason for this celebration of your birthday. You will know later." The same day, he initiated me in Sri Vidya. I had lunch with many children. Something big had taken place on my birthday without me being aware of it. Avadhoota Nadananda later told that the initiation was as per the instruction of Guru Mandala. He told that 14 years he has been waiting for a worthy successor who he could adopt and hand over the wealth of his *saadhana* (spiritual practices; in this context, the bank balance of years of spiritual practices). The debt to one's guru will be complete only when one finds a worthy successor and hands over his acquired spiritual wealth, he mentioned. For fourteen years he has been suffering from cancer and had decided to put a full stop to his journey of this existence and many times it became a comma or semi-colon! He had lost hope of finding a successor. A day before Datta Jayanthi, the Guru Mandala brought me to him. He was told "we sent Mohanji to you" and guided him as to what to do next. Everything was flowing as per their plan and in a way, we both were just instruments or in other words, projection of their world which is ours too. We did not have extensive communications on spiritual matters except that of the world wide release of his Autobiography and the service projects that Ammucare and Manav Seva Samithi could work together on. I attended the inauguration function of the seva that Guruji and team does every year at a place near Kurnool. That was a grand function where they heal the pilgrims, with a special oil which Guruji himself prepares, who walk many miles to Sri Sailam for Ugadi. Numerous volunteers did service day and night. I was privileged to inaugurate this function along with other dignitaries. This was in March 2016.

Shirdi and entry to Gyanganj

We met at Shirdi in June 2016 to inaugurate the restaurants Madhuban and Ahimsa Vegan. A few days before we met at Shirdi, he called me and said "I need some time with you alone when we meet at Shirdi. Something important needs to be done. Can we go for a walk in the streets of Shirdi—just you and me?" I said "Sure Gurudev." We walked in the streets of Shirdi. He said "we shall not go into the Samadhi mandir weathering the rush of people. Those who want to see us will meet us outside." While walking towards the Shani temple, he stopped. He pointed towards a lean saint with his matted hair rolled conically over his head and exclaimed "Here he is! He is the one we have to meet today." He took out Rs. 100/- from the cloth that he was wearing, gave it in my hands and said "go to him and give this to him". I walked towards the saint with matted hair and offered him the money. He accepted. I remember briefly touching his hair. Then we walked away. Later, Guruji said "That was Bhruguram Paramahamsa, the saint who took me to Gyanganj. He is the guru of Bhagawan Nithyananda. My mission was to connect you to Gyanganj directly. When you gave *dakshina* to the master from Gyanganj, that connection is established. My job is over. They have taken over. You belong to Gyanganj now." He also told that Shirdi Sai Baba was the 37th Pontiff of Gyanganj and Avadhoota Nadananda the 48th. Everything was so unbelievable to me just like a fairy tale. I accepted with utmost surrender all what I heard and all what I was asked to perform. Avadhoota Nadananda was in one word INNOCENCE and nothing else. He walked the earth like an innocent child. He went about performing his entrusted tasks without asking "WHY", and thus served the world and Gyanganj totally and unselfishly. He is a master beyond comparisons. I knew I was in safe hands. I have come home at last. Even though a couple of times I questioned my eligibility for this honour, I quickly realised my lack of eligibility to assess my eligibility and the wisdom to leave it to wiser and better hands such as that of these great masters. The best medicine for ignorance is surrender into the safe hands of great guides, just like the logical remedy for darkness is some light.

The Celestial Kappar (Begging Bowl)

Guruji keeps the celestial *Kappar* that Mahatapa Babaji of Gyanganj used and handed down through the tradition of masters into the hands of Avadhoota Nadananda by his Guru Avadhoota Tara Mayee. If I am right, this Kappar was used by 7 great masters of Gyanganj from Mahatapa Babaji including Bhagawan Nithyananda. He has kept it sacred, away from the eyes and touches of curious seekers. One time when I visited Kurnool, I expressed my desire to see the celestial bowl. He obliged. He handed it over to me and it was indeed a divine experience to hold the celestial kappar that great masters carried in their hands for centuries. I touched my third eye with it and handed it back to Guruji. He wrapped and kept it safe. On October 10th, he took the divine kappar again and allowed my mother to hold it. Later, my mother and I were allowed to give him *bhiksha* (ritualistic alms that is offered to renunciates) in the celestial kappar while we were at Kurnool. This was an unbelievable blessing for both me and my mother. Guruji receives every type of food in the same bowl and he will mix everything together, adding some water to it, as Sai Baba used to do. Whatever food he gets in the bowl will all be mixed up and meshed together in a pulp form and he eats them with detachment. All flavours are mixed together. I had a desire to receive some food from that kappar which would mean as a great "Prasad" (Celestial offering/gift). Guruji read my mind and while he was having food, he gave me a handful of food from the bowl. Devi, my wife was also sitting with me. He gave her some food as well. Thus, he fulfilled a great wish of mine to eat out of the celestial bowl of Babaji. Food from that bowl is celestial nectar. He does not use the kappar every day. He keeps it safe and away as it is far too sacred for him than anything else.

Back to the fast track

Things have started to shift rapidly. Mohanji has started dissolving. Guruji visited Mookambika to relive his time spent with his Guru Maa Tara Mayee. On Guru Poornima, while I was in London, Guruji was in Mookambika. Bhruguram Paramahamsa appeared in the early hours and informed him the permission of Gyanganj to "step down". Guruji was asked to transfer his powers and spiritual bank balance to me, anoint me as his successor and declare it to the world. Even though all these are predominantly of spiritual significance and should be performed in silence and solitude, Guruji decided on a grand program. The Guru Mandala also asked Guruji to confer the title of "Brahmarishi" to me. Mind you, I never asked anything from Guruji or any masters till date. I realised that whatever comes to us without asking, amounts to sheer eligibility and grace. Guruji wanted to see me urgently. As soon as I returned from London, I came to Bangalore to meet Guruji. He was like a wonderful father waiting for his dear son. He personally went and bought vegetables, made curries and fed me. I experienced unfathomable love! He kept repeating "My Mohanji has come back to me. I will give you everything I have. You need not walk anymore. I walk towards you, for you." Later I wrote a blog about this as per his instruction and guidance.

The date was fixed for 2016 December 14—Datta Jayanthi which would also become the first anniversary of our meeting on earth. But, as per the instruction of Guru Mandala, it was later changed to 2016 October 10th, the day of Vijaya Dasami and also the day of Maha Samadhi of Shirdi Sai Baba[4]. All the arrangements

---

4 Sai Baba of Shirdi was an Indian spiritual master, who lived in Shirdi, Maharashtra, India for many years. He attained Samadhi on Vijaya

were made by Guruji himself. He supervised everything, went into micro details in planning and ensured no stones were unturned. There were three programs put into one. My title ceremony of Brahmarishi, The transfer of spiritual powers, and the release of books, including Autobiography international edition volume one in English and its Malayalam translation. Some people tried their best to disrupt this program, as we expected, considering the divine nature of the grand function. But, as Guruji stated, "this is neither my decision nor yours. What the Guru Mandala planned will also be executed by them. Terrestrial beings can do nothing". Everything went picture perfect. It was the most enchanting program that I have ever witnessed and participated in my life! Guruji transferred his spiritual bank balance to me and declared "I am bankrupt now. Mohanji will take the light forward, guided by the Gyanganj. He compared this transfer to that of Sri Ramakrishna Paramahamsa[5] to Vivekananda as well as Sri Yukteswar Giri to Paramahamsa Yogananda[6]." October 10th evaporated like a dream. In the early hours, Guruji performed a fire ceremony with only camphor and no wood. It was just me and him assisted by Sujatha Gaaru. He transferred his powers to me through that ceremony. The fire which was towards him turned towards me as soon as his

---

Dasami the 10th day at the conclusion of the nine days auspicious celebration of Mother Divine, Shakti, celebrated during September or October, as the day may fall per the Vedic calendar.

5 Sri Ramakrishna Paramahamsa, an Indian spiritual master and mystic who lived during 1836-1886. His disciple was Swami Vivekananda who is known world over and was a key figure in the introduction of the Indian philosophies of Vedanta to the Western world.

6 Sri Yukteswar Giri, a kriya yogi, a Vedic astrologer, a scholar of the Bhagavat Gita and the Bible, an educator and an astronomer was the guru of Paramahamsa Yogananda. Paramahamsa Yogananda was an Indian yogi and guru who introduced millions of westerners to the teachings of mediation and kriya yoga, and became a world renowned figure through his book, *Autobiography of a Yogi.*

transfer was complete. He gave me a flower in hand asked me to take a circle of the fire and offer the flower into the fire and walk away. In the afternoon, at the public function, he issued a certificate conferring me with the title of Brahmarishi[7]. Even the design of the certificate was supervised by Guruji himself. When I arrived he jokingly said "I have prepared a certificate for you, but will not show you until at the function." When I asked him the relevance of a terrestrial certificate for a celestial ceremony, he said "to make this title authentic and for the sake of sceptical people who may say against it or even say that it never happened." He also released all the books on stage through different people who he handpicked from the audience. Later, when he left the stage, people cried. He came back and danced with the audience. He created such a euphoria which will be remembered by many through time. That event was incomparable.

Today, I stand here, looking back in wonder. It is not even one year since I first met Guruji. How many events transpired until now! My whole status changed. His status also changed. What a grand collaboration! One person asked me "are you aware of the responsibilities that you have taken over?" I said "I do not need to know that. Those who entrusted the responsibilities to me will ensure its smooth completion as well. They are powerful. They are focused. They will take me through and make me do it well." This is the truth. I am just an instrument. None of the thoughts, words or actions is mine anymore. There is no mind anymore. Guruji keeps saying, I am your elder brother, not your guru. But, I see him as my preceptor, guide, and above everything—as myself. His love is beyond comparisons. He said "I am where you are. I shall be with you always." He means it and he proves it. I have no doubt or worry whether he would be with me in times of crisis. I am sure that he will not allow anymore crisis in life.

---

7 In Hinduism, a Brahmarishi is a member of the highest class of seers or sages—a highly evolved soul who has attained the realization of the *Brahman* or absolute reality.

It will be a smooth flow as the life will only be for the benefit of the universe.

I write this with deep surrender to the masters who guide me, to Avadhoota Nadananda and the eternal Guru Parampara[8]. I do not exist. Only they exist. May the right words and the right deeds happen through this existence and may I remain faithful and useful to the universe.

With immense love and gratitude to all those who are reading this,

Brahmarishi Mohanji

---

[8] Guru Parampara—The spiritual tradition or lineage of Gurus or Spiritual Masters

Abhayanadam

HESITATINGLY, I HAVE started writing the second part of my '*Autobiography of an Avadhoota*.' Since completing the first part, the response from people, my disciples, devotees and even some unknown people, has been encouraging. Even if a single person gets inspired and changes his attitude towards life, I will consider myself to be a successful writer. I have tried to put the experiences I had during my childhood and in long life as a guru, sanyasi, avadhoota and a social worker. Life long I have tried to live for the betterment of others. I have been a lonely traveler from my birth, and even now, I move alone in the crowd of my disciples, devotees and well wishers. In my long journey, I have encountered people from all walks of life, few to remember, few to forget. Some people helped me, some harassed, some criticized and some just moved along side me as a witness to my pain and pleasures.

When I thought of writing this part of my autobiography, the first face that appeared in front of me was my beloved Guruji, '*Avadhoota Tara Mayee*,' who is everything to me and every moment with me—rather in me. A black and rough stone in her hand, she made it a smooth and beautiful sculpture. Because of Amma's ability of transforming mud to gold, few kept that idol, in the altar of their heart and worshipped as Guru. That is me and my story.

It is my privilege to mention at least one person, who has understood me and travelled physically, mentally, and emotionally with me for more than thirty years sharing my unconcealed pleasures and pains, my spiritual brother Swami Abhayanand Saraswathi. Without his loving help, writing, correcting, editing of work, could never have been possible as I was strictly instructed by my doctors for bed rest after my third cardiac attack. Even though he stayed in Gujarat or Uttarakhand or Bengal, we communicated daily by mail or phone to edit and finalize this work. As he is a part and parcel of my life, I will never say thanks to him, as nobody says thanks to his own head for a good or positive thought. In fact he deserves the credit for the book in this shape, as for correcting my mistakes in spelling, grammar, idioms, reshaping of paragraphs, deleting and adding few lines as per his likes. He has that much freedom with me to correct my words, even me.

Few words on my disciples who served me whole heartedly during serious illness. They pressed me again and again to complete the writing works so soon, as my memory fades due to long medication. They not only served food, shelter, cloth at my convenience, but took care of my medicines in time even when I was deeply immersed in writing works. Of course, with my permission, they even blocked all roads of other disciples, not to reach me physically or even on cell phone avoiding visitors and discussing them on the importance of the work I do, and to keep me stress and strain free, enabling me to write this autobiography in its full value.

I tried to pen down my experiences and emotions in its true spirit and value. Let time, decide the value of the words of an Avadhoota in front of you.

Contents

From my Heart with Gratitude ix
Abhayanadam xviii

1. Advent Of An Avadhoota 1
2. Seeds Of Divine Love 4
3. The Belt And Beat 9
4. A Kiss And Blackmail 15
5. The Money Lender Child 20
6. The Yellow Shorts And The Mystic Hug 25
7. A Few Scattered Memories 29
8. Impulsive Genius Of A Humble Caretaker 37
9. Oh! You Are That Boy 42
10. The Inexplicable Days 49
11. Death Of An Artist 54
12. To Know Is To Be 59
13. The Use And Throw Guruji 70
14. Where You Are, There I Am 77
15. Another Purascharan At Narmada 82
16. Beginning Itself Is Ending 87
17. Again At Narmada 92
18. In Search Of Unknown 96
19. Liberation Of A Soul 99
20. From Here To There And Back 108
21. Again At My Father's Abode 111
22. The Must Forget Faces 115
23. The Parasite Guruji 121

24. Bhagavadajjuka—The story of a prostitute and a Sanyasi ... 127
25. Experience Oneness ... 132
26. Mud On My Face ... 139
27. Oneness As Fire And Heat ... 144
28. Anantham, Atmabandham ... 149
29. Being In Awareness ... 155
30. Beware, They Are Watching ... 165
31. A Bittersweet Experience ... 169
32. A Dream Comes True ... 172
33. A Joke Of Six Lakhs ... 176
34. A Runa Paid Off ... 184
35. Activated Inabilities ... 188
36. Hungry For Affection ... 194
37. Curry Leaf Inspirations ... 207
38. Faceless Crowd Aimless Mob ... 213
39. Forget It—It Is Your Mistake ... 219
40. Pouring Milk Onto A Neem Tree ... 223
41. Put Small Fish, Catch Big One ... 227
42. The Return Journey ... 230
43. Three Stories To Remember ... 235
44. An Emotional Sunset ... 239
45. Butterfly—A Messenger ... 243
46. The Hamsa Gaanam ... 247
47. Break Not The Mirror If Thy Face Is Ugly ... 252
48. Vyavahara ... 257
49. Be There Where You Are ... 260
50. To You, For The Motivating Assurances ... 264
51. The Waiting ... 266
52. Meeting Mohanji ... 268

Parting Thoughts ... 279
Sparks Of Oblivion ... 280
Glossary ... 337

Advent Of An Avadhoota

STRUGGLE! HE IS my co-born, my sibling; waiting outside when I was born. My mother once told me that I looked like a stillborn baby. A fat body, blue in hue. And to everyone's consternation, I was born mute, taking more than the usual time to learn or understand, seemingly lacking in intellectual faculties. The newborn boy they said, did not cry—the first ritual a human being has to do when he enters this world. Though I didn't weep, everybody else did, and my parents particularly. The infant was motionless, cool, glossy blue in color and almost corpse-like. The only sign of life was just a hint of a sparkle in the eyes. All the indications were that of an *Avadhoota*, one who may be dead to the world, but really the one who 'lives' in the true, ultimate sense. Everybody tried to make me respond to some stimuli from outside, but failed to elicit the ritualistic cry or wail of the infant. When such odd characteristics manifest in isolated cases, people instead of leaving it to its natural course, in their impatience plant undetectable *samskaras* in the child's physique that may even prove to be fatal to the child concerned. The situation has not improved even in these days of modern education, with advanced techniques of delivery etc., we still remain under the influence of arbitrary practices. When Avadhoota-like beings manifest—the *samsaric* people see them as ordinary beings. But not as variations in the manifestations of Almighty Nature. Seeing the infant not responding to the outer stimuli, the village midwife overconfident in her knowledge, gave it a slap. When there was no response even to this, she followed with a pinch to the soft, tender skin and yet another slap. He responded now, but with a laugh of sarcasm and opened his sparkling twinkly eyes to look at the midwife, or rather at '*samsara*.'

So from day one, I was already starting to get punished for others' ignorance of their own deeds. That was the first slap I ever received in my life. And the slaps continue to this day with me, even now, getting blessed by slaps from ignorant, insignificant, and immature disciples and devotees, through their words and deeds. But now I never weep, as the tears too have dried up.

I have struggled my whole life—for others of course, and never for myself. Because I live for others, and for them only—though I never speak yet sounds haunt me, though I never walk yet I fall down, and though I never die yet I am reborn every moment. The action of inaction-ness is my nature, but not the directionless-ness as seen so commonly among those born with silver spoons. Silence is my language, deeds are my words, experiences are my sentences, and being is my living—that is my song, and the rhythm of my life. To live, be alive, always for others, and only for others. If I serve, I breathe, and if I do not serve, I die.

Struggle has become my companion at every step of life. When I look back into the lovely lanes of my past in retrospection, I see myself as a *sadhaka*, as a *sanyasi*, or as a *guru*—yet I am none of those, but am the yearning of the all-pervading Spirit itself that wants to confer the best of its creation to its children. But the child, alas! It runs behind the ice cream-seller. The foolish world cries out for love in search of love everywhere, but none hears the voice of the spirit calling out loud, running through the streets with his bosom wide open, to give that love. Because the definition of love of the spirit is entirely different from the way the world defines love. The world wants to get love but upon its conditions only, and that is not possible for the spirit to offer—since who possesses the bottomless vessel necessary to hold that water, which that love will require?

The base required to hold the water of Divinity is just sacrifice. Every moment must become one of *saadhana*, the *Saadhana* of

Service. Every step must become a dance, like the *tandava* dance of Shiva, of destruction for a new construction. Every sound must become a song, a poem, the Song of Silence. Even every glance or look must become one of affection, affection towards Nature, the Mother Goddess. Every thought has to become like a '*shastra*', the science of existence, or the existence of self.

Seeds Of Divine Love

IF THERE IS the expectation of a remarkable change or transformation to happen in anyone's life, for it to manifest, there must exist some unknown inspiration behind bringing up the latent karma inside. If the sown-in seeds of spirituality are unable to sprout in spite of birth and life in a spiritual background, it means that the seeds were sprinkled in barren land in hostile conditions. When I look back in memory lane, about how I was brought up and shaped as a human, the person who identified and nurtured the dormant divinity and spiritual potential within me was the grand old lady of my family, the younger sister of my grandmother, known as '*kunjechi*', to whom I shall be ever grateful. She was responsible for sowing within me the seeds of divinity, the love for knowledge, and nurturing in me the faculties of grasping and understanding in childhood itself. She was about seventy years old when I was a young lad. Though I was born and brought up in a religious, orthodox environment and though I did not dedicate myself to it, I developed into a banyan tree of divine bhakti towards the Almighty. I am sure that had she not ever narrated stories of *Prahlada, Dhruva* or of *Rama*[9] and his brothers, I would have

---

9 The Ramayana is an ancient Indian epic poem which narrates the struggle of the divine prince Rama to rescue his wife Sita from the demon king Ravana. Rama's closest aide or disciple was Hanuman. There are several short stories contained in this epic which is nor-

never become an ascetic. She would discourse to me, repeatedly again and again at my request, the stories of *Veer Hanuman* that captivated my heart, and which I memorized from repetition. I loved that '*muthassi*', the grandma very much, except for her dress code. In those days no stitched upper garments were allowed to be used by a widow, and hence a '*dhavani*' was to be used as upper garment by ladies. With every breath she would hum the mantra '*rama narayana, rama narayana*' with mesmerizing emotion and intensity.

The pond or tank attached to the cluster of buildings in our ancestral home, was the common but private to the cluster, bathing facility for all concerned, where we all mostly bathed in. It always remained filled with water to the brimful, and the steps that led down to it were slippery. The discarded oil and soap gathered together to give out an odor, which I never liked in my childhood. Once grandmother went to have her bath and when she had not returned after a long time, everybody grew worried and started making enquiries and searching for her. But to the relief of all, she returned to appear in front of the courtyard shivering in wet clothes, but still chanting in her characteristically charming way. My concerned mother asked why she had been so late in returning. Grandma said with a smile that she had slipped, and fallen down into the pond. Since there was no chance of survival if one fell into that pond since it was so deep, my mother asked again, "*Kunjechi*, how then did you come out of the water?" Grandma said, "Narayanan pulled me out from the pond." Hearing this, everyone standing there laughed at her, even mockingly. One of them was even shameless to the extent of saying, "If Narayanan touched you then you should do *punyaham* (purificatory rites) before entering inside the house." This was because the name of the servant at home was also incidentally Narayanan. With a smile, grandmother replied, "*Ninte Narayanan alla, ente Narayanan aa*

---

mally taught or told to children in households by their parents or grandparents.

enne rakshichathu." (It was not your Narayanan, the servant, but my Narayanan—the Lord, who saved me). That incident had a major impact on me, and left in my heart an everlasting imprint as an example of staunch faith in what we believe and do. Actually, it was an eye-opener for me. Thus early in childhood itself, the seed of staunch belief in the existence of divinity with all its glory began sprouting in me.

In those days, the bark of a certain tree was used for soap, and the paste of *'chemparathi'* (hibiscus) was used for washing hair. One day, my uncle who worked in the military, brought home from the town, a bathing soap with a wonderful fragrance. I was very fascinated by it but even after repeated requests, it never came to my hand for use. I was not able to use it even once and was a bit frustrated. The old grandmother *Kunjechi* placed 4 *annas* in Kochu Narayanan's hand and asked him to get a soap with good fragrance. On his return from the town, he brought a good soap of my choice and I was very happy. Without anyone objecting, I went with my eldest sister to the pond for a royal bath, as soap was a great luxury for children. Grandmother was also bathing there at that time. While applying the soap to my body I felt as if I were in high heavens. I handed over the soap to grandmother but she refused to use it saying that it was made of *'apavitra'* (impure) things. I felt sad at the thought that I had made a scene in the family for that *'apavitra'* soap. Grandmother enlightened me saying, "Never allow a fascination to grow in your mind for such things not meant for you. You are like *Ravana* who had a fascination for *Sita* which turned into an infatuation, and as a consequence he got himself killed by *Rama*." That made me feel bad and I threw away the soap in the water, because it was due to that object that my loving *'muthassi'* had called me *Ravana*. In fact, I had really wanted to be like *Hanuman*, and now I was being called *Ravana*. This was the first lesson I had from her on *'aparigraha'*. She taught me so much through her example.

Upon the sole power (I came to realize later in my life this as spiritual) of continuous japa of *'rama narayana'* brought her *'anayasa maranam'*—a death without pain. I observed that she possessed nothing of her own, but lived life happily till her last breath. I am obliged to her a lot for the teachings and stories which helped me understand and shape life in whole, and when those seeds grew to a big tree, an ascetic was born. Even now as I share those old stories with others, I feel the importance of grandparents in a child's life. Though at that time I was a child and unable to appreciate the greatness of the effortless teachings of that old lady, later after becoming a sadhu and gaining an understanding of the elements of life, and becoming guide and guru to someone, I certainly did realize the power of the simple '*sanskaras*' that she had conferred upon me.

A young man and woman may wed and beget a child together, but it is merely a mass of flesh. It is the grandparents who with the wealth of valuable experience gained from their long span of life that can transform it into a human being. Today the meaning and relevance of grandparents and parents in life has deteriorated so much that when a young man gets married, he immediately starts thinking that their responsibility is now over, that they have no more use, relevance, or right to live, and so they should think of dying, or must vacate the house, or go to an ashram. But when I recall the contribution of this old lady to my life, my heart weeps out in agony for the present day generation. Actually due to too much of exposure to consumerism, they have forgotten to take a few lessons in love. Love, respect and regard for our grandparents is actually our own self-respect. If you do not respect them, it amounts to saying that you too are a product of those valueless human beings; that you too are undeserving of any respect. So grandparents mean not just a lot, but everything to us. Hopefully, the younger generation will realize the 'ultimate reality' one day too, from the morals of the stories told to them, and from the values instilled in them by those old grandparents. Those will never go out of context, as the children of today seem to imagine about their grandparents. If the basic building blocks of these children, or the foundation provided by their grandparents, are weak, one cannot expect any epic out of their lives. Of course one may live a life of a rich slave with millions in the bank, but be a mean beggar at heart.

It is the values of regarding, respecting, and loving one's family elders that are the real rejuvenating factors in life. If they are weak and there is short supply of love, the life that follows will be an undesirable one. So I dedicate these words of mine to the names of all those unassuming grandparents who gave us great saints, scholars, devotees, leaders, philanthropists, or any great human being, out of their experience.

The Belt And Beat

A CHILD MUST BE thought of as innocence personified. His naiveté should never be mistaken for mental deficiency, and this is true whatever creed, breed, or country the child belongs to. Children represent the purity of the soul itself. A child is imparted education by the world and starts gaining the so-called empirical knowledge, of knowing how others may behave, how to retaliate, and how to make itself 'intelligent'. The meaning and purpose beneath such education is to learn how to differentiate, but not how to integrate. In spite of towering scientific attainment, the man of today is not ready to spare even a little time to understand the mindset of a child, which is created quite differently than the careless understandings of the so called matured man. The result is seen amply on the streets. The highly tantalizing things created to attract innocent children show what kind of ideas we have about a child. The mesmerizing, instigating, and mind-diverting toys, clothes, art-objects, and entertainment, all demonstrate how the world wants a child to develop—into a good consumer, but not necessarily a good human being. The innocent child as he is naturally very friendly to others, will give even his dearest things to his friends, for which he may suffer at the hands of his elders. It may be that the elders are not in a position to understand the mind of a child. Certainly the ways of education, medicines, kinds of toys, food articles, and the upbringing of a child are indicative of how mean humans become at adulthood, to exploit their own children, the future of the world, with all adulterated and cunningly poisoned articles.

I remember an incident from my life, where I was rewarded with agony, for manifesting a natural expression of love in reciprocation of an act of innocent friendship. I remember it was during my high school days, living amongst my *Nambudiri* clan famous for its naiveté, which the whole village took advantage of. And for that, they were stamped as simpletons. I was never interested in learning this art of dividing the heart on imaginary grounds. I rather deem anyone who teaches their children this art, as the real enemy of humanity. I cherish and appreciate such an act of a child giving any such thing away to a poor classmate or urchin or to anybody, anything of its choice. The parent should feel proud of that child because giving a thing that we possess if others need it, shows real humanity. That tendency flowers in us only due to God's grace. People who do not have the grace of God only want to keep everything for themselves. People blessed with that grace feel bliss in giving, and this joy in giving is a sure indication of whether we have God's grace. Especially in *Kaliyuga* the easiest way to get close to God is to give . . . give . . . give.

Since I was not made that way, I was the last one to understand such mean-natured people. At that time, I had just been brought back to my native village home from the strict and rigorous life at my sympathetic uncle's place far away from my parents, and the reunion at this time when I was longing for parental affection, was surprisingly happy. I felt a little distant initially due to the pangs of the separation from my parents, my mind in a little aversion since they kept me away for a long period of five years from my village home. My rapport or tuning in heart was far deeper with my elder sister than with others. I was enrolled in a school in the nearby town to pursue my matriculation. I had to walk a distance of four miles every morning along with my sister who was also pursuing her education in that same town. As time passed, I slowly developed friendships with a few in my class. Even though I was a stout boy, I was of sturdy build. So I was admitted as a cadet in the National Cadet Corps (NCC), which fulfilled the need of channelizing my physical energy with time to play as well as to instill self-discipline, which my military uncle very much appreciated due to his military affinity. He would therefore gleefully provide me with the articles needed for the NCC cadet uniform etc., even without my asking. He expected and encouraged me also to excel in it so that I could be pushed into the armed forces later if needed. But the tragic point which disturbed me was that this uncle also started staying with us in our old house, since he was single and alone with no one to take care of or to rear. The problem was that he got involved in each and every aspect of the house. As I stayed with him for a long period of five years, even without my knowledge a slave-like mentality developed in me, and a fear and loathing for his approach to life which was filled with meaningless rigor. My sister however was shrewd to escape him, and sometimes showed the courage to revolt against him. By that time the financial condition of the house had also improved and the uncle also contributed financially now and then for the household needs. So it was quite natural to accept his 'military rule' at our home.

    I had a classmate, Mathew, in tenth grade, a village boy like me, who also walked daily to school from his village five or six miles away. We were good friends, who sat on the same bench, and ate together the lunches we had brought, sitting on the steps of the river flowing in front of the school. We often shared the curries we brought (of course he was a non-vegetarian, and I once shared a fish curry from his lunch box), and played together. We studied and did homework assignments together, and so you could say we were intimate to each other. We wore khaki shorts and white shirts as our school uniform. Those from well-to-do families wore belts over their shorts after tucking in their shirts, while others just tucked in their shirts remaining beltless. But when we attended NCC sessions, the rule was to wear the belt provided by the institution, and just tucking in the shirt without the belt was not allowed. Though the belt provided was a little worn out and old, I was not mindful of these things, and neither were the instructors.

But once my military uncle saw me shabbily dressed in the worn out belt, he brought a plastic belt to wear over the shorts.

The belt was very attractive, and looked like a snake, and caught everyone's eyes at school. Uncle had bought it from the city for me, and I liked it too. I went around the school with my friend Mathew showing it off to others as if I were a 'hero.' In the village as well, I was very proud of such a rare possession and started roaming around flaunting it to other village boys younger than me. But the poor boy Mathew had lost his heart to the belt and was eying it. In those days, plastic products were very rare. Uncle told me he had purchased it for two rupees. A few days passed with me thus zooming. One day my friend Mathew came to me with an offer to swap this snake belt, with which he had become possessed by now, for a double-color pencil. This pencil had one end blue and the other end red, and it was another rarity which I was seeing for the first time, and it became an object of fascination to me at the very first sight. He had bought it only that day from the market. We mutually agreed to exchange our respective possessions. Thus the double-headed color pencil came to me and the snake belt went to him. That is the mindset of children. Without thinking about consequences, they do things and get into trouble.

Two days later, when uncle noticed that I was not wearing the belt, he roared, asking—"Where is that belt?" After many years I was seeing him in such overbearing anger, because I rarely gave him occasion to yell at me, which he liked very much to do. So, that day he had got a golden chance to jump upon me, like a hungry lion. Now I realized the mistake I had made in my sympathy, and the fear grew in my mind, engulfing my heart. First I thought of telling some lie and escaping from the scene. But how could it be possible, as was I not the grandson of *Satyavadi Harischandra*[10]?

---

10 Harischandra is a legendary Indian king who is known for speaking truth and being truthful under all circumstances, in this context being used anecdotally.

He shouted, "Where is it?" Hearing the shout, most of the family members appeared on the verandah and stood like silent spectators where I was trembling like a goat in front of a roaring lion. No one dared to intervene and ask or pacify or protect me from that precarious situation, such was the command and authority of my uncle in our family. My throat started choking up, and I said, "I exchanged it with my friend for a red and blue pencil." Then all hell broke loose in a moment—the military uncle lost his temper, took a one-foot ruler from his desk top and started beating me black and blue. That foot rule was very heavy, made of wood and looked like a baton, and he beat me with it till I fell down unconscious with pain. I was crying like a mad dog, and no one but my courageous older sister, who was more close to me than my parents, came forward to rescue me from that devil's hand. Many welts formed on my body and started swelling.

So going to school next day with those welts from Uncle, they became a topic of discussion. There were talks at school among pockets of friends that I got a sumptuous feast of beating from Uncle for exchanging the belt. Mathew also came to know about this, as one of the boys from my village had heard of the incident and informed him. He came to me with tears in his eyes soliciting, and pleading sorry and said, "Because of me, you got very badly hurt yesterday." He wanted to reverse the exchange. But by now my heart had also grown in maturity from that incident, and I was resolved to face whatever was impending. He said "You take this and return it to your uncle," and was just removing that belt from his shorts to return to me, when I stopped him from doing so and told him not to worry. I said, "My friend! In life we have to be ready to meet, face, and confront such situations, when they are certain acts which our heart asks us to do for its happiness." I did not accept the belt, nor did I return his blue and red pencil. I kept that pencil with me safely for a very long time as a memory in my wooden box.

A lot of water had flowed through the Ganges since then, years have passed, and times have changed. On the day, before going to join my *Guruji* at *Mookambika*[11] and entering into the life of a sanyasi, as I was searching for some of my old papers and books, I found that blue and red pencil kept unused till then in that wooden box. That brought back memories of the friend and the associated incident. By now he had married and settled down. I felt some sense of kinship with him and thought of bidding him farewell. I went to Mathew to convey to him my decision to leave the temporal home in search of the permanent one. He felt very happy meeting me after such a long time and was also one of those who appreciated my decision to tread the path of godhood. Mathew was leading a family life and taking care of an agricultural land for living. He introduced his wife to me, who served food to both of us. We spent the whole day reminiscing the school days we had spent together.

I took out the blue and red pencil, which I had purposely brought, from within my shoulder bag and handed it back to him. Both of us had tears in our eyes for some time. Sometimes, the impressions of incidents from childhood, however insignificant, may serve as life changing ones. Even though at that moment, the incident was insignificant to me or to anyone with a worldly view, today as a sadhu knowing the unimaginable intricacies and subtleties of human life, it offers me many insights that I can impart to my disciples, who too can take recourse from my own life's experience for theirs. So I wanted them to be penned down here with the intention that they might induce in the reader, an outlook on life, if they too have to face similar situations in their lives. I would thus like to dedicate this chapter to those children who may have met with such situations.

---

11 The days spent by Avadhoota Nadananda with his Guru, Tara Mayee, in the forest in Mookambika which is a temple city in Kerala, southern India, is described in volume 1 of the *Autobiography of an Avadhoota*.

A Kiss And Blackmail

They say love is blind. I would rather say it is blinding, because in the name of love, every '*jeeva*' here is engaged in blinding each other, when in fact it is not love but sensual infatuation. While the eyes of people still remain unopened, and their eyes lack even the basic skill to see, they insist on maintaining that what they perceive with their limited ability in the unreal '*jagat*' is the truth, and preach and try to establish that as the reality. This is like a bird trying to assert that there is no space beyond where it cannot fly. When they finally realize that the darkness around was due to their own deeds, they acknowledge that it was created out of ignorance. But they forget about the need and necessity of unmaking or dispelling the darkness that they themselves created, and left the succeeding generation to keep groping in the same darkness with shame.

It was when I was in my tenth class (matriculation) in a nearby town. My older sister and I (we were both in the same class but in different schools), another girl studying in the ninth class, and her brother, and an eighth class student- this was our group, and we walked together daily a four or five mile distance from village to school and back. We would even wait at both ends for the others to join us, if anyone happened to be late by chance.

I was a good-looking young boy of 14 of 15, light-skinned, and a bit more handsome than the others. I tried to add to my attractive looks by applying burnt matchsticks to the just-appearing moustache, carefully managing to make it look a little blacker each day. Some days my oldest sister would scold me for this type of daily makeup. During the long walks, we used to converse on topics, which sometimes we were not very knowledgeable of.

The girl in our group was what people would call pretty. She had a vulture's eye towards me, which I noticed only a few months later during one of our group's daily walks together. She would come to me on the pretext of seeking help on some homework or this or that kind of flimsy grounds. I tried to avoid her company, sensing my composure getting disturbed and irritated. But it was in vain as she tried to get closer by inches, day by day. I was starting to get very nervous in her very presence near me. Running after girls was never in my nature. I do not know whether those were symptoms of love, or perhaps it was just a teenage crush or something that she actually had towards me.

It was during one of the *'utsavams'* (annual festival at our village temple), that I was returning from the temple after having *darshan* as a neat, devoted *Nambudiri* boy with dazzling *tilak* adorning my forehead. It was yet to be dark, even though the sun had set. I was passing through a narrow path between lush green paddy fields which are characteristic of Kerala. Both sides of the road were elevated and the path was like a walled lane. I saw from a distance, the girl approaching from the opposite direction and I thought that she too may be going to the temple. During such annual festivals at temples, sometimes passionate youngsters would meet and exchange their feelings of love. She stopped in front of me for a while, and asked me to accompany her to the temple and back as it is getting dark. I declined, and tried to move forward in the direction I was heading. I also reciprocated out of the surge of youth and embarrassed her and thanked her with a more sophisticated kiss. As we both lacked nerves even to talk further, within a moment we separated and flew off on our own ways.

After the festival, the school resumed and our group's walking together as well. As this adolescence-related disturbance was now allowed to enter our hearts, the effect was a considerable change in the way we glanced at each other and our dealings during walks to school. Now I could see a difference in her eyes and behavior towards me. In the meantime, my uncle gave me a pen which he bought specially for me from town during his recent visit. It was a self-inking pen with a gold plated nib. One had to just press on the back of the pen and dip it in the ink, and the pen would refill itself. No extra filler was required. I with a gait, demonstrated its greatness among my friends, and this girl too tried her hand in writing her name in my notebook. But somehow she had lost her heart to the impressive pen, and it seemed that she had decided to possess it somehow or the other from me. See the weakness of a human being—she loved that insignificant pen to the point of infatuation, and courted me in order to obtain it from me. My answer was total refusal as I too liked it very much, and for me it was proving to be an object of dignity.

From the very next day itself she stooped to employ arm-twisting tactics of milder kinds. I too regarded it as the exclusive female prerogative of distracting and extorting from males. When she understood that I was also a stingy miser and a class apart, she came all the way down to use the exclusive weapon of the fairer sex—blackmailing. The next day while we all were walking together she served the notice ultimatum to me. She said, "If you don't give me this pen, ok it's no problem, but I will tell your older sister that you kissed me forcibly on the *utsavam* day. And I know very well that you cannot lie to your sister, and one of my friends is ready to pay witness too." I was extremely afraid that if by chance she let the cat out of the bag, and the news reached my uncle, an unmarried army man with an extreme hate of such things, what would be my plight? Moreover I held my sister in high esteem, and she too had deep love for me. If this shrew let loose her tongue, plenty of mine was at stake. The fear of being depreciated in value by my sister and uncle, was eating into my peace.

This was the first shock treatment I received from nature—to be extremely alert in all dealings with women later on in my life. To one not valuing dignity, such things are as child's play, but to me it is dear as life itself, from the beginning. I fell between the proverbial devil and deep blue sea. I was not in a position to imagine my uncle's reaction, especially after hearing the news of this kiss. And also a sea change came upon my heart. What was definitely noticeable was that when previously I'd had a mild appreciation of her beauty, now I was seeing her as an ugly goblin. Today and at this advanced age, I have come to believe after a careful scrutiny of things, that it had to be a subtle way of teaching by Providence to completely erase out of my heart any chances of future infatuation. This would have been the hardest of hard things to accomplish through our own efforts as *sadhakas*. Thanks to the beauty of grace a great feat was done with just an insignificant jerk. But no one must consider that I have a hating heart for women. If they do, they will be in grave error, for my object of worship is verily the Universal Woman. I worship women, not exploit them as others do.

Now I tried to avoid her company from that day onwards, but it was not possible. If I went alone to school, my older sister would question me about the reason. So I was in a fix. Daily, as a rule, that girl kept reminding me about the pen. Whenever I would reply with a refusal, she with seething blackmail would retort, "I will tell your sister." One day I was reading through the spiritual column of a newspaper about a story, in which a vulture was flying in the sky with prey in its mouth when another vulture spied it. That vulture then started to fight to grab that, with both vultures fighting a long fight till at last the first one thought that because of the rotten rat in my mouth, the enemy is behind me. Then he dropped the rotten rat down, and the enemy also left him in peace. This story struck me deeply, and I immediately decided to part with the object of my agony so that I could remain in peace. So finally one day, just before the final exams, I handed that pen to her with the irrevocable warning that if she faltered again, it may take her to ugly consequences to her disadvantage. Thus I, saved my image as a 'good boy' and got the first lesson on how an infatuation for a split second can take us to the gallows.

I did choose to put this down because it offered me a lesson in interpersonal relations, that you should not take anybody at face value if you want to walk the way of divinity. In my case it was a mere pen, but we have examples where great knights had been brought to their knees on account of infatuation. True love never blackmails, for love verily means sacrifice. Forget it, if it is infatuatio, be ready to pay the price. The art of loving whether it be for a mother, father, brother, sister or wife, requires a lot of sense of sacrifice. If you do not know that art, go the way of compromised living which is what the west is exporting to India now free of cost—where Radha and Krishna are not considered as icons of love but valentines.

I respect love, support love, sponsor love, encourage love, help love and at times redeem lovers too. But I am at logger heads with exploiters, and blackmailers of both sexes. We have epics on love, temples for love, great gurus to teach love, and friends who helped lovers. But for us it is a shame to take lessons on love from perverts like valentines. Resort to our roots, know and be aware of love, live for it, and die for it because it is an eternal element and so worthy of it. It only evolves inside anyone into pure selfless devotion towards God and Self. Only one who knows the value of *atma*, who knows the worth of this human birth, who has self-respect, only such a one can love others. To reach that lofty ideal, we must first serve humanity selflessly for a long time, and especially the deprived section of our contemporary society.

The Money Lender Child

I WAS BORN AND brought up in an unassuming, simple but orthodox *Nambudiri* Brahmin family who were erstwhile Samantha rulers. Once the republic was formed, the *zamindari* abolition bill was introduced and trashed by the bystanders of our holy fight against British rule, and we thus lost all our lands. Our family was reduced to the quandary of hand to mouth existence, since previously the income was from the land. During my elementary school days, I remember it may have been perhaps in class 3 or 4 that my oldest sister bought me a small clay 'bank' in which to deposit the coins I would get from visiting relatives, and sometimes from my mother or any elders. Usually it would be 1/4 *ana*. (One *ana* is 6 *paisa*, and 1/4 *ana* was a big amount for the child concerned). There was a wooden box-type table, which elders used for writing purposes in those days. Since the upper part was broken, it was given to me, and I used it to store my slate, pencil, one or two text books of alphabets, mathematics, etc.

I was afraid of my sister, who might take my pencil or slate away. I kept the small clay bank in the inner corner of the box. My oldest sister gave me a *kaal ana* (made of copper, which had a hole in the center, looking like a *vada*) and dropped it into the slot in that 'bank' as my first saving. Then I went around showing it to other elders, father, mother, older brothers, and even to Kochu Narayanan (who was the *kaaryasthan*—caretaker or manager of the house) but none except my mother offered to contribute to my 'banking.' During one of his visits, my father's younger brother gave me 2 *kaal anas* and I, with utmost care, put it into the 'bank'. My thinking in those days was that if I put any amount in the clay bank, it would multiply itself. Once one of my friends had kept a small peacock feather (as a lucky charm) in my text book and told me that this feather would 'deliver' and if it happened, we would do well in our studies and that the teacher would never scold or beat us. With that foolish thought of an innocent mind, every night, just before sleeping, I would open my small wooden box and take out the 'bank' and shake it to hear the sound of the *anas* I had deposited.

One day when I realized that my bank was not showing any signs of getting full, I felt very bad. But on *Vishu*, a special occasion of the Hindu New Year, children used to get some gifts of money, say 1/4 or 1/2 *annas* from elders. On *Vishu* (New Year day celebration in Kerala) day some of the elders gave me 1/4 *ana* each, and I added these also to the pool with much devotion, as if I was doing some great deed. As usual one day I was shaking the clay bank to find out whether the deposited coins had multiplied or not, and seeing this, my oldest sister got annoyed at my foolishness and gave me a small shove to tease me. The bank in my hand fell down and broke in pieces. It was not just the bank, but my great dream itself that she broke. Even though the bank was broken, my mind was not upset, as I could now find out easily whether the amount had multiplied or not. With all the curiosities of expectancy, I counted the amount and the heavens were descending in my house, it was 3 and ½ Ana. I felt as happy as if I had earned some very big amount. Then my eyes went over to the broken clay bank. I started thinking about a place to safely store the savings, that 'big amount' that I had so meticulously saved, safe and secure from the eyes of my sister or brother, but was not able to think of one. Since I was starting to feel sleepy, I kept this issue pending for the time being. I put the coins in the pocket of the shorts I was wearing. Usually those pockets would be full of things like colored paper, or a beautiful dry leaf, or one or two '*gottis*,' a broken whistle which my older brother had given me during last year's temple *utsav*, or a small pencil stub. Whenever my oldest sister washed my clothes, she would throw away such 'useless' things, but again I would gather them up again and kept them. Only that evening, had those pair of shorts been washed, so the pockets were empty. I used to wonder sometimes about why those people scolded me for keeping the so-called useless things in my pockets, though to me they were valuable.

When I woke up in the morning and checked my pocket, the 3 and ½ anas were still safe in there. But I knew a bath from my older sister was due soon, and then worrying that she might throw away this 'big amount' considering it useless too, I removed the coins from my pocket. I carefully packed them in a piece of paper which too was not mine, having torn it out of my sister's notebook (since if I had torn out even one page from my own book, they would have scolded me, so I thought I would let my sister get the scolding) and kept the packed amount in the corner of the wooden box.

As expected my sister called me for a bath. It was a Sunday. No school! At first I was a bit angry with my eldest sister since the previous night she had broken my 'bank' locker and now even on a holiday she was insisting on a bath. I did not enjoy the morning baths of my childhood days, as I never liked the smell of the water. The pond in which we bathed in, that was just in front of the grain storage room of our ancestral home, had been built by the *Maharaja* of *Travancore* and gifted to one of my uncles. It was always full of oil with a dirty smell of soap.(due to the tradition of bathing after massaging the body with oil). In those days, soaps with good fragrance like those today, were not easily available on the market, nor were they ever purchased for the household. I went around the house in search of a place to escape to. The old house was constructed of teak wood, without proper ventilation, and so had many dark corners to hide in and I went and hid in one of them. My mother who came in to get something from that room, found me hiding in the corner, and asked what the hell I was doing there. Without replying, and in fear of being beaten in the morning itself, I ran away from the room by reflex, to where my eldest sister was doing some cleaning, I escaped my mother, but fell into the clutches of my sister. She caught hold of me and took me to the dirty pond for a wash. By this time Kochu Narayanan was getting ready to go the market which was about 5 miles from the house. An idea clicked, slipping out from the hands of my eldest sister, I ran to the room where the wooden box was kept. I carefully took out the money from the wrapping and brought it to Kochu Narayanan, asking how much a clay bank would cost.

He told me that it might be around ½ *ana,* and again with much care and utmost reverence to the money, I took out 2 *kaal anas* and handed them over to him to purchase a mud bank. My mother, elder sister and elder brother were witnessing all this. While taking this amount and paying it to Kochu Narayanan, my brother came forward and asked me, "Why don't you give it to me as a loan instead, which I will repay during the *utsavam* at the temple." He added, "You give me 3 *anas* and I will return you 4 anas during *utsavam*. (That one ana might have been the interest on the loan which I was supposed to get back from my brother). Without a second thought I gave the 3 *anas* to my brother.

But till date, even though we have all become old, and the eldest sister—the witness of the loan payment—has passed away, my brother has forgotten to repay my 3 *anas* with the interest of 1 *ana* as he had vouched for. This was my first banking business in life that ended in bankruptcy. In the evening Kochu Narayanan brought the small mud bank and even though it looked nice and better than what I had before, there was not a single 1/4 *ana* left with me to deposit in it. I kept the bank in a corner of the room that was always dark, and I don't know where the bank is today or where the money has gone.

Today I remember the state of mind I had, when I was as one possessed with the thought of that miniscule amount of money for days together, absorbed and totally immersed with the idea of increasing, multiplying, and safeguarding that small amount, and letting it disturb my whole routine of studies. It goes to show that the power of desire is so great as to create the delusion that an insignificant thing is an all sustaining one. And the *jeeva* forgets its real purpose and keeps engaged in penny management. When money is lost, it feels as if life itself is lost. The teaching we get right from childhood is about money—get money, save money, grow money and die for money. Our knowledge about the true nature, value, meaning, and use of wealth is totally a science of ignorance. Now our scriptures do not deny the importance of money—if so, there would not have been a necessity for *Bhagawan* to marry *Laxmi* and love, respect, and safeguard her the most. That itself is a good indication as to what place, importance, respect, and attitude our Rishis, the founding fathers of the Vedic way of life, had about wealth. There is no question of diminishing or undermining the value of that element and factor called money in our existence. But our understanding and attitude towards it makes us its slave. So before the twilight of life descends on us, we should try to understand the real place of wealth in our life. Perhaps an event like when my sister hit my elbow breaking my clay bank, may happen to you too, to make you realize and un-awe you about money, to make you wonder about how you wasted your all-precious life pursuing it. The attitude towards wealth described in our Vedic system is more pure, deep, divine, and life supporting like Laxmi-Narayan and not greediness to wealth in today's world which makes us only losers, and never ever gainers.

So, my appeal with folded hands to the parents of today is that first, you gain the proper knowledge from the proper source in the proper method about wealth, and then impart that knowledge to your children, along with the wealth itself. Wealth without knowledge is going to end up becoming a noose for them, which will choke and kill them—is that the gift you want to bequeath your loved ones? Think before you indulge. *Dharma* does not minimize the importance of wealth, but gives it the most prominent place. That is why *artha* (material wealth) is second to *dharma* in *purusharthas* of *dharma* (duty), *artha* (wealth), *kama* (desire), *moksha* (liberation). Then how can one say that God is against money? He is against your attitude towards money, for is not *Sri* His all respect-worthy wife, and our Mother?

The Yellow Shorts And The Mystic Hug

IT WAS *CHINGA* masam (August—September). *Onam (*a major festival celebrated in Kerala*)* was very near and in that season, one *chettiar*, a wandering hawker from the neighboring state of Tamil Nadu, would visit our village with bundles of clothes. Onam is a very special and major annual event for Keralites, and new clothes are purchased for the festivities, houses renovated or beautified etc. But as mentioned previously, our family was facing a huge financial crisis at that time, with difficulty in making ends meet. I was not expected to have knowledge of the intricacies of the situation, as that would the natural disposition of an immature lad. Maturity does set in, with the flash within of sensitivity to feelings of others, and I relate here the first episode of the onset of that maturity.

As usual that year too, the *chettiar*, known as Lakshmanan Pillai, arrived with his bundles of new clothes. Such people pass through the streets hawking their wares, and thriving by exploiting the weaknesses of the innocent children who crowd around them, much to the dismay and dilemma of the parents. It is a delightful situation for children, but a pathetic one for their poor parents. These commercial traps have been developed from the tactics of greedy businessmen, and every one of us are still lured by them till death.

Children used to get new sets of clothing during Onam as it was presumed mandatory, and every parent naturally wanted to see their loved ones wearing new clothes. Lakshmanan Pillai headed straight to my mother's sister's house, adjoining my house with one court yard shared by both the houses. He started displaying his entire art of exploiting the sentimental weakness of children and their parents. Standing on the verandah of my house, I saw in the hands of my cousin sister Amminy, a beautiful new frock, and alas! She came over to me showing her new frock with great excitement. My older sister, the one who was two years older than me, was also standing by me. She and I both were also expecting to get new clothes that day. So, this hawker understood from our faces, that we innocent children had fallen prey to his tactics, and now came to our house to encash it. Lakshmanan Pillai opened his bundle and started showing his stock of clothes, or rather cane of worries.

From childhood itself, I have always liked the color yellow. My gaze stopped on a pair of yellow shorts that he had in his stock. Without pausing to think, and in a flash of a moment I laid my hand over and I picked it up or rather grabbed it. My mother for the first time was giving me a lesson in discipline; but it did not go down my throat. She told me (and even now I remember the distress in her voice from having to refuse due to abject poverty) to place it back, and told me that we would purchase it during Lakshman Pillai's next visit. I was not ready to accept her forlorn pleas. My sister didn't seem to be in a hurry to select anything. But I was adamant that I must get it right then. I saw her head hang down from the painful inability to fulfill the desire of her loved one. My mother went into the kitchen and called up Gowri, the maid. They were saying something which was not clear to me. My mother came out and asked Lakshman Pillai, "What is the price of the pair of shorts?" It was only one *rupee* and four *anas*. Gowri appeared in a few minutes and passed on the amount needed into my mother's hands.

Happy to get the pair of yellow shorts in hand, I displayed them to my sister, in great glee. But the poor girl's heart was otherwise, not able to enjoy her brother's achievement. Her face hung dull, sunk in despair as she could not get new clothes. But even though

I was extremely happy to get my desire fulfilled, yet the look of despair on my sister's face broke my heart, and is still green in my memory even today. My happiness started evaporating; I thought I had committed a sin. It was wrenching my heart.

To add to that sorrow, my oldest sister informed me in the evening that my mother had sold four coconuts to arrange for the required amount, i.e. one *rupee* and four *anas*. She chided me to not be adamant for such things without knowing the situation, and to not put our parents through suffering. I ought to have first enquired whether money was available at home or not. That moved me, and that day saw me, a boy becoming a man. I felt my eyes grow wet at my sister's disappointment. I felt she was more entitled to this than me. The jubilant mood from getting a new pair of shorts, even in yellow, which I liked so very much, had now gone to hell. It was a regret for a lifetime. It is the first time I started feeling a sense of responsibility, and a feeling of love for others, which is a sign of the dawn of maturity in a child. And for the first time I felt too, that sense of love and concern for one's sibling, with the face in my mind's eye, that of my younger sister when she saw my shorts. I kept quiet for some time, and with a feeling of guilt consciousness, placed those shorts in the small wooden box where I used to keep my books, pencils and even my *kudukka*, the clay bank. A strong feeling worth mentioning engulfed me, which prevented me from wearing the shorts, rather it looked like a monument of foolishness. So I was not at all in the frame of mind to wear it on Onam day. Thus that Onam, the beginning of the year, was for me a kind of awakening. In the middle of the day my mother saw me in old shorts and asked, "Why didn't you wear the new one?" I said with a sinking voice of shame, "Maa! My heart did not accept, for I have hurt my sister, so until she too gets a new frock of her liking, I will not touch it. I beg pardon—sorry Maa for my foolishness. I swear, I swear, I will not do it again." Shaking with tears, I touched her feet. On hearing this she took me to her bosom. Even today I feel that priceless warmth of love, the special reward of love worth a thousand lives. That hug and the experience went so deep in me. My mother planted a deep kiss on my forehead, and all-purifying pearls of love ran down from her eyes over my head. And as a memento of my foolishness or ignorance, and the start of the functioning of the faculty of maturity, I kept the shorts wrapped in a piece of newsprint, inside that wooden box. And love for such things were gone from my mind, once and for all. I remember that the shorts were in the box even when I got to my tenth class, but I forgot about it thenceforth. Even today, whenever I see yellow clothing, I remember the mistake I committed.

A Few Scattered Memories

ALMOST TWO YEARS had passed since I completed writing the first part of the Indian edition of my autobiography—*The Pyre of the Destined*[12]. It was in May 2011. I received many calls enquiring about the second part of the book. Of course when a book is named as first part, the expectations for the next part is only natural. I was incapacitated for a long time due to cardiac problems and kept on hold the writing work. My memory also seemed to be fading, or at least a little of its fertility. But the extremely good care given by the dedicated Maram family, I am feeling better now, little recovered too. When the mind is gathering courage, one has to apply and put it to use in order for it to multiply, otherwise though one may wait for courage to grow to fullness, yet it may not happen. Therefore let me try, and as for courage, even if you apply yourself with just a little, it will keep on increasing on its own. So I have decided to write down to the extent possible, but this time around, I am not in a position to write about my experiences in chronological order but a few as scattered memories.

Even though my poverty ridden boyhood is not sweet enough

---

12 The autobiography of Nadanandaji was initially published in India as two books namely—*The Pyre of the Destined* and *Roaring Silence*. The books have since been published in two volumes under the title, "*Autobiography of an Avadhoota*".

for much remembrance, it does hold in its womb the gems of messages that surely have universal applications. My boyhood (though not childhood), despite being caught in a whirlpool of circumstances from ignorance of child psychology, did pass off with colors just due to the grace of the guru.

I venture here to recall, and believe my memory to be accurate, that it may have been around the age of 10 or 11. My studies had become a concern, and a rather uphill task for my poor parents to accomplish. After exploring a lot of avenues within their reach, and with no other option in sight, I was separated from them and sent to stay with my maternal uncle for my studies, far away from home. Since they loved me very much, for them too, the separation from me was unbearable agony. I hope and expect it to be so for any parent in this world. Until the point children acquire and develop the ability to exist independently of the parents, separation will be unbearable for both, and in many instances dying together may be the destiny. Destiny spares none, this is a truth everyone must remember well unto their heart. The element called destiny, whenever it gets a chance or you give it a chance to play, will not spare anyone even from Lord *Narayana* himself to a pauper like *Sudama*[13]. But the irony is that the so called edifice of destiny is raised and erected, from our own actions.

I had just completed my 4th class. Late one afternoon during summer vacation, when I had woken from a daytime nap, I saw many of my family members sitting together and they seem to be deep in discussion on something which was beyond the undeveloped comprehensive faculties of a 10-year old. Even with that little ability of comprehension, I was able to make out to some

---

13 One of the stories of the Bhagavatham text—Sudama is Krishna's childhood friend who is from a poor family and comes to visit Krishna with a handful of puffed rice as an offering. The offering pleases Krishna and he turns into a wealthy man. The lesson of the story is not to be greedy and always remember the Lord before having food.

extent that they were talking about money matters, loans, their repayment etc. What else is there in this world to talk about—only two things, one is about money or wealth, and the other about women, and if those didn't work out for you, then you immersed yourself in wine. This is the internet (www) age. In the evening that poor innocent girl, my older sister, was appointed the bearer of the bitter message of my moving to my uncle's for future studies, the present location having failed to produce the features in me, or the future that they had expected or envisaged. My uncle was retired as a Major from the military, and was then a school teacher teaching the *Hindi* language. So the Major was going to control me, the minor. I was wondering why I was being sent away from my parents. But what could they have done—they merely wanted to distribute something amongst the children, and since they only had a lot of miseries, they distributed those, and well in advance. I learnt from my sister to my surprise, that my older brother would also be parting for studies, along with the oldest brother. I felt sad, as I liked the ancestral house a lot—it was an aesthetically pleasing atmosphere to me, a lover of nature by birth. The surroundings of countryside with lush greenery, pure air and pure hearts, a small river flowing in front of the house, my little friends, especially *Lakshmi*, my pet cat—too many to count. The vague but scary picture of my family's poor financial condition was, and is fresh even now, in front of my eyes. I presume, because I have a lot of time to ponder on it now, that this may have been the reason for the reshuffle in my family setup. The following week, I was asked to be ready to go with uncle. What could a small boy of 10 years, grasp about the commitments and situations of a big family? After a four year-stay with my uncle, I returned to join another school for matriculation that was five miles from my native village. But I noticed that there was now a perceptible difference in the intensity of kinship between my older brothers and I, and an unrepairable gap of emotional emptiness and loss of intimacy that had now come between me and my elders, especially my parents. This absence gave birth to the spiritualistic tendencies that have brought me this far.

Those five years, wow! I was groomed into becoming a man in a very demanding atmosphere of very strict discipline. Even though all who retire from service in the military or police are taught to disorient themselves from the military mentality, all of them without exception want to continue living the same way. And my uncle followed this too, obsessed with his military discipline even after retirement. He taught me English, especially grammar, based on the book by 'Wren and Martin'. Looking back to that iron age of days with my uncle, I feel that whatever is memorized or learned in youth remains almost evergreen since our 'memory chip' was pure and without virus in the beginning, in technical terms, virgin. Only later we download for free from others, even parents, all the viruses called *samskaras*, impressions, tendencies, complexes, attitudes, habits—the memory card! So I very well remember the agony, tortures, harassments that I was offered, asked, taught, expected to know, trained to follow, obey, and adhere in order to maintain the 'military discipline'. This method has to date, not produced, not even one person, whose life can be called a role model, one worth emulating, and those adopting such methods have not even been able to train their own children. I used to have a fully packed time-table of routines from waking till going to bed, with dos and don'ts written in big letters. One such was posted in my room in his house, with another around my neck like the ID card of today, while ID cards have value, but not the humans owning them. As far as worldly comforts were concerned, I was well-provided for, with better food, modern clothes, etc., but even though I had those comforts, something was missing—there was a sense of vacuum—the affection, the love, a pat, that warm hug of my mother when I returned from school, the soft word which a child by nature always expects and likes to have all along, always. But nature likes a child to become a man, and not for a man to be childish. And so, the so-called universal disease of homesickness attacked me. Sitting alone, I used to cry at nights, thinking about my mother or my home in the village, or my ever-loving pet Lakshmi the cat. It is natural for every child to pass such a phase in life, even more than once, but the difficulty is the lack of awareness in the parents, who are the cause for this child to enter this world.

Everyone knows the technique well, how to produce a child but they least care about learning the art of raising a child. Once I slipped into homesickness, just like it happens to anyone who is thus afflicted—absent-mindedness, attention-deficiencies, etc., followed. But a child-less man, who has not had a single lesson in child psychology, resorts to idiotic teaching methods to hide his shameful ignorance. Those stunt a child. So I used to receive a lot of the medicine from a madman—severe corporal punishment—beating by hand, and when the hands grew tired, beatings with sticks, and kicks even with their holy legs. These were for my blunders in studies, especially in mathematics, the worst science invented by humans to make the whole world accountable. The very first week itself (after leaving home) a fear complex or insecure feeling developed in my mind and to my wonder they remain even now, those impressions in spite of my deep spiritual understanding, attainments etc. The same scary picture, is created even today.

This is to drive home the point about learning at least to some extent, the lesson of child psychology as taught by our rishis, not by the modern world, so you may be successful in presenting to the world a good human being, and to the hope that no child ever receives the treatment I did. Somewhere in the recesses of the subconscious mind, those impressions of insecurity still exist. But with an entirely different meaning. They are still tender. The intention here in writing this is not to cast blame, charge, accuse, or devalue anyone but to make you aware about what childhood is, its phases, how well it can be handled. This I have learnt from my own life. Just like blotting paper, a child's mind absorbs all the plusses and minuses inevitably prevailing in its environment, and the circumstances which he or she has to go through.

Like a caged bird, I used to look at the sky for hours together (in the absence of my uncle) and wonder about my fate. When I see them from here now, they were all merely empty emotions, but gave me very deep anguish. It has been so for every child I have come across, especially during my short stint with Vanavasi Kalyan ashram in Dehradun.

Even though the mind of that child was disturbed, his studies went well. During summer vacations, I was taken to my village for a few days to stay with my parents. To be frank, I hated my mother, father and other elders in those days, as some unknown force compelled and convinced me that all these people were nobody to me. During my college days, when I read child psychology, I understood about all those sensibilities. Slowly those negative psychological feelings which had been burning like a fire inside a contained furnace, empowered and turned the direction of my consciousness levels, and I started loving 'the Mother Goddess' for refuge. When I was in the 6th class, I got a small, pocket-sized picture of *Durga*, the Mother Universal, from one of my classmates. I used to hide it between the pages of my textbook. As there was no pooja-room or shrine in the major uncle's residence, there was no daily worship system. Occasionally he would invite some *'purohits'* to do some kind of *poojas* which were yet unfamiliar to me, and I was not sure for what purpose. But everyday after bathing in the river, on his way back home, my uncle used to visit a temple on the river banks. I used to follow him daily and I remember it was an *Ayyappa*[14] *Mandir*. I use to get a banana or *trimadhuram* as *prasadam*, but to my wonder my uncle never allowed me to eat it. I had seen though some of my classmates having *darshan* at that village mandir and eating that sweet *prasadam*. My uncle had a different logic, or let's say worm in his mind—"The prasadams that these *poojaris* hand out, are not at all hygienic." Keeping the *prasadam* in my hand, and walking the long distance back home was a tragic parading event for me.

Regarding the picture inside my textbook, a faith slowly took root in me, and later grew to become a practice, that if one was seeking relief from the miseries of this world (in my personal case

---

14 Lord Ayyappa is a Hindu deity fused with the energies of Shiva and Vishnu.

it was the seeking of a remedy), then that refuge could be found only in the form of mother, a friend, a savior.

After the examinations ended, in the summer vacations, there used to be tradesmen or *paperwalas* going around neighborhoods who would buy paper and old books. Some smart mothers used this opportunity to seek out better bargains for used textbooks. When the new academic year began and I was purchasing new books, I noticed one day that my mother had done away with my old books, following the annual ritual. When I came to know of this, a floodgate of turbulent emotions opened up. I did not realize that even without my knowledge, somehow I had developed such a love for *Maa* that I was feeling the same old heartbreak I had experienced at the time of leaving my parents to stay with my uncle. I felt like I had parted from someone most near and dear to my heart—the feeling was not for the loss of the book, but for the Divine Mother's picture which had been kept inside. I cried and cried and cried. After two or three days, some intuition came, and meeting the old *paperwala* on the street, I spoke to him with tears in my eyes about my photo. He was moved, and said, "Don't worry my dear boy, I will do my best to find that picture of the Mother for you. And true to his words he did put in the effort to find that picture, and give my Mother back to me. This was my first kiss of grace by the Mother. It was a happy moment of a deeper transformation taking place in me. As a small boy it may have been just an act of adoring but when I remember it now, aided with the knowledge of the value and ways of grace, how closely *She* was taking care of me without my knowledge. The next day when he brought back the photo to me after searching through all his bundles, he said, "Look, I have worked for four or five hours to search and find this. You must compensate me for this with a good amount of money when you are grown up, and in a job." I did grow up, and did get a job, left that job, and became sanyasi. I doubt now the exact meaning of those words: whether they were the words of the paperwala said with love, or whether they were those of the Mother with some hidden meaning. I feel it may have been Her, but his payment is a sweet due yet! In the pace of my life, I have failed to remember him and repay his debt. This may be the first *runa* needing to be paid! During those five years I lived a dull life, except for the days when my sister or others visited from back home.

My pet cat Lakshmi was a very affectionate friend during my childhood days. I was in the 6th class when one day I received a postcard in the mail from my mother. That was the first letter received in my life. I was so happy to receive a letter, and that too from my mother that I broke down while reading it. The letter brought sad news of the death of my pet Lakshmi. I felt as if I had lost everything—yes, when a true friend is lost it feels like almost everything is lost. More than my parents and elders, I had loved Lakshmi and I am sure I too got the same affection from her, as she would sleep, eat, and play with me everyday during my childhood. Lakshmi appears to me in my dreams even now.

Impulsive Genius Of A Humble Caretaker

EACH ONE OF us may have experienced more than once in our lives, that unconventional wisdom wins over conventional wisdom. But that does not amount to making a rule that a conventional approach is of no use. This unconventional wisdom is also a mere gain of one's conventional efforts from a previous birth. When I think of this fallout, an incident comes to mind.

Kochu Narayanan, the loyal and dedicated *karyasthan* (care taker) of my family had a lot of influence in my life in the area of social activity. He acted in all capacities as manager, servant, friend, and advisor to all and sundry in our household, and who served our family loyally over three generations both in its days of glory and days of doom. He had a spotless reputation among our family members. In my childhood he was like an ideal to me as far as engaging oneself in action without a grudge was concerned. He was at work in our house from early morning up until late at night and was systematic, disciplined and a good organizer too. I loved him deeply, as he helped me more than my elders in everything a child needs. Due to the curse of untouchability prevailing in those days, I was not allowed to mingle with him freely or sit near him. I never cared about the rules though, and got scolded by my mother on that regard. On holidays, while he worked at the field, I would sit by him, fascinated to see the sweating drops emerging on his body and falling down every moment. He too kept me engaged with his folk stories. His two sons, Subhash and Santosh became my friends. They would accompany their mother, who used to help my mother while she worked in the yard cleaning rice, *dal* or such things. Even during the days of our dire family financial crisis, the group of servants were content to live with the entire family, within the constraints of their means.

Kochu Narayanan was very well-versed in the stories of the *Ramayana* and *Mahabharata*. One day while taking a small break in work to chew betel leaves or *paan*, he asked me, "Could you tell me, my respected young master, why *Ravana* had ten heads? Was there a meaning behind it?" I was in my matriculation. Even though I was well-familiar with such stories from the basic scriptures of our culture, I was not prepared however to face such posers. I rattled my brains for an answer, but nothing clicked. I went around asking my mother, oldest sister, brother and a few others, in all innocence but also with a sense of prick to status, in search of a suitable answer to his question. But everyone had their own babblings—while some answered vaguely, others just laughed.

My inquisitive curiosity turned to dismay! Finally I decided to seek the answer from Kochu Narayanan himself and went to him in a dejected mood. He said, "You got no answer?" He laughed for a moment and told me, "The ten heads of Ravana imply that Ravana possessed the combined intellect of ten persons." I was delighted to hear the answer and amazed at the intellect of that illiterate villager. This incident opened my eyes and cultivated in me the habit of reading between the lines.

Whatever work was entrusted to him, Kochu Narayanan did wholeheartedly, and in a systematic disciplined way, for he had been trained by our old grandfathers. So he was like the connecting thread of the old customs of our forefathers. I used to spend most of the time with him, observing how he did his tasks, in the field, in negotiating purchases, in accounts, and in everything. One thing that I however was not able to digest by instinct was that his food was served to him on the verandah of our house. Sometimes, I used to insist to mother that I be served food alongside him. This transgression earned me lot of scoldings from all my family members. In those days it was unimaginable that a *Nambudiri* boy sit near a person from the *Chettiar* community for meals. But I was adamant in having my food sitting by his side, and despite the negative comments from other elders of the house, I ate food sitting near him at every opportunity.

Even as early as my matriculation days, I was starting to gain awareness and enlightenment about the changes taking place in society, and had begun reading books on the social structure of that era, of the terrible practice of untouchability and the eradication of that menace among people. After a few years, I happened to attend a *satsang* of a *Swamiji* in a nearby town, in which he spoke on the concepts of the four-fold ways of the *Vedic* way of life. The edifices called *varna* and *ashram* were the dictum of the great *rishis*. Though society was divided into the four castes, no caste was deemed greater in dignity or respectability than the other. All had equal responsibility to contribute to the collective welfare and evolution of the society as a whole. But as time passed, certain elements of society began over-reaching their rights, and with selfish motives started to deliberately distort the very rules that had been designed for their own welfare, exploiting or disregarding them. The result was that both the *varna* and ashram systems began collapsing into ruin. Society is still unaware of the real magnitude of the loss that was thus incurred. Some intellectuals say during the course of a single day, a person's life may contain all the four kinds of tendencies and in stages and steps, we unknowingly pass and perform all these actions. The *Swamiji* said further that when doing *puja* in the morning for example he could be called a *Brahmin*, when managing the family affairs with authority he would be a *Kshatriya*, when purchasing the daily needs or engaging in trade a *Vaishya* and when doing petty work a *Shudra* But this explanation was merely superfluous. When I read up in detail and contemplated on this, I understood the importance of the verse in the *Bhagawad Gita*—'*chaturvarnyam maya srishtam*, *guna karma vibhagasa*[15].' The citizens constituting the society were classified and compartmentalized only on the basis of division of the work to be done for a smooth functioning harmonious society. This classification was not according to *guna*. The *gunas* of a person indicate the inherent disposition, and the karma from the previous birth now manifesting as inclinations. They are the means and resources provided in the current birth, as equipment for the journey towards the final goal of a human birth. Due to foolishness, or rather ignorance, I was under the impression that Lord Krishna was a socialist, or '*samatva vadi*' or advocate of a classless society. No society however materially advanced it may become, can ever see the face of peace and happiness if its citizens are not classified and educated to live in mutual dependency with equal rights over the resources at its disposal,. This dictum of the *rishis* is beyond dispute and anyone however great and intelligent he may consider himself, should not work against it or he would be misleading his own fellow humans to hell. He would be the real demon.

By the time I left home to lead the life of an ascetic, Kochu Narayanan had grown very old, but even then he frequented our house to do a little work and oversee other workers in a supervisory role. He felt extreme anguish at my leaving home, and tried in vain to convince me with the worn-out story and argument that God could be realized even while living at home. His logic was very different, "You can very well do *tapas* staying right here at home. Why then do you want to run away from us all?" I paid homage to his love for me, and made no attempt to argue with him or convince him otherwise, due to his pure-hearted and good intentions.

More than twenty five years later in Delhi, I met his son Subhash, the closest friend of my youth, with whom I had so many

---

15 Bhagavad-Gita Chap 4.13—states that there are four orders of classes namely Brahmana, Kshatriya, Vaishya and Shudra were created by the Creator/Creation (maya) according to the quality of the individual (guna) and work to be carried out in the society (karma).

shared experiences including acting in plays together. From him, I learned of the demise of his father Kochu Narayanan, the moral and emotional pillar of support during my childhood and youth, the one who had taught me about self-discipline, hard work, and even about viewing situations with a positive perspective. He had been a good friend, mentor, advisor, and older brother to me. Here I do offer my prayers for him—"May his spirit rest in peace."

Oh! You Are That Boy

A FEW MEMORIES OF childhood never fade. I was in class six, staying for my studies with my ex-military uncle, far from my loving parents. As I was new to that school, having joined there just one year prior in class five, I did not have many friends.

In those days I had to wear shorts with suspenders in the European style, in accordance with the wishes of my uncle. The suspenders held up my shorts which were a bit over-sized, my future-minded uncle having purchased them with my growing age and chubbiness in mind. But they had a defect in that the left shoulder belt would keep slipping out frequently. It was a nuisance in that it needed very careful handling to maintain and keep in place. And except for when I was in school, these were the shorts I would most often be wearing while playing outside or at home. There were no upper garments to support the shorts, and my left hand was almost always engaged in the duty of rearranging the belt again and again. One of the pockets on the shorts was a little ripped as well, and as a result whatever I put in could easily fall out.

One day while playing in the courtyard of the house where I stayed, I found a small *gotti* made of glass. It had quite a unique look and therefore it became a precious thing to me. The thinking among children is that the value of something is more depending on how rare and uncommon it is, and so I prized this *gotti* since none of my friends had anything like it. This special toy used to be found inside soda bottles. Blue in color, and though smeared with dirt from the courtyard this new asset was precious to me. I gave a good bath to this new friend and after drying it by wiping it on my clothes, placed it in the safety of my shorts pocket, forgetting that the pocket had a hole. I would keep checking in the pocket again and again, to make sure it was there—in the manner of a worldly creature who, even after it has been proved and established that there is not a single drop of happiness in the world, still hangs on with the hope that he will get it someday.

The following day I was returning from the village after successfully completing a mission of purchasing a bar of soap from the store, for which I had been sent by my uncle. While putting the soap into my pocket, I found to my deepest dismay that my darling gotti had dropped herself out through the hole in my shorts! I felt as if the sky had fallen, and went around looking for my good friend, but even after long searching failed to locate it. I had completely forgotten that I had been sent on an errand. Not only did I not return with the soap, I was extremely late too. I had to face my furious uncle whose daunting words were, "Why are you so late?" At first I kept mum for a minute, but when I told him about my search for the lost *gotti*, he flew into a rage. He beat me again and again for keeping him waiting for the soap, and as his evening bath was delayed because of me. What can one do in a world where elders are ever expecting children to behave in ways developmentally beyond their age, but children expect elders to behave below their age by showing understanding and sensitivity. Even in this era of science, adults are direly and pressingly in need of lessons in child psychology. Though they are failing badly in properly preparing and educating themselves to raise a child, this illiteracy never stops them from producing children. Not only is the work of producing children not suspended, they do not bother to take the time to learn how to properly bring up a child. I was thinking in my mind thus—see how cruel this fellow is, I have lost my most cherished new friend, the valuable *gotti*, and this man is not having a bit of sympathy for me, and punishing me for coming just a little late. This situation was like the tale of the old woman who went to see a mahatma complaining that her water-buffalo had not produced any milk that day. When instead the mahatma gave her *Vedantic* advice, the woman went about saying that the *baba* did not have a bit of concern regarding her buffalo, and kept talking like an idiot about something else.

Of course, within a couple of days I had all but forgotten that 'friend', in the way that the modern, educated young widow of a millionaire who died young, goes back to normal and prepares to find a better husband. After now obtaining some other petty thing to play with, I did forget my old darling. But just as it happens in the typical love triangle, to my wonder one day at school, I saw that my lost darling *gotti* was now in the possession of Saudamini, a classmate of mine. She had stumbled upon it by chance, and was playing with it in all innocence. But my greed came to fore when I saw it in her hands and I accused her of stealing it. I asked her fiercely to return my *gotti*, but with the confidence of an Indian well-aware of her constitutional rights, she replied, "I found it on the roadside near that village shop, and so this is mine now, not yours." And had I not too acquired it in the same way from the roadside a few days back, so what right could I have upon such a thing? I was failing to remember and acknowledge this logic. She was certainly within her rights but I, a *kaliyugi jeeva,* had started asserting my ownership over it.

Today when such incidents spring afresh from memory, as a sadhu I now have a new understanding from within on the foolishness of humans chasing after and fighting for perceived rights on *gotti*-like things, which we have lost from carelessness. The state of affairs of the 'learned grownups' is not too different. Though the objects, characters, and situations have changed, the basic elements that ignite a conflict or quarrel remain same— the lack of love for others, the narrow-mindedness and short-sightedness, and no faith in the virtue of forgiveness.

Even after repeated requests, Saudamini was still not ready to 'return' the *gotti* to me. I was angry but it did not occur to me how idiotically I was behaving, and nor was I able to accept or digest the fact that it was only my foolishness and carelessness that was the cause of loss. Depressed at not getting back the *gotti,* and stinging with the humiliation of not being honored as a boy after repeated requests, I pulled at her dress in anger and struck out at her. Not only did her dress tear off, but my long nails made a cut on her cheek, which started to bleed. Sensing now the gravity of the situation, I grew afraid and slinked away to the bench in my classroom. By this time the issue of the 'war' between us had reached the headmaster's ears. Since I was a relative of a teacher (my uncle) who taught in the same school, I had been getting special consideration in the school so far. But this time, that did not work. The headmaster appeared in the classroom along with my uncle, and I was rewarded with legitimate beatings in front of all the students for my unlawful quarrel. The headmaster and my uncle took Saudamini to the office room to apply dressing to the wound caused at my hands.

In the evening a good 'reception' awaited me at uncle's home. Not only did I get a fresh feast of beatings from uncle, but was also ordered to go to Saudamini's house to apologize for the incident. Dinner that evening was also not to be served to me till I went and said 'sorry, pardon me' to Saudamini. As I nurtured a strong ego—that protected 'ego'—was not willing to yield to disgrace. Thinking to myself that only the evening's meal would be denied but not lunch, I took double the amount of food at lunch. I thought that this way having no dinner would not matter, at least for a few days. Seeing this my uncle was perhaps smiling within, and left me to the test, knowing that a boy will always be a boy and that is very difficult for anyone to win over hunger. I was no exception, for in this world 'Hunger is the king who rules without a throne'. And the situation was worsening due to the diplomatic pressure mounting on me, from the goodwill of the victim's family. In any case I lost my battle, which did not have any valid moral strength anyway. So I went to her house with head hanging, to offer reluctant apology with the flags of antagonism hoisted down.

Saudamini was playing by the verandah with her younger brother, and with the same *gotti*. Her mother was sitting nearby. Saudamini displayed graceful acceptance of my apology, showing that women too will always be women, gifted with the angelic ability to forgive easily. She demonstrated the all-forgetting, generous nature of womankind which alone sustains this world in spite of all its flaws. I felt really ashamed of myself. As if nothing had happened, Saudamini invited me to join her in playing with the *gotti*. I went near her and said 'sorry' for whatever had happened in school. I could still see the dressing to the wound on her cheek, so deep had been the scratch I had inflicted from my act of greed.

At that time I was unaware of why the Mother is worshipped as '*baala*', and why the earth itself called '*kshama*'—it is only because of that divine and all-forgiving nature inbuilt in every woman, and if by exception this quality is absent, she is called '*abaala*'. I felt repentance at my doing, and I hope it was a play by my Mother whom I worship, to teach me about motherliness. From that very moment, regard and respect for the whole of womankind leapt up and increased in my heart. The incident with this '*baala*' is an undeletable chapter of my life which contains in it lessons of deep significance.

When we keep our eyes open to every incident we come across, there are a lot of lessons contained in them that we can learn from. But if we arrogantly decide to keep our eyes closed, not even an efficient and skilled teacher can teach us anything. After all, she was suffering all that pain only for a *gotti*. I wept and her mother came near and told me not to cry and tried to soothe me by saying that it is was not uncommon for children to get cuts and wounds while playing. Saudamini came forward and offered the *gotti* to me. There were tears, nay, purifying waters of the Ganga I must say, in her eyes too. I told her, "Mini, do not cry. I am sorry for whatever happened. I tender an unconditional apology. You keep the *gotti* with you and play, I don't need it." I stepped back and walked a few steps away. Saudamini came running to me, put her hand around my shoulder, and asked, "Did uncle beat you too much?" Even today I can remember those sublimely sweet words of concern ringing in my ears. She said, "Now I say sorry, for it was because of me and this useless *gotti* that you got beatings from headmaster and uncle". Saying so, she threw away that *gotti* onto the ground nearby. I walked back home. Both of us were classmates and studied together till the tenth class. The black thick scar, of my nails was always on her cheek, and whenever I saw her face I felt bad for my misdeed. Though at that age I was unable to appreciate the intensity of the warmth of love, and the value of the sacrifice in the tiny heart of that girl because of my immaturity, today, I feel fulfillment in writing this as a tribute to that angel of love. If I make the mistake of regarding this incident as small and insignificant, as perhaps most other people in the world might, I will not have earned or learned anything by becoming a saint.

Years passed by. After leaving school I never again saw Saudamini or remembered the foolishness of childhood. But when I was in Mookambika, one day I was sitting on the banks of the Sauparnika, a couple came to meet *Maa*, my Guruji, and with them was a child. When I saw the young woman with her child and husband, and with a scar on her cheek, I immediately recognized her, but due to decorum I did not ask anything. She too seemed to have recognized me for without speaking, though with a trace of doubt, she started rolling her fingers on the marks on her face, as if asking me for verification. I could easily recollect the black, thick mark on her cheek. Now I decided to clear the air and asked her, "Are you not Mini, do you remember me?" She shook her head to indicate that she did not. Of course, I was now in *kashaya* robes and had changed a lot, and besides who would remember such silly incidents of schooldays in an ever- changing life. I asked her, "Do you remember the incident behind the thick, black mark on your cheek?" She burst out crying," Oh! You are that boy!" Her husband was looking at our faces with puzzlement on his face. Then I narrated to him the whole story.

I felt happy to meet a known face in that unknown forest. They informed me that they were in Mookambika for the *aksharabhyasam* of their little boy. They invited me to attend the ceremony and with *Amma*'s permission I joined them. I gave their son a small blue similar *gotti* (which I bought from a shop near the *mandir*) to celebrate the occasion, telling him not to fight for it as his mother and her friend had done in their school days. I do feel immense solace in remembering this as a tribute to that pure tender heart which taught me the lesson of forgiveness, and a lot of gratitude at the feet of my Mother Goddess who came in the form of a loving child to teach me the greatness of mercy. If any reader deems this trivial, or a meaningless childhood incident, I say to them—get lost.

The Inexplicable Days

WHEN I MET him for the first time, I was scared to look into his face. He was jet black in complexion, with a long beard, a well-built body and rough looking, but a radiant smile on his face. His manner was very calm, welcoming, and loving. The Hindus called him with the name Sreedharan, and the Christians called him Thomas. But nobody knew for sure whether he was either of those, though they did recognize him almost as a different species of being. I never enquired of him where he was born and brought up, and he never told me too. He had been in our village since long, working for years as a menial laborer in the agricultural fields. He possessed nothing other than a couple items of clothing, a bundle of *beedies*, a box of matches, and a few packets of *ganja*. While at work or at rest, and except when sleeping, he would sing extempore songs of his own composition, which rose spontaneously as a flow from within, and as a gift from nature. A peculiarity of his style of lyrics was that if he began singing for example, with a word beginning with the letter 'a', then the rest of the song would only comprise of words starting with the letter 'a'. The language was neither chaste Malayalam nor Sanskrit, but a synthesis of both. For example—"*aksharam archana aalinganam anubhooti anjanvum ahah, ariv aarum aksharam aanu akhilam*"—which was difficult to interpret. He resembled Yogi Vemana of Andhra Pradesh, who sang such songs. At the first hearing, the song would sound absurd, but an entirely different meaning would emerge upon contemplation on the words.

He once told me his story, about the beginning of all of this, on an evening at the village temple ground where we met daily. He narrated,—"Once I was traveling from Mangalore to Trichur by bus. It was almost dark. The monsoon was in full swing. In those days I worked as a laborer in a coffee plantation in Mangalore. All of a sudden there was a flash of lightning in the sky, followed by the booming sound of a thunder bolt. It must have descended right upon my head for I totally went out of body and mind consciousness. The lightning passing through me generated a lot of heat inside my body my head throbbed from a burning sensation. The suffocating uneasiness lasted a few minutes and then all of a sudden it started cooling down. I felt some kind of newness, not of course freshness. I noted that a few lines in the form of a song just emerged from my lips, and I started singing loudly on the bus. Then onwards I have been singing songs, which come out spontaneously from within. I never consciously compose the words or think about the meaning. I just sing or murmur whenever the waves of exhilaration spring from inside. I feel it must be an echo of some profound experience which is happening deep inside." I wondered about this man who was totally illiterate, and did not even know how to write his name. I tried to write down his songs, as I felt they were unusual in meaning and worth transcribing, and who knows who might benefit from reading them in the future. But he never permitted me to do so, as he felt this was a sacred offering to Mother Nature and hence should not be written or printed.

I observed, as has been the tradition with great poet devotees or *bhakt kavi*s, that every song ended with the words '*sreedharan shakti*,' his mark, (*sabda shata, samaveda, sabdam cha sreedhara shakti* ...), this is an example of the concluding line from all of his songs.

Since he sang the word '*sreedhara*' in all his songs, I felt this should be his name, and started calling him by that name. All day long he toiled in the fields of landlords, and earned just thirty rupees. In the evenings he would reach the small village tea shop where he would purchase a lot of *'vadas'* or deep-fried lentil patties, and distribute them to everybody sitting there, and even to the dogs and cows. A few poor villagers would await his arrival every day to avail of the free *vadas*. From the remaining money he would purchase two or three bundles of *beedies* and match boxes, and a few packets of *ganja*. Then he would buy himself a cup of tea and with a couple of *vadas* have that as dinner. After bathing at the temple pond or the small river nearby, he would sit with his *beedi* bundles and *ganja* to begin his evening routine of filling *ganja* in the *beedi* and smoke and sing till late night. I used to sit by him till the temple closed for the night. Every day I tried to memorize at least one song of his. For this routine of coming back home late, my mother used to scold me since I had sat near an *antyaja*, as well as a known *ganja* addict, and for eating *vadas* made in the village tea shop, which was considered unimaginable transgression by my so-called higher caste- labeled *Nambudiri* family.

My friendship with Sreedharan grew deeper with time. There was something different and special about his face, words, and deeds. Sometimes it was difficult for me to analyze or understand his words. One day it happened that the temple did not open for morning rituals even after sunrise. By sunrise the morning pooja was usually over. The temple was managed by endowment (*Devaswam* Board) and the priest had not paid his salary for more than three months. The priest therefore closed the main gates, keeping the key with him, and did not open the temple in the early morning as usual. A few villagers including me went to his house and tried to pacify him in vain. The villagers were even ready to collect money between them and present it to him as salary. But he was not at all ready to agree to it. He was adamant that the endowment executive officer must visit the temple and settle matters. When the talks failed, I had no other choice but to sit in front of the mandir in *dharna* declaring 'fast unto death' till the re-opening of the temple and resuming of *pooja*. I sat on a towel spread as *asan* in front of the temple east gate, and to my wonder Sreedharan also sat in *dharna* at the west gate. Most of the villagers assembled and started shouting slogans against the endowment and priest. In the meantime, a few elders from the village went to the town to meet the *Devaswam* department authorities to settle the issue. At around 2 pm they managed to bring the officers to the temple premises and the priest was also called in to discuss the issue. After a few heated arguments between priest and endowment authorities, and villagers versus priest, the problem was finally settled. During the whole episode of discussion, I was chanting some *devi stotras* (without getting involved in the talks) and Sreedharan was singing his songs sitting at the western gate. When the issue was settled, and the priest ready to assume his duties, the village elders first asked me to enter into the temple chanting *'deviyei, devi devi ammoi...'* For a minute I was silent and then going to the western gate, I took hold of Sreedharan's hand, and then hand in hand we came back to the eastern gate. Even before the villagers could not fathom what was happening, I entered the temple premises holding Sreedharan's hand, who was an *antyaja*, who was forbidden from entering into temples in those days, shouting *'deviyei, devi devi ammoi...'* (Mother Devi, the mother of all). Now the villagers realized what had happened—a *Nambudiri* boy (from a highly respectable Brahmin family) had entered the temple holding the hand of an *antyaja* (from a lower caste family). There was chaos among the villagers for a few minutes and they were divided in opinion on what had just happened. I tried arguing with them in a few words to prove my point that there is no valid yardstick of authentic nature in deciding how anybody is 'great' or 'small' in front of the 'Mother of the Universe' and that it was time to change the age-old blind traditions, which had become just a practice of prejudice by the privileged class. This was the first successful social activity I managed to do, and then onwards the temple was thrown open to all classes of people. The so-called 'high profile' village elders started treating me as a rebel born in their village to destroy the traditions, and they even planned to drive me out of the village through their petty, dirty politics. They called me a communist, or born demon, or idiot or whatever name they wanted. But the majority of the villagers who wanted to walk along with the changing times, were with me.

The days were nearing for my departure to Mookambika in

search of the real 'Me'. Sreedharan felt very happy when I conveyed to him of my resolve, that I had decided to move on the 'path of God.' On the evening of the day before my leaving home and the village to lead an ascetic's life, Sreedharan and I sat in front of the temple for a long time. He was singing a song about *sanyasis* and for the first time he allowed me to write it down. It was full of deep philosophy, telling me the dos and don'ts of *sanyasa ashram* in a nutshell. The next day Sreedharan gave me a ride to the bus stand on his bicycle, and bid me farewell. That paper on which I wrote the 'farewell song' was with me till my stay in Rishikesh after *sanyas*. When I studied the *Paramahamsa Upanishad* during my Rishikesh stay, I wondered how that illiterate outcaste villager could have had such an effortless grasp of the so-called classified deep details of such an exalted system of our scriptures. Like any other memory, memories of Sreedharan too have started fading away into oblivion with me going farther and farther away from my past.

Once I discussed this with my spiritual brother, Swami Abhayanand, as to how an illiterate villager was able to possess the knowledge of a scholar very well-versed in scriptures,' to which Swamiji said, "Perhaps he may have been a *'yoga bhrashta sadhak'* in his previous birth. It is not a matter of wonder, as such things often happen in spiritual life. There are innumerable instances of such silent saints. In order to gain knowledge, scriptures are not the only source. Intuition, inspiration and grace can also do the trick. One should not get entangled in one's activities, but try to be a witness to them and understand them. If possible one must try to grasp any knowledge they deliver by chance. For that we must be vigilant, because it can happen at any point in time."

Death Of An Artist

EVERYDAY A FEW teenagers would assemble in a small rented room on the bank of the river. Some of them were painters, some poets and playwrights, and some were drama artists. Though they came from different backgrounds, what they had in common connecting them were poverty and no definite source of livelihood. None had regular income, except for a couple of them who worked as elementary school teachers. They sometimes staged a few theatrical events in the villages, enacting plays that either they themselves had written, or plays they translated from work by famous playwrights.

I too was one among these young men in the 'glory' days of my youth, and had written some poetry as well as translated a few famous plays of Brecht, Samuel Beckett, Utpal Dutt, and Badal Sarkar into English from the original languages. Our group with its modern outlook was trying to do something unique, which is a common tendency in this modern age. Nobody is willing to carry on the successful establishments of their forefathers and ancestors, or follow established customs, or complete the well-meant but unfinished work etc. They only want to add their share of undigested vomit in the form of opinions and ideas on dharma, religion, dogmas blah blah . . . blah.

Our group of young men organized plays in that small village as well as in nearby towns. A few of us were existentialists, a few communists, and few were neutral, but no one really had any faith in a well-tested or well-established school of thought. We used to assemble every evening in the room, and all being birds of the same feather, we shared our pleasures and pain with each other. The day we received some money from a magazine for publishing our poetry, play or article, or from sale of a painting, or even from writing a banner, that day would a cause for celebration. On other days we would starve, as none of us were attached to our homes or liked to depend upon them for food. The amount any one of us received for our respective work would then be spent collectively for purchasing plenty of *kallu and kappa* (toddy and tapioca curry), and everybody enjoyed the food sitting together, either chit-chatting or discussing only art-related matters.

Occasionally I would earn twenty five rupees for a poem published in a local weekly, or rarely a hundred or hundred fifty for a semi-classical song or poem broadcast on All India Radio. Another artist received what was considered a good amount of five hundred or thousand, upon sale of his oil paintings. As he had some family commitments, he sent the lion's share of his income to his parents in his village.

Those were the days of my youth that seemed wonderful. In my struggle to establish himself, even though it was for a short period, I spent most of my time in that company, visiting my home only for a few hours. My own people spoke ill of me for mingling with young men of different castes, and for dining with them. But that never bothered me, and I just ignored their comments.

By that time I had obtained a job as sub-editor for a weekly in a nearby town, with a daily salary of ten rupees. Five rupees were spent every day on bus fare to the office and back, and two rupees for food. The chief editor of that weekly was a well-known activist of the communist party who introduced me to books by left-leaning authors. I read Marx, Engels, and such authors. I had now lost touch with the circle of friends from the previous small town, and many of them had also flown far away in search of greener pastures. I now found myself in the company of editors, movie directors, critics, and established writers of that time.

One time I received an 'award' of two hundred and fifty rupees for a poem I entered in a contest organized by another magazine.

This was the first 'big' amount I had received in my life. In fact, I had wanted to purchase a sari for my oldest sister who loved me more than any other in the family, even my parents or other elders. In a very happy mood, I went in search of those remaining from the old group of friends to share the happy news of the award, and to celebrate my achievement with the usual *kallu and kappa* party. My friends told me that this time the regular 'cheap' toddy party would not do, and they purchased a bottle of brandy and good eatables. In an hour or two, all the money had vanished in thin air. I felt terrible, even cursing myself that I had failed to get a sari of a hundred rupees for my sister. Sitting alone in the room in a corner, I wept for my mistake.

Even though he was poor, a well-known film director happened to be a close friend during my days as sub-editor. A staunch communist who lived like a hippy, he had managed to convince a financier to back his movie, and with the help of a few friends and well-wishers he had succeeded in it as well, winning a few international and national awards for his classical work in cinema. He had a habit of incessantly drinking liquor and smoking *ganja*, and moved around carelessly with others, but was a gem of an artist in the field, because of his unique perspective on life and his work. But the relentless onslaught of time makes no exceptions, even for one possessing unusual, unimaginable, and incomparable intelligence or talent. The dictate is that as long as you live on this planet earth, you have to follow the rules of an orderly life, or else pay through your nose. He paid little heed to orderliness in life, and time too did not grant him any respite either for escaping, and took him away from the field of art, and from the friends who loved him. They cursed him plenty in choicest words of filth, because they did not understand that time knows not the value of art, and neither does an artist know the value of life. His intelligence had not helped him in any way to make his life orderly. A few days later, when one of his films was released, he was appreciated with many awards and he and his friends were deep in enjoyment celebrating his award money in a hotel's terrace garden. Swinging in intoxication, he had sat on the parapet wall on the third floor of the hotel and fell to his death. I was not there on the spot, but heard of the news through the media, and was unable to even react for a few days, such was the shock. It was a big struggle to recover from that unexpected loss.

In the meantime, the weekly in which I was working as an editor went into a very bad financial crisis, even fighting for existence. The management finally decided to end the publication, and I thus lost my job and had to return to the village, or rather back to the wall. My disposition had changed too during the past few years due to change of social groups. I was no more in a mood to return to that old group of remaining artistes in the town. Even when I did so rarely, it was to attend a few programs they arranged. By this time I had translated a few plays into English, from the Bengali and German originals, and myself authored a collection of one-act plays, that was compiled and published. I kept myself, or rather liked to remain confined to a room in my old home in the parental village, limiting my activities to reading or writing, or to simply sitting in the agonizing darkness of that hundred-year old house, most of the time brooding in melancholy.

A group of friends in the village decided to form a group, and try their hand at staging the small plays I had written. We began staging small plays, based on contemporary social issues as themes. Those plays were based mostly on folk art, exploring possibilities of presenting pressing social issues in a simple way, minimizing makeup and expenses by using traditional formats. Our youth group comprised of my good friends, or distant relatives from my parental village. It was during this period that the sea change occurred. Whether it was the tepid response to my much-labored work, or whether it was destiny that did not wish me to indulge and entangle myself in meaningless and unproductive activities for which I was not meant—but the heat of repeated defeats in undertakings began at last shaping my inclinations into spiritual ones, into being a *dwija* (twice-born). The *dwija*-oriented impressions were now starting to surface and manifest, overpowering the erstwhile earned *samskaras*. Naturally and without any effort, I was being drawn to spirituality and identifying myself more and more with it. I had failed at staging my plays, because the future had already written a different script for me to act in. How could I possibly succeed with my Director being the much more powerful play-writer? When I recollect the turns He made me take in life, I cannot but pay Him tribute with my tears. My tears of gratitude are the only price I can pay in return for the unconditional and immeasurable grace that has showered upon me, for His driving me into *sanyasa*, the only true and real life anyone could aspire for. This became clear to me only after I started seeing things of this world in the light of His grace. That life of a playwright or director did not last long, and finally abandoning life as an artist, I decided to leave home and village to play the role of a beggar on His stage, the world. And as per His script, I am playing and enjoying it to my heart's content. Certainly the art or artist in me died, but as the obedient actor of my wonderful Master, I was transformed into an eternal artist. Thereafter I stopped acting in the drama of the world, for He placed me under His eternal contract. I love to dance to His tunes, and I love to deliver the dialogs written by Him. I act, and He is the lone spectator. We are just the world.

To Know Is To Be

IT IS NOT an easy task for a disciple to stay with his guru for long, unless he is willing to dissolve his limited ego into the limitless ego of the *gurutatva*, especially during the training periods. Otherwise his limited ego will revolt at every step, preventing the *saadhana* from taking a definite shape. Once the disciple allows his own *laghutvam* (limitedness) to merge with the *gurutvam* (limitless, expanded state) of the guru, it will annihilate and remove the boundaries of ego, his life now flowing easily between the two banks, of disciplines of this world and of the world he wants to attain. But for this to happen, the disciple must undergo vigorous training with utmost vigilance. Of course, if he understands that this tedious training is only for the advancement of his own future spiritual life, then the difficulties involved in the training will not make him lose heart. But instead, if he gives more importance to ego obeying its commands, then he will likely end up in regret, cursing and saying something like—"Oh, why have I given control to an unknown person, who keeps imposing more and more of meaningless rules and regulations."

Life with a guru is like walking on a razor's edge. The quantity and quality of merits earned in our previous births decide the nature of the life with our guru. As the scriptures say, one gets a guru only because of one's *poorva janma sukrutham* (previous meritorious deeds) and only that can lead him to liberation, and free him from the clutches of the cycle of rebirth.

If one's mother and father are to be considered the first gurus, it follows then that the spiritual guru must be an advanced and improved combination of both mother and father roles. But ever since the invasion of certain sensual elements in society, which made enjoyment the primary goal of life, and which cooked up the theory that spirituality and world are distinct and separate, spirituality has become the enemy of the householder's life. It has now become the norm to think of spiritual life and worldly life as two non-intersecting and separate spheres.

Since the past 900 years, gurus have been separated from mother and father. When the father and mother receive the rank of guru they are happy, but when a real guru is brought in, they grow fearful of losing their own importance. When I left my home village as a young innocent boy to live with my guru, I was not educated (and these days no one is) about the true relationship between a seeker and his guru, and unaware of the dangerous pitfalls involved. It is only the guru who can be real mother and father—only when we get a guru do we actually 'take birth' and find our ultimate mother and father.

Since no one's parents want to lose their offspring, the donkey who will work to realize their own broken dreams and unfulfilled ambitions in the future, the parents choose to totally black out the guru from life. We are not aware of the consequences of this black-out philosophy. A famous example is that of the parents of Gautama Buddha. The parents of post-independent India seem to be comfortable with the possibility that their son may turn out to be a liar, cheat, rowdy, pervert, drug or sex addict, and may even enable and support his ventures. But the same parents become sleepless with worry if the son displays an interest in spirituality. That is what happened with me as well.

I was raised with an extroverted and materialistic vision of the environment, parents, brothers, sisters, and friends. I did not have enough lessons in *guru shishya sambandha*. It was only after my initiation that this changed. When I began living with my guru, who I addressed as *'Amma'*, and ONLY BECAUSE OF GOD'S GRACE, I came to realize the meaning of love. I experienced my guru in all roles of friend, brother, sister, father and more than all as mother. The love and affection I enjoyed from '*Amma*,' surpassed what I had experienced from my own parents. I was still in the tender and impressionable teen years then, foolhardy and with naive expectations of life. Worldly relationships which had been fed to me (taught) to me by this world were really hollow in meaning. But when I joined her, my guru, a world by herself—it was in her that I saw the real world, the Universal family.

As stated in the first part of my autobiography, I lived with my Guruji or *Amma*, in the dense forests of Kollur, not far from the famous Mookambika temple in the South Indian state of Karnataka. In those days, Amma camped under a big tree in the forest, a few yards' walk after one crossed the Sauparnika River. It was always dark there due to the dense vegetation, and day and night didn't seem too different. The lush greenery and unpolluted air made for a most inviting and elevating environment, my only source of anxiety being the wild animals. Once after reading the fear in my mind, Amma said, "Fear them not—love them, and they will love you too. Love every being and you will be loved, hate and you will be hated." I learnt the lexicon of love and affection from her. In the nights we stayed only under the tree. Amma slept carefree, not bothered by the ants or insects or even by the odd scorpion and snake that sometimes visited our 'bedroom' beneath the tree under the open skies. But before getting ready to lay down to sleep just near Amma's holy feet, I used to clean the ground there, every day. She would watch this with a wry smile, then finally one day said, "If you must clean, why not clean up the entire Earth, and not just this six-foot piece of land that you are using for your pleasure." I was a bit taken aback at first, but after that remark, I stopped cleaning that spot near Amma. Never did even a small ant bite me, nor was there ever any disturbance from a forest creatures either.

For ages, the Sauparnika River has been revered as a *teertham* (a holy bathing place) by devotees visiting Mookambika. They carry away its holy water in containers to keep in their homes. And as other people living there do, we too used it. It is a small but elegant and beautiful river flowing down the Kudajadri Hill (where *Adi Shankara* had done *tapas* to bring her down from the top of the hills). We would be at the river for our daily ablutions, bathing, drinking etc. Whenever we went down there to bathe, I would wash Amma's *'alphi,'* which was the only cloth she wore, and give her a good bath as well. She taught me a saadhana that involved sitting in neck-deep water. Fish would bite at my body while I sat for long periods in the river doing my *japa*, with no body consciousness. Once Amma said, "That is good. They (the fish) are getting something to eat. Be there. Similarly when you enter *samsara,* make your body useful for the welfare of others. This was the way of her training. An *avadhoota* must be carefree about his body and not have any attachment to it, as it is merely an instrument of service to others. She inspired me with the courage and ability to serve with no self-interest or sense of ownership of body, even when it was suffering acutely.

Once a shop owner, who was running a small teashop near the Mookambika temple, came crying to Amma. His business was doing poorly, the shop was in shambles, and he was sunk in debt. For some time Amma kept silent. One evening Amma asked me to follow her, and entering the dilapidated shop, she went into the kitchen. She started urinating in front of the wood stove (in those days firewood was used), and as if nothing had happened, she started walking out. I felt very uncomfortable at this behavior but dared not ask her for reasons behind her action, in fear of getting a few blows from her walking stick. But I was astounded when after a few months that shop keeper visited Amma to convey with gratitude that everything had turned around. His business had gained momentum and improved hugely right after Amma's visit, and he had now constructed a permanent structure. He had brought a few *daal vadas* but Amma did not accept them and said, "Never offer a bribe or pay for the favors received from me. Just toss the *vadas* into the Sauparnika, and let the fishes lunch well today." For a human being living in today's computer age, such things appear absurd, but keep in mind this: what science can see and offer to the world is infinitesimal. There are fourth-dimensional activities of people like Amma, whose actions, words, and movements cannot be brought under scientific scrutiny.

But each word, gesture, action, and movement coming from an elevated soul such as Amma is always result-oriented. Any prejudiced scientist attempting to decipher or codify actions of such souls will be making futile efforts in vain.

Even an *Arjuna* needed to demonstrate his achievements by winning the Mahabharata[16] war. After staying with Amma for about six months as a *sanyasi*, my mind started comparing the life of a householder with that of a *sanyasi*. Amma had never let me feel unloved, her love was divine rather than worldly. Yet I had been feeling some listlessness, and yearned to see my parents in my native village. It may have been homesickness, and perhaps a desire to show them my exalted state as a *sanyasi*. Amma observed my mood and asked, "What is going on in your mind?" I told her of my intention to visit my parents but she laughed at my foolishness, and asked, "Do you realize what you are saying, my boy? After leaving home and parents to become a *sanyasi* (I have only just initiated you into *sanyasa*) one is not supposed to look back or meet them, as there are chances to develop attachments." I was not aware of this. But being an ignorant youth, my mind was disturbed from thinking of my village and parents. I was sitting near Amma under the big tree that was our shelter, when she called me near her and embracing me said, "My son, you have had millions of parents in previous births, do you remember them or cry for them? This *sanyasa* is verily a new birth to you. Being a '*sarva sanga parityagi*,' a *sanyasi* should never look back, homeward. Look! I am here as your mother, father, brother, sister, friend and guru. I am everything to you here, worry not anymore. Kill that very thought with the sword of *asanga*." But I was in tears, trying in vain to control them. Amma then said, "Look here at me, and

---

16 The Mahabharata, one of the two major epics of ancient Indian written in Sanskrit language, is a narrative of the major war between the Kaurava and Pandava princes. Arjuna was one of the five Pandava princes and Duryodhana was one of the one hundred Kaurava princes. The famous Bhagvad Gita was imparted to Arjuna by Krishna.

wipe out your tears." I looked up at her, and there was no limit to my wonder—standing before me was the mother who had given birth to me! I was lost in deep silence, and then fell down at her holy feet, holding them for a long time. With a laugh Amma said, "Foolish boy, I will be with you forever and ever. Do not cry any more. Remember, none is yours other than me. Be with me, I will always be with you." It has been only that assurance of Amma that has kept me living through this painful life of bitter experiences and serious illnesses.

The ways of teaching of my guru to her *sishya* were different. She never lectured to me, but taught me by pin-pointing practical ways of doing things, which I had to observe, study, and apply to my life. As she doted on me, she would never allow me to go to collect *bhiksha* (daily food), and she would bring it from the temple herself and feed me with her own hands. When she brought the *bhiksha,* she would do the *pancha maha yagna* of first feeding the ants, birds etc., then me and only then would she herself eat (detailed description given in the volume 1 of my autobiography). With that wonderful experience, I learned the lesson not to eat anything without sharing first (*yagna*). Continuing to this day, I follow the same practice of taking food only after feeding all—servants, guests, disciples etc. during all programs convened in the *ashram*.

During one heavy monsoon season during my days by the Sauparnika, the river was overflowing and it became impossible to cross. We sat drenched under that big tree in the open with no shelter other than sky. It continued to rain throughout the night. Looking at the river I worried how we would go to the other side to collect bhiksha. The rain finally stopped, and the sun came out but the earth as well as the trees were soaked. I was shivering a little because of drenching through the night.

Amma walked over twice to the Sauparnika to see if the water flow had reduced or not. The floods would usually come as a flash as the water coming from the hills moved downward quickly. It seemed impossible to cross the river as the flow of water was in full strength. I was feeling hungry too. I could hear the temple bell inviting *bhikshus* and *yatris* to collect their due of *bhiksha*. My Guruji glanced my face and shivering body. She looked around, put her hands in the tin *dabba* in which she collected food for us from temple. I knew that it would be empty since she washed it every day after we ate. But to my amazement, she took out four bananas from it and gave me three, keeping one. She asked me to eat and held on to the one banana she had in her hand till I had finished eating the three bananas, and as soon as I was done, she crushed the banana in her hand and put it back into her tin *dabba*.

I was wondering, and did not understand what was happening. By now my stomach was full, but I felt bad that Amma had not eaten the banana which had been in her hand. I looked into the tin box, and was astonished to discover that it was now empty! Months later, when I was getting ready to leave her for *tapas* in the Himalayas, Amma taught me how to accomplish this feat, if food ever became unavailable, or in an emergency for survival.

Gurus will never allow their children to suffer mentally, physically or in any other way, being dearer to the guru than *prana* itself. Disciples may receive scolding or an occasional beating for wrong doings, but really only for their own benefit in both materialistic and spiritual life. From lack of maturity or poor intellectual capacity, we disciples may foolishly and ignorantly jump to conclude that the guru must be unfit, seeing him or her always in a negative mood. It is important to keep open our eyes and be attentive, so as not to miss the lessons being imparted.

It is unwise for someone to attempt to fathom or appraise a guru with a mind ill-trained in well-established, well-tested, and proven methods of investigative logic, or knowledge of human behavior and evolution. Supporting an ignorant and arrogant mind is like supporting our own evil *Duryodhana*[17]-like son, just because he happens to be our son. Such a Duryodhana will not only not let us live in peace, but will also destroy all our 'ancestors', or our *poorva punya* (accumulated merits), a two-fold loss. The

---

17 Duryodhana is a villainous character in the epic Mahabharatha.

adventure of estimating the guru is like trying to measure the ocean with a spoon, or using one's fingers to count the stars in the sky or like measuring the earth with a broken yardstick. It takes the disciple to an oblivion of non-belief or half-belief, a state of doubt that is verily destruction (*samshayatma vinashyati*) which will result in a series of hell-like, helpless existences (births) of negative experiences. The scriptures say, '*vishwaasam (belief) bala daayakam* (strength provider)'—only a staunch belief in the guru and application of the teachings can take anyone to realization. The *sishya* or disciple should take care lest the bacteria of doubt infect the element of faith in him. Maintaining that faith is itself a full time job for a *sadhaka*. That faith should be like the breath in the body. I would like to part my experience with such a situation in my life as an ardent sadhak, but prone to ever ready misleading, misguiding, exploitative, and manipulative elements, energies, powers, and factors around.

I had been standing on the banks of the river Sauparnika for a long time, looking into some incomprehensible void without any outward consciousness. When I came back to awareness, it was about sunset. Amma used to go near the Mookambika temple often—it was her practice to paying obeisance from outside the temple, in consonance with her state of awareness. On such walks in the evening, she never took anyone with her, and would ask me to be at the riverside doing *japa* or *dhyana*. On one such visit, a person from the Sri Ramakrishna Yogashram came running to me saying that someone had tried to hurt Amma with a stick. I immediately ran fast towards where Amma was sitting.

She was sitting by the roadside just holding her right hand with her left. When I asked what happened she simply smiled. A few people were standing around, and from their facial expressions I could easily make out that something vile had happened. But Amma did not say anything even though I kept pressing her. One among the people standing there said, "Swamiji, Amma was trying to take a few bananas to feed the old cow standing on the other side of the road, but the shopkeeper hurt her with a stick." Amma used to take bananas or anything she pleased, from the shops to give to cows, dogs or to children moving around the road. Never previously had any of the shopkeepers objected, denied, or resisted her actions, as all knew very well that her mere presence near their shop would be like a great benediction or blessing on them. In fact they would be thrilled as they knew business would shoot up with such doings of Amma. It seemed that this shop was new and the shopkeeper was unaware of Amma's way of doing things with others. I got wildly angry, and felled the shopkeeper with a few blows. Amma came running to stop me from doing so, but by this time people standing there had lifted him from the road. They showed me his right hand which had gone stiff like a log of wood. One of them said, "As soon as this man hit Amma, his hand got paralyzed. Now he is not able to move it." The shopkeeper was crying out to her to pardon his mistake. My anger was not coming down. In fact I wanted to thrash him further. Amma was annoyed with me and said, "Why are you bent on punishing this poor shopkeeper- after all it was only a natural reaction. See his hand!" She seemed unperturbed, as if nothing had happened. Unmindful of her own hands, and with all *'karuna bhava'* Amma went to the shopkeeper, and taking his hands in her hand, massaged them gently and lovingly, then said, "All this happened on account of a few bananas, which I wanted to feed that hungry cow. Go now and feed that cow a few bananas, and keep doing it every day, you will soon be all right." He obeyed, taking a bunch of bananas and fed the cow. From that day onwards I heard he was doing it without fail, as if it were an order from Amma. His hand had become normal now. Just one day's forbearance made the shopkeeper a devotee. I often argued with Amma about such actions of hers, like lifting eatables from shops and feeding them to others. Her logic was rather unusual and profound, "Nothing is personal or can be owned by anyone in this world. Everything belongs only to the One *Iswara*. Anyone unwilling to share with his fellow beings or with needy persons, materials such as food or clothing that really belong to Him (hoarding because of greed), will surely suffer and be reborn as well to live a life of suffering. So my act was in order to help create this awareness in that man, and to bring him out from his illusion. None of you could understand that I only do such acts to others for bettering their lives." I felt ashamed that I had not understood the secret of the vision behind my Guruji's actions.

Once one of the families in Mookambika, who were Amma's staunch devotees, invited her home for *bhiksha*. Usually Amma never accepted such invitations, subsisting only on the food distributed in the temple for *sadhus* and *yatris*. But to my astonishment, she graciously accepted this invitation and asked me to follow her too.

They had prepared a meal fit for royalty with all devotion (rice, *sambaar*, curry, *paapad* etc.). After serving the meal on a plantain leaf, they prayed that Amma should commence eating. But to my wonder, she mixed together all the food on the leaf, and divided it into five portions. She then made the usual whistling sound and then who knew from where they had appeared, but a dog, cat, and crow came into the dining room. Giving them their share of food, she then took one portion outside to feed a calf waiting there. She re-entered the room, and then lastly gave the fifth part to the Brahmin who had served the food on the leaf. From the expression on the Brahmin's face, it was clear that he did not appreciate this action, especially since the dog had eaten directly from Amma's plantain leaf. Amma asked him to share his portion equally among his wife and other family members, and he did so.

After this was over, she then sat near me and instructed me to begin meditation, "Sit there and meditate. Don't move." More than two hours passed thus. My mind was gripped with the desire to drink some water. Finally she asked me to get up and follow her. When we reached the bank of the Sauparnika, Amma gave me a big kick from behind, and I fell headlong into the river. I heard her, "Drink, drink as much as you can. So that in the future there should be no thirst at all during your *saadhana*." Without drinking even a drop of water I emerged from the river and came up to Amma, tears overflowing my eyes. Amma said, "*Bete*, during *saadhana* never yield to other diverting thoughts that try to enter.

Hunger, thirst etc. are all only mind's play, in order to keep you in body consciousness. Forgetting body, mind and intellect, try to be just a witness to what is happening. Never make a pretence of saadhana. Let it happen, and be a witness."

She had taught me this valuable lesson in a very practical but unusual way, the memory of which will always be evergreen.

The Use And Throw Guruji

THEY ACCUSED ME of being an escapist. They said I was a runaway from *samsara*, afraid to face worldly life with all its minus and plus points. Some of those 'lion-hearted' people, or rather 'loin-hearted' people (who were in *samsara* from the urging of their loins) said I was unfit for married life. Some insinuated that I had taken to *sanyasa* due to a failed love affair. Everybody had his own story to tell about me, commensurate with the level of reach of his consciousness. Their preaching and comments, edited and updated regularly, and unsolicited advice and criticism, were devoid of any true value. I waited, and waited for long to prove to these people who I really was. It took more than thirty years to show them my real face—the face of an *avadhoota*, who lives always only for the sake of others, in every moment and breath. Finally when they read my previous book, my autobiography, 'The Pyre of the Destined,' then of course some of them changed their minds and called me up to say, "Sorry, we were late in realizing your real face." It took more than thirty years for my life to unfold to that point. As to the circumstances of the unfolding—the what, why, when and where: it involved living in bitter hardship in the Himalayan hills, most often with nothing to eat except for Ganga water, and with the barest minimum of clothing and shelter. It involved intense '*tapas*' in deep silence for years and years, till the reaching of the ultimate reality. I returned, filled with energy, to fulfill the wishes of the people who were deep in *samsara*. Now all of them, whose 'wills' and wishes have been fulfilled because of that accumulated energy of mine, are keeping silent. I have had so many such experiences with people—people who have 'used' my energy to fulfill their needs, and then thrown me out of their lives, is this not true?

During my stay at Kurnool, in Andhra Pradesh, a disciple came to me one morning, accompanied by his weeping wife. I was engaged in *pooja* at the time. Getting up from *pooja*, I asked them the reason for their gloom. The disciple told me that his wife's brother had met with an accident while driving his car, and was in serious condition. Without a second thought, as I always did in such situations I decided to go with them to see the suffering person and pray to the 'Mother' for his well-being. I took a banana which had been offered to 'Amma' during my *pooja* and left my room with them.

His body was fully broken, and the doctors were not hopeful of him returning to normalcy. I requested permission from the attending physician to touch the patient and offer him the *prasadam* of banana which I had brought. The patient was surrounded by his wife, children and other relatives. I asked them to keep a distance, and except for his wife and another relative, everyone else then left the room. Touching the patient, I prayed to my Guruji and to the 'Mother Goddess' to save him so there would be no tears on the faces of his wife and children. I fed him a little part of the *prasadam* and left the room.

In the evening I received a call from his wife who in an elated voice informed me that the patient, who was to have had an unexpected demise, was now sitting up and drinking tea. After some time, the attending doctor also called me up and asked, "What in heaven's could be the reason for this miraculous recovery?" I told them that these were not miracles. If one had staunch faith and strong belief in 'Amma' such things naturally happened. But the doctor was not one to buy my story—he needed irrefutable, scientific, step-by-step explanation of this incident. I told him, "See, that man was suffering. Sufferings are the result of negative actions. I had transferred into him some of the accumulated positive earnings of my positive actions, from my long *saadhana* in the Himalayan hills. Thus the negativity in that suffering person was totally removed through the positivity I poured in, in my act of touching him. It is as simple as a glassful of water changing to milk—when one continues to pour milk into the glass, after some time the water will change to milk. But for this, the healer must have a heavy stock of positive energy. Then the doctor countered with another question, "Swamiji, when you are healing a person who is suffering because of his '*karmas*', are you not going against the laws of nature?" I replied, "Yes, of course, it is. But I am here to weigh the utility of that person to his family, society, nation etc. against my use to society. As he is more useful to his family and to the society through his physical body than I am, I made the choice of transferring energy. I am 'useless' to society in this physical body, since my work arena is in the astral planes where this physical body is totally useless. Moreover being in that transcendental state, I do not have a family setup wherein I could have channelized energies towards a higher purpose. So the energy conserved in my physical body can be used for a genuine, needy, and deserving person. In going against the laws of karma, since I am taking his '*karma phalas*' upon myself, I have to suffer for as long a time as that person was supposed to suffer." Laws of nature are not changed but something is paid from outside as a helping hand. To perform my duties, the physically accumulated energy is immaterial. Moreover I hope you know that no energy can be saved. Just like electricity cannot saved, if you do not use it, it will go to waste. Money, mind, and time all like that too. My logic is not to waste the accumulated positive energy at the time of my death." The doctor was silent for a few minutes at hearing this and murmured, "It is difficult to understand people like you." The big issue with the scientific education that is spoon-fed to today's youth is that they appoint themselves as the all-knowing custodians of society, when actually they are mere pawns in the hands of the distant capitalists who are greedy, corrupt and anti-humanitarian by nature. The youth of today are all being driven by the greed of the perverted industrialists, in the name of good salary.

I suffered for eighteen months as a result of that karmic transfer. The person was discharged from hospital in a week or so after having recovered fully contrary to everyone's expectations. But then onwards I started suffering with back pain, body ache, and other symptoms and syndromes. That person did develop a faith in God, and in the existence of an invisible power governing the universe, and in me, of course, and became my disciple.

A few such people are however *avasarvadis*—hardcore opportunists, or victims of greed due to their new exposure to wealth, with hearts of clay. They used to come to me, make use of and exploit me, or spiritual entities like me with hearts of butter, looking for us in temples, pilgrimage centers etc. Then they would run away from the scene once and for all. This came to light when a few years later, we were considering starting a project for rehabilitation of street children and economically deprived children. For their medical and educational needs, and for providing them nutritious food and other essentials, I was working hard to generate the resources and necessary funds. To kickstart the project, the plan was to construct at least a few thatched sheds for the time being. Though in the figurative sense, I was dancing on the streets singing the songs of the poor, all these people who had benefited from me, clapped their hands and enjoyed the dance but never thought of dropping a single penny into my desperate begging bowl. At last, the same few disciples who have all along been with me in all my foolish endeavors, pulling me back from the quicksand of social service, now came forward to create a 'trust', an organization which is now taking care of the project. I had been running here and there, and 'pick-pocketing' my disciples for amounts to face the needs. I now requested the very same person, who had got a new lease on life thanks to me and the Mother, to also donate a little to the Trust to meet the construction needs according to his ability. He very politely and diplomatically told the treasurer of the trust that he would definitely donate a good amount. But to my surprise, nothing has been delivered to date. The work is now complete and the work of rehabilitation of the poor commenced in small scale but that 'rich' man never turned up, nor even enquired about it, in fear of being asked to donate something for his downtrodden brethren of society. When I think of people like him, the only conclusion I can make is that they are really contributing in some way to the work of nature, by adding to the burden of sins so that *Kaliyuga* comes to an end earlier than expected.

Though this was not a demonstration of a lack of sense of gratitude, it definitely showed how human beings attach an enormous importance to money. If I gave you a 500 rupee note, you will definitely value it and may say, "Oh, my Guruji has given me 500 rupees." You might go around saying you received such an amount from Guruji as *prasadam*. But you may not have the intelligence to value the *aashirvadam* or the help given to you in the form of spiritual energy. This lack of appreciation is because you yourself have no knowledge about the mechanism of obtaining such energy. So how could you respect or feel that invisible energy accumulated by Guruji through long years of tapasya? You may casually say that you recovered by the ashirvad of Guruji, but without really understanding the meaning of that *aashirvadam*. The materialists have taught us to value money as the only higher energy but it is not so. Money is the last corrupt energy in this creation beyond which no corruption exists. So one should not make the blunder of assigning ultimate value to money among all energies. The power to bestow *aashirvadam* accumulates from living a life of *saadhana*, while money is accumulated by wasting the life through years and years of lies used for your selfish purposes.

P.S.: As soon as I completed this chapter, a few of my disciples heard a reading of it and raised a relevant question through one among them. "Guruji, tell us, are you expecting something in return when you do such *sevas* for others? If so, is it not hypocrisy?" This was a genuine question. In reply I said it was not done out of expectation but was an effort to create another *aashirvad*-giver like me for the coming generation. Since this body will not be available to the coming generation, I have to find someone else possessing capacity for the same kind of tapas, and teach him how to acquire the same *aashirvad*-providing energy to deliver to his contemporary society. When a hen lays an egg, you have to feed and take care of her, and wait for the next day to collect the next egg. If in a hurry however you cut open the hen to get that egg, you will lose all eggs in that one act. So I expect that you people will join together to prepare someone to become a *sadhak*, *tapasvi*, or *sadhu*, so that he will be able to bless your children in the way that I have tried to bless you wholeheartedly. If you destroy the system itself, then who will be there to make your children aware of possibility of *aashirvads*, blessings etc. So other than expecting you to keep the system intact for the future, I had no expectations from anybody when I did *seva*. I studied, digested, and was trained well in the practice of the dictum, '*karmanye vadhikarsthey, ma phaleshu kadachana*' of the Bhagawad Gita, as early as the tenth class. Also 'give and take' is the law of nature. When you accept some favors from someone, don't you repay him? If you cut the tree after you have eaten its fruit, what will your children then do—will they have to now plant a new tree in order to eat fruit? If so, they will no more be bound to call you their parents or honor you. You will not deserve any divinity, having created a situation like the law of the jungle. Hence, think not only just about getting blessings for yourself, but arrange some similar system of *seva* serving others to save yourself from the grip of the hands of *runa*. If I really had been after money as you esteemed souls seem to think, by this time I would have been at least a *crorepati*, married to a Keralite damsel, with chubby children to play with. But I have never cared to hoard the papers of the Reserve Bank. So I expect that one thing from all of you in return. I am sure you people will not like your children going childless, and for me too it is painful to see the sanyasi system going extinct, for then the curse of rishis will be upon me and on you all too. So just observe my day-to-day life, try to analyze my words and deeds, and then decide and conclude for yourself what it means to you in your life. This is all the explanation I can offer." That disciple sat quietly for some time and said, "Sorry that such a thought came to me, it was from ignorance. Now it is clear to me. Sorry for doubting you." I said that lack of awareness, and ignorance of something were entirely different things. If you are unaware of certain things, awareness will be provided and the previous mistakes pardoned. But if you argue ignorance to escape your mistakes, the punishment will be compounded: this law must be kept in mind for all religious and spiritual matters. Lest one day you be forced to pay through the nose for simple oversights.

Where You Are, There I Am

THE FORESTS OF *Mookambika* were densely vegetated and replete with different kinds of wild animals, snakes, and birds, all the ingredients of a wilderness. The river Sauparnika flows between the small temple village and this dense forest, separating them. There exists no habitat of permanent nature in that forest, and few people other than a few meditating *sadhakas*, or a few nature-loving pilgrims. It was early in the morning, and the temple bells were yet to ring to invite the devotees for the *aarathi darshan*. After completing my daily routine of bathing etc., I was awaiting dawn. I was sitting on the bank of the Sauparnika across from the temple, thought-free, not meditating but immersed in myself. I could see Amma (my beloved Guruji, Avadhoota Taramayee) on the other side of the river looking towards me as if beckoning me. By reflex I crossed the river and reached hurriedly towards her but to my surprise she started walking away in long strides as if escaping from me. She turned in the direction of the shukla theertham and I too followed her.

Amma then sat down on a stone near the shukla theertham, remaining silent, and I too followed like an obedient dog sitting near its master. Yes, I was always content to be that, though never did she regard me that way like a rough master might treat his dog, but always doted on me, pouring her affection with a gentle look or a tender touch, and fed me like a loving mother. Suddenly Amma spoke—"*Ab tum sanyasi hogaye na, mera peecha chodkar door jao.*" (Now that you are a sanyasi, you must quit following me and you must move away, far from here). It was a shock to hear those words, how could that be? Why was Amma repeatedly asking me to leave her? Perhaps reading my mind she said—"*Yei, tum ko jaana hei. Door kahin jaakar apni saadhana karo.*" (Yes, you have to leave and continue doing *saadhana*, but far away from here). I desperately tried to convince Amma with tears in my eyes that I was not in a position to leave her. She replied saying, "*Rona dhona sab bevakoofi hei. Aaj nahi to kal tum ko jaana hee hei. Jitni jaldi ho sakey apane pairon par khada hokar dikhao, vahi meri iccha hei.*" (All this weeping and lamentation is foolishness. One day or the other, of course you will be leaving me, my only desire is that you stand on your two legs and become independent as soon as possible). And actually at one point I did entertain many thoughts of the Himalayas, even wanting to go there, but those had been the moods and fancies of a novice *sadhaka,* and they had all gone with the winds after my long stay with Amma. I was like a six-month old babe in these days, not wanting to leave Amma even for a few minutes. When she had given me everything I needed— love that of a mother, discipline that of a father, affection that of a brother, sister, or friend, and the mentoring of a guide, how would it be possible for me to leave her? For Amma was everything to me, at every moment. She stood up, and moving swiftly like a whirlwind, vanished into the woods. I wanted to get up and run behind her, but it was as if someone had chained my legs—it was impossible for me to get up or move. I was not aware how many hours I sat thus, as I slowly began losing external consciousness. Neither meditating, nor in deep sleep or dreaming, I was aware of the being of the 'Self.' I was experiencing the song of silence inside me vibrating all around, forming the echo of *omkara* from within. I was not visualizing anything in that state, nor as a witness, but was in the depth of experiencing a scene enacted by me. Around me hovered hundreds of people with faces identical to mine. They all appeared to be carrying a stretcher-like thing made of bamboo, like the one that Hindus use to carry a dead body to the cremation ground. I looked around—everybody had the same face as mine. Some of them then came forward, lowered the stretcher near me and lifting my body on it, placed it on the stretcher and tied it with some rope-like thing. The others who were like my replicas in *roopa* (form) and *bhava* (devotion), started to dance around me who was laying down on that chariot. Now the scene abruptly changed to one of darkness, where those hundreds of my replicas were now dancing wildly holding flaming country torches. The *thaalam* or rhythm sounded familiar, it was the *thaalam* of dissolution, wild and furious, of drums beating all around me. Then just as suddenly, everything stopped, and there was the deepest silence with nobody near. I was clueless and baffled at this experience, when suddenly I felt the comforting touch of a palm rolling over my head. I knew it must belong to none other than my Amma who had affectionately caressed my head for a few seconds. And there was not even a trace of the entire incident: I was still sitting at the same spot, shukla theertham, where I had been sitting since dawn.

I glanced around to find Amma sitting nearby on the same stone, looking at me. I was wondering and groping for an explanation as to what had just happened a few seconds before and looked to her face questioningly. Amma said, *"Onnumilla, oru anubhavam maatram, nee peydikkanda, nee evide undo, njanum avide undu"* (That was nothing but an experience and there is no need to be afraid—for wherever you find yourself, I shall also be present). I was not satisfied with her answer and needed more explanation. But the temple bells were ringing inviting sadhus and pilgrims for collecting *prasaadam* and so Amma picked up her tin container and stood up to move towards the temple. I remained there, lost in thought, trying to interpret my experience. Seeing this, with a smile Amma asked if I had got anything out of those visuals. I pouted and shook my head. Amma giggled a little and asked me to repeat whatever I had visualized just a while ago. Composing myself, I slowly recounted them in sequence. She then started her explanation, asking me, "Tell me how many you's, did you see in the visuals?" I replied,

1. The first me was on the pyre.
2. The second me—there were a lot of me's dancing.

3. The third me was watching the other two me's—the one on the pyre, and the many who were dancing around.

4. The fourth one who was witnessing all the other three me's.

"Exactly!" Amma exclaimed and said, "Yes, that is indeed what you saw—the four you's of 'you'. What this implies then my boy, is that the first 'you' laying on the pyre was your body in which the ignorance was living till now. It is now dead. Secondly, the many you's dancing around were all the impressions of the previous births that want to re-enter the body, but unable to do so. They were trying to make the physical body get life again, but failing. The third 'you' watching all these, was the liberated 'you' after taking the sanyasi order but not freed fully. The fourth 'you', the basis for all these three you's, is the real You. It is just a spectator and not the partaker of any of these things. Only in his presence do all the other three come into being. It is the one ever perfect, and unaffected by such things."

I was spellbound and asked Amma why I had 'returned'. She replied saying that it was because I had *rishi runa*, debt owed to the *rishis*. This was why she was asking me to go, and to give the same message to the world. She told me that when one of my disciples came to me to experience the same oneness of *atma*, I would be fully free of that *runa*, and until then I would have to remain in the world. I told her that was too much of a punishment, now that I clearly knew and had experienced that I was not the body but the spirit, and asked why I should again be left in the lurch in this world. It would now be much too painful for me to live in this world. Amma replied that I would not be able to help that, it was the order of the Lord. Unless I made at least one person understand this, I could not be freed from *rishi runa*, and even the great Adi Sankaracharya had not been able to do that. So I was to go out into the world and to preach to them the truth that they were not their bodies but the spirit, and try to stop them to the extent possible, from running too much behind sensual enjoyment.

I was becoming intimidated at all this, at the thoughts of how I was going to pass the days from now on, and who I would impart all this to for getting freedom from *rishi runa*. Amma came near and caressing my head, said, "Don't worry boy, install me in your heart. I will be with you wherever you are. I will see to it that it gets done." I still await the one who will be able to get it from me, while I linger around here among the householders. So far no one has come, and the weighty wait still continues.

Another Purascharan At Narmada

I RETURNED ONCE AGAIN to the Narmada, with the intention to stay there for three months to do another *purascharan* on the *Srividya Shodashi* mantra. It was just past *Guru Poornima* and I had been at my Jammu Ashram for a few weeks. That year I was not in the mood to go for *Chaturmas deeksha,* and thought that I should use the Chaturmas for another *purascharan* instead.

As usual I came to the Markandeya Sanyas Ashram, where I met Swami Ramanandji Maharaj, the head and founder, and well-known, universally accepted scholar of our time. He loves and accepts me as one among his inner circle associates. I conveyed to him my intention of doing the *purascharan,* and asked for accommodation. With great affection and respect, I was allotted a room. It was to be shared with somebody though, and he was helpless regarding this, since there were a lot of *sanyasis* staying there to attend Swamiji's daily classes on *Vedanta*. I have noticed that, in no other ashram in India do so many *sadhakas* congregate at one place, and receive proper and exact guidance for interpretation of spiritual texts. They are mostly young *sadhakas* who want to study, but sometimes even *mathaadhishas* (head of the mutt), who want to groom their successors, send their disciples here to get proper exposure on spirituality. But I was not keen on sharing a room with three persons, being sure that my *japa purascharan* would be undisturbed only I stayed alone. So with the help of another known swamiji, and Ramanandji Maharaj's consent, I began searching for some other suitable accommodation. Finally after two to three days' search I found a place on the other shore of the Narmada. This *ashram* was in the name of Anandamayi Maa, world-renowned saint of our time and well-known both in her own capacity as well her association with the Nehru family as their guru. She shed the mortal coil only in the eighties. The head of this *ashram* was one Swami Atmaswaroopananda, a direct disciple of Maa Anandamayi, better known as Kedar Baba among Srividya *sadhakas*. As directed, I approached him to make my request for accommodation. We were sitting in an open area facing the Narmada. Our conversation at some point went to the topic of my *saadhana* and Himalayan life etc.—whether it was out of curiosity, or an intention to test me, I am not sure but it did happen. This ashram is in a peaceful, picturesque location affording solitude, away from crowds and markets. Maa Anandamayi's Mandir, Shiv Mandir, and the few rooms have been carved out of the hill. I sent a mental e-mail praying to my Guruji, to make this *baba* grant me permission for stay, as the chances looked bleak. If Maa Narmada and my Guruji, Maa Tara didn't will it, no amount of convincing the Baba would work. Baba was at this place rarely, staying mostly at the Indore ashram, also in Maa Anandamayi's name. During the interview, all of a sudden Baba asked me, "Are you from Gyanganj?" I kept quiet, as I was not supposed to reveal my identity. In a ploy to divert his attention, I brought Baba's notice to a *sadhu* sitting on the other shore, washing his hands and legs. I asked Baba, "Can you make that *sadhu* get up without calling out to him, or without any gestures?" Baba shook his head, saying, "Oh! That would be impossible!" He retorted asking me in turn, "Can you? Can you do it?" I replied, out of reflex, "Baba, aren't you saints always saying that it is all one *chaitanya* that pervades everywhere equally? If that is indeed true, then the chaitanya that 'I' am is also sitting there in the form of that *sadhu*. And if that is so, if I stand up, then that sadhu must also stand up." What prompted me to do so? I closed my eyes for a few seconds, then opened them again for a few seconds, looking intensely at the *sadhu*, whispering in my mind, "Get up, I say. Get up, get up." When I did this, that *sadhu* also got up mechanically, and sat down as soon as I sat as well. Baba, now disturbed, stood up and did *namaskaars* to my feet and asked, "Now please tell me, how is this possible?" I replied, "It is just a simple matter. I merely sent him my thoughts by vibrations, accompanied with an instruction, to get up. He got up. Before I sat down, I sent the same vibrations again telling him to sit. That is all." A few minutes passed with Baba in silence. And he then granted me permission to stay there for my 12th *puracharan*!! Baba called his Brahmachari (Kanaiah), and instructed him to make arrangements as per my needs, for stay in the cave beneath the Maa Anandamayi temple. Baba had previously used it for his *saadhana* and it was connected to a room on the bottom storey, just under Maa's feet. I was happy to get this suitable place for *saadhana*. It was the day of *panchami* and I decided to begin *saadhana* on *ashtami*. I came back to Markandeya Ashram and gave Swami Ramanandaji Maharaj the good news of my getting a place of my choice, with the necessary conditions for proper *saadhana*, and returned to Anandamayi Ashram immediately. Though Baba had been planning to return to the Indore Ashram the next day itself, at my request he agreed to delay it till *ashtami* day. On *ashtami* morning, I took my *sankalpa* at the Narmada, and with Baba's blessings, started my *japa purascharan*. He then left for Indore giving instructions to the staff to cater to my needs as if they were his. In addition to me, there were only two or three other persons staying there. One of the servants cooked food for all. I had only one meal a day, and just a cup of tea in the morning and evening. I tried to maximize the time spent doing *japa*. Even though the cave had electric lighting, the small gap in the door was enough to let in air and light. I used to do *japa* every day for at least fifteen hours.

Maa's grace had been evident through it all, right from securing the place to finishing the *purascharana* satisfactorily: a seamless flow of grace from the two mothers, Maa and Narmada. Everything went smoothly and just as I wished on those days. Every morning I would sit on the river banks for *japa* till the sun got too hot, then would return to the cave and continue the *japa* till lunchtime. In the evening I would again start *japa* to carry on till late night. Over a month passed thus. Baba returned to the ashram from Indore and I had discussions with him on my incomplete research work on *Srividya*. The research was on the vibrations of *bindu*. Baba helped me a lot with inputs in theory, plenty of encouragement with due appreciation. Thereupon I decided to continue the research work after completing the running *purascharan*.

One day we decided upon doing daily *Sri Chakra Shodashi homam* in the night time, till the completion of the *purascharan*. Brahmachari Kanaiah and Baba started constructing a big *havan kund* in an open area near the ashram on the Narmada bank. On an auspicious night, Kanaiah and I initiated the homam, since Baba was absent. I would recite the *Shodashi Mantra* and Kanaiah would offer the *aahutis*. Later, this Brahmachari became a good friend during my stays in Omkareshwar and Indore.

Once when I was walking through the ashram courtyard, I fell down due to the surface being slippery. My left hand was badly injured, and hurting as if it had been broken into pieces. One of my disciples, Dr. Raoji, was called in from Dhar (near Indore). Suspecting a fracture, he insisted that I go to Indore with him to get an X-ray. I was reluctant as that would definitely disturb my *japa saadhana*. So Dr. Raoji plastered my left hand, asking to keep it for three weeks. But there was no sign of the pain coming down after some days of nursing and medication. And though it was becoming almost unbearable, I persevered with the *saadhana* through the pain.

Unto Grace! I completed my *purascharan* in ninety days, in the prescribed time. I began getting ready to leave for my Jammu Ashram, but Baba was not happy to bid me farewell and let me go. He was persuading me to stay with him at Indore Ashram for some time more, where I could make use of his big library for my research. As I too was not in a hurry, I conceded to his loving insistence. I accepted his proposal with courtesy and stayed at the Indore Anandamayi Ashram. One of my *Srividya* disciples Swami Brahmendran was also staying at that Ashram during those days.

He was very helpful to me, in all aspects. I was introduced to many devotees of Baba, and a few of them including Ashok Dubey and Purushotham took *Srividya Deeksha* from me. Everyday I spent many hours in the library, taking notes. One day Baba put forth the suggestion of my starting daily satsang and offering classes on *Soundarya Lahari*. Baba would talk on literature by Maa Anandamayi. We implemented this, and for a month or so, a good number of Baba's devotees attended.

In those days I was troubled frequently by stomach pain. While I had been at my Jammu Ashram previously, I had suffered for long with peptic ulcer. The pain was increasing so one day Kanaiah took me to a doctor at a nearby hospital. Endoscopy or colonoscopy showed that the ulcer had worsened and so medication was started. My stay in Indore thus extended for a few more days.

In the Jammu Ashram Navaratri was always an important annual event. As Navaratri was nearing, I insisted on leaving for Jammu and left that week itself.

Beginning Itself Is Ending

AT THE END of my last life and at the moment of the 'I' leaving that body, perhaps there might have been the desire to be reborn as a guru. Surely that must be why that in this birth I have manifested as an *avadhoota*, wandered on this planet for so long. Common knowledge says that the sun 'rises' and 'sets'. But in reality it neither rises nor sets. It has and will always be present—giving out energy as light and heat to all beings till the end of creation. An *Avadhoota* is like a sun too, working to nature's orders. He functions like a night watchman to the world. He keeps himself awake, while reminding others to be alert to their possession, and not descend too much into the darkness of sleep, lest they invite theft. His message comes purely from the light of his spiritual experience. He wears a placard warning against wasting life in mere sensual enjoyment, and chasing after money and power to protect a very perishable body. The *avadhoota*, in doing what has been entrusted to him by the Almighty, is the luminary not only shining the moonlight of wisdom, but also providing the rejuvenating warmth of affection to the beings of this transitory world tormented by desires. The reality of his being is always connected with the ultimate existence known as the Supreme Being. It remains ever-shining even after the physical body made up of the five elements, merges into the respective sources.

I was in Jammu ashram in those days, prepared for a long stay for my last and fifteenth *purascharan* of *shodashi mantra* of *Srividya*. The work related to construction was almost over, having being done on a day-to-day basis, due to scarcity of resources. It had not been possible to start out with an overall plan because of shoestring budgets, and the rooms had been constructed like *kutias*. But my lone *sanyasi* disciple, Swami Omkarananda, arranged for a good amount of money to build a convenient room for me with an attached bathroom.

When the room was ready, I had an urge to do a *mauna vrata* for at least 41 days and to do a purascharana, sustaining myself just on fruit and *thulasi jalam*. Madan Lal Sharma, Omprakash and their families took care of arranging for my basic needs. I used to lock the room from the inside, and asked them to lock the door from the outside as well. From the back door, I could come out for a stroll into a vacant enclosed space of just about a hundred square feet, adjoining my room. The disciples attending to my needs had made arrangements to place some fruit in plastic covers in the open space daily, which I could collect during my stroll at nights.

I did japa averaging around sixteen hours everyday. The reduced sleep and food, increased water intake, and a few yogic *kriyas* such as *pranayama* etc. kept me healthy and I continued my *saadhana* peacefully. I had a rich collection of reference books on Srividya and other scriptures which I had already read, but whenever I had free time I engaged myself in reading them and taking notes. I experienced a lot in those days during the night time *saadhana* sessions.

One day, when it was almost dawn and I was about to conclude the night *japa* and was readying for a break to do the morning rituals, I heard the sound of footsteps, as if someone was walking just outside the cave. At first I ignored this, thinking this a hallucination from lack of sleep. A few minutes later, I again sensed a silhouette, along with the sound. When we face such situations, they can provide insights to us on what we are on the inside. So at first I was a little scared and perhaps it was a physiological problem from not taking enough food etc. I confess I felt some kind of fear, a rootless kind. But the intellect kicked in, and I now wanted to verify what was actually outside. In spite of the cautious fear, the *gyana shakti* in me did not allow it to grow out of proportion. A voice from within told me there was nothing to fear, and to look outside. I popped my head out, and saw somebody's feet. I wondered who could have sneaked into the room without my knowledge. As far as I remembered, I had bolted the door but perhaps I might not have secured it well, so somebody might have come in. Then I tried to make out who it was. Because the low-ceilinged cave-like room did not permit me to stand up inside, I could not stretch my legs fully. There was just barely enough space to crawl in and out. Crawling out, I called out asking who it was. I could now see somebody- it was a woman, an old lady of splendorous countenance. There was a familiar smell about her, and she wore South Indian style attire. Because it was still dark and winter time, with some struggle I tried to turn on the lights on, but they would not come on. Now growing more perplexed, I squinted to identify her. Oh, my goodness! To my greatest astonishment, the lady was none other than my beloved and all merciful Guruji, Avadhoota Tara Mayee, standing there in front of the cave with a mesmerizing smile. I tried my utmost to say something to express the feelings and emotions that surged, but the force of love that had erupted upon her unexpected *darshan* was choking my throat. Her gesture seemed to say, "Don't worry, I have received your words from the heart, no need for any words to be uttered." Like a tree that had been cut, I just fell down at her feet, my eyes raining tears. I remained that way for a few minutes. Then abruptly the thought arose that I must offer her something, and getting up I went to look for some fruit etc., but she made a gesture of dismissal, that she had no need for such things, that she was satisfied with the *bhajan* that had been my offering, and raised her hands to tell me to carry on. Desiring to touch her hands, I advanced a little, but to my disappointment she vanished into thin air.

After a very long time, I had again had such a satisfying *saakshatkaaram*. And right at the time when my heart had been longing for love and guidance, she had appeared and poured it on me. I was in tears thinking that she had disappeared, before I could talk with her about my saadhana. I was shaking in tears and holding my head, when to my surprise, she reappeared and passed her hands on my head. Her touch totally refreshed and reassured me, and I did a *saashtaanga namaskaaram* to Amma. She patted my back lovingly and in her silvery voice said, "*Kya re, fir se ek baar shuru kiya? Bahut acha. Yeh jeevan poora ek saadhana mayam banao. Sanchita oorja se samaj ke logom ka kalyan karo.*" (You have started another purascharan? That is excellent. Let your whole life be one of *saadhana*. And with the spiritual power you thus accumulate, you must serve society.)

Then Amma reached out to again touch my body, and with that touch I lost myself in 'my Self'. For some time I didn't know where I was—I had lost all body-consciousness and complexes. I sat thus for a pretty long time, not wanting to disturb and lose that state of bliss never before experienced. When I came back to myself, it was sunset the next day. A whole day had passed in ecstasy. I had not been asleep, but sitting with body bent towards the wall of that cave.

Almost one month of *saadhana* had passed, and there were just a few days remaining for completion of the *japa purascharana*. I had been so caught in the powerful spell of that experience of enlightenment after the *darshan*, that I was unaware of its impact on my health. I learned later from expert sources that such experiences very much debilitate the body. It is not advisable to aspire for such experiences, because that everlasting ocean of bliss is seen only after traveling a very long way. The body also must be prepared and ready to drink as much of that nectar as possible. And if one has any work of the world in hand, it is better not to think of touching it for the time being. My body had weakened to the extent that I now felt incapable of performing the *homam* that was supposed follow the *purascharana*. I had to forgo it this time as well. My spiritual brother Abhayanandji had once told me that if ever I felt unable to do *homam* after the completion of *japa purascharan*, I could instead do a *dasaamsa japa*, which the scriptures permitted. That meant that I had to extend my stay by a few more days. I continued *the japa* and completed it on the 50th day. I slid a piece of paper outside the door, requesting that they open it on the 51st day. There were a lot of disciples and devotees assembled outside that morning, waiting for me with *halwa* for *prasadam*.

Finally I opened the door and came out, had darshan at the Shiva Mandir and Devi mandir in the ashram premises, and then sat in front of Maa for a few minutes. Chanting out loud the Om mantra, I broke my *mauna vrata,* and ate some of the *halwa prasadam* to conclude the 51 days of eventful *saadhana.*

After the experience of the protective hands of my beloved Guruji during the 51-day saadhana, there have since been many more such experiences, but the understandings from those were different from the one of this time. This one had brought a considerable change in my body capacity. It had happened seven years after my Guruji left her body, so I was filled and carried away by a lot of emotions, when she manifested in front of me to bless, protect, and guide me in keeping to my course. I am certain that at the time of my leaving this body as well, my Amma will be with me. After this incident, when a wave of similar emotion arose in my heart even remotely, I did not welcome it. In spite of that I once more had a severe attack recently, which I will narrate in the later episode '*Hamsa gaanam*'.

Again At Narmada

I WAS VERY HAPPY to again find myself on the banks, or rather the lap, of Maa Narmada. I have not been able to fathom the reason for this deep affinity and identification with Maa Narmada. On the very first day of my arrival at Omkareshwar, I went in search of the old Avadhoot Baba, who used to stay in front of Vignanshaala on the Narmada banks (there is a mention of this in the previous volume of my autobiography). Not finding him there, I made enquiries from the ashram inmates but none were able to provide a satisfactory answer. Let alone caring about, people barely pay attention to this type of person. This was because he was so unassuming and had made himself so inconspicuous, such was his state of detachment and *akinchanata* (making oneself so insignificant). But in today's world, people value only recognition and identity of some kind or even any kind—if you give them the 'Best Cheat' award they will happily take it, because of associated fame. I felt very pained at this.

However when I came out of the ashram, to my wonder I now saw him at the same spot collecting dry leaves, unperturbed and with least concern about the outside world. I went near and offered him my pranams. He scanned me with his eyes for a few minutes, and serenely and silently continued collecting dry leaves! Mustering some courage, I asked, "Baba, where have you been? I have been looking for you the past three days." He remained silent for some more time, and then with a captivating smile he spoke, "You too were on a long journey it seems! Very good. I am happy that you have completed your Gyanganj journey successfully. And I knew that one day you will return here to the Narmada." Apparently he was not willing to answer directly my question about his whereabouts. I said, "Baba, by the grace of the Guru Mandali, the *yatra* and stay at Gyanganj were successful. I did higher studies in Srividya, and gained some metaphysical knowledge from there as well." He interrupted, "I know, I know, but what do you have to do with me? You may go now! Let me carry on." I submissively said, "Baba please don't do that, don't send me far away from you. I wish to be near with you." But Baba, refusing categorically said, "Never. Our ways are different. There is no use being here with me. For me there are no dear and near ones except these dry leaves. This is my way of life, and my message too!" He busied himself again with the same work of collecting dry leaves. I thought that perhaps he was not in a good mood and so was avoiding me. I was just turning away when he said in a booming voice, "Son, it is not as you think. I remain always unruffled and calm. Nothing can break my *sahaja samadhi*. And I was not avoiding you. I just wanted to convey to you the truth that though the energy of existence and the Guru Parampara are the same, we are travelling on different paths. So why should you disturb me, or I disturb you?" He glanced at my face lovingly. I said, "Baba, what you just said is correct. But I am merely a child in front of you. Just a few years' *saadhana* and a visit to Gyanganj are not enough to fulfill the work entrusted to me by destiny. I recognize you as one of the senior *acharyas* of Gyanganj. I thought that being in your presence would help me gain more experience and knowledge which would be useful for my work in the future." Looking at my face with the same smile again, he said, "Son, this time is very bad. People around here are very selfish. If you come and sit by me, definitely you will also be labeled the way I have been. They will call you too mad! Better that you hide your identity for some more time. Go, go away from me." I returned to the ashram in very damp spirits.

The spiritual life at the Markandeya Sanyas Ashram continued smoothly in discipline. As I had been journeying continuously to many destinations for years together, my matted hair and beard had grown forest-like. Some of the swamis of the ashram who were friends and well-wishers, first suggested and then insisted that I get rid of the matted hair and beard, and have a clean shave on the next *poornima*. Since long I had also been irked at maintaining the *jata* and *dhaadi* (matted hair and beard). So on a *poornima* day, I had a clean shave after removing the matted hair!

During those days one *Vaishnavite sadhu* in white clothes, from Maharashtra, was introduced to me by another known *swami*. His name was Keshav and he was in charge of the cooking in the ashram. He was a good *bhajan* singer and we would both sit on the Narmada *ghats* at night and sing Maa bhajans together. Slowly our acquaintance grew to a deep friendship. I had a strange dream one day and it repeated for a few consecutive days. I would see this vision—I was in an unknown village. On one side of this village were a few hills covered with vegetation, and on the other side was the sea. There were two teenage boys approach me and then disappear. I felt these boys were known to me since long! I tried to decode the dream but failed. Was it some message? My mind was a bit disturbed and soon I was possessed, or focused upon the dream. One day again I went to meet the old *Avadhoot* Baba. He was sitting under, and leaning against a small tree, gazing at the Narmada. With a sardonic laugh, he said, "Oh! You?! Now you look like a hero, or rather a *Mathadhipati*! Look at you now—clean head and face, *vibhooti*, *kumkum* and all. Your look has totally changed! Now what has brought you to me again?!" I told him about the repeating dream. Baba kept quiet for a long time. Then suddenly he spoke, "Yes, definitely it has a message. Your destiny is telling you to locate that village and meet the boys. They are in search of a Guru. Go find out. You are destined to take them in your fold." I told him in all innocence, "Baba, I have no idea how to locate that village, and how to reach those boys." Baba smiled- "You are behaving like Hanuman who forgot his strength. Your stamina, the accumulated energy, and your willpower will take you to the next destination. Someone will come to take you there, wait. Wait for a few more days." I sat there quietly. Baba was also immersed in deep silence. Breaking the silence, he said, "See, the small fish in the Narmada forget the way to reach their mother and are lost. The mother fish await the arrival of the small ones and asks a friend fish to help her reach her children. The fish-friend helps in the search, and after some time mother and the children fish are united. Remember, you are like that mother fish. Go and do your search, you will find them. Now you must leave! Do not sit here anymore." I went back to the ghat in front of the ashram. Contemplating on the story Baba had told, I sat there for a long time.

In Search Of Unknown

ONE DAY WHILE I was sitting on the banks of the Narmada, I told Keshav about the dream. He heard it with due respect and said, "Oh! I think I know a village similar to your description. But it is in Maharashtra!" I requested him to take me there. But he stayed silent and would not answer. After two days, he said, "See Swamiji, the last few years I have been very eager to get initiated into *sanyasa* through proper *deeksha*. After completing the rituals, I shall definitely take you to that village." I thought it is not in propose bargain, because it involves a lot of commitments as a guru of this kind. So I posed an empty smile in the vacuum and kept quiet. After two days he came to me with the same request but this time the protocol was changed entirely, so, I just thought whether give and take is a part, way of life. What is wrong in doing Sanyas Sanskar to him-"It is all okay? Then, we have to fix a "good muhurtham" (auspicious time) for Sanyas Deeksha. Next Guru Poornima I will do it for you. First you take me to the village and help me to find the boys I am in search of", He agreed. I was having only twenty eight Rupees with me. Keshav told me that he will take care of the traveling expenses. He said, first we will go to Shirdi and then next day, we can proceed to our destination.

During my college days one of my friends gave me a photo of Shirdi Sai Baba. I read small books on Sai during that period. But as I had never visited Shirdi earlier, I was happy to go there. From

Indore we have started journey to Shirdi by night private bus and reached there next day morning.

Even though I was going there for the first time, I felt as if I knew this place since long! We kept our belongings in a locker of Sansthan and after bath we went to Sai Baba darshan. Keshav went to verify whether it was crowded or not. I was sitting alone on a bench in Lendi Garden. An old man came near and asked, "Baba, have you taken breakfast? Have this!" he offered few bread pieces to me. As Keshav was very orthodox vaishnav, neither he took food at night in hotel nor did he allow me to. I was hungry. I accepted the bread offered to me by the old man (a Baba devotee), while I was eating, Keshav came to me and said that there was no rush at the Samadhi Mandir and so we better go now. "Abhishek" (Holy ablution) was going on and that the Samadhi Darshan would be possible now. After I ate the bread and washed my hand and face with the water from the Kamandal and followed him to Samadhi mandir.

Abhishek was in progress. We had a good darshan to my heart's content. As there was not much rush we got a lot of time to be at the Samadhi Mandir. We came out and sat in the open courtyard for some time. Keshav told me that we better move now only then we may be able to reach our destination by night. We went to the bus stand. I was not knowing where I was going. We got a state transport bus to Alibag, which was ready to take leave. Journey to Alibagh was very pleasant except that Keshav did not to allow me to eat or drink anything from the hotels. On the way, around afternoon, the bus took a halt for lunch and we got some boiled ground nuts. We had it for our lunch.

We reached Alibagh by about ten at night. It was raining heavily there. Keshav updated that we had to travel yet another fifteen kms to reach the village. By chance we got a bus, and by mid night we reached our destination, the village of chowl, which I was in search of. Due to heavy rain we got drenched completely. We again took an auto rickshaw and reached a small Hanuman Mandir about 2 kms from Chowl naka. Keshav rang the Mandir Bell and from the nearby house an old lady with her two sons, young boys, came out. They were all known to Keshav. The old Lady went into her house and brought some "Bhakari" (Roti made of Rice) and few pieces of Jaggery which we had for dinner and spread our clothes to dry and tried to sleep.

Liberation Of A Soul

I DECIDED TO CONTINUE my stay in the Indore Ashram for a few more months. My research on the vibrations of *Srichakra bindu* was in progress, with some perceivable results in the desired direction. After the butterfly incident, Baba had also transformed into a good friend and helped me a lot in making the research a success, for we had both taken shelter in the same *shastra*. In the evenings for about an hour I would lecture on Srividya or allied subjects and in the nights I would either read, write, or practice certain mantras. The first phase of my research was almost over, and the manuscript of *"Secrets of Sri Chakra"* was now ready.

In the following days, I was taking it easy and relaxing, engaging more in contemplation than in thinking. My *saadhana* at night used to be *sahaja japa* with observation.

With these amendments to my routine, I was regaining the energy dissipated in the butterfly adventure. A different kind of clarity with some depth in feeling, was descending from within. One day while I was reclining in a chair in the room, and brooding on some emotional aspects of Sri Vidya, I suddenly heard the jingling sound of a woman's anklets, somewhere around me. I turned my head to look, but there was nobody there. I thought it was a hallucination and did not pay much attention. The next night I heard again the same sound outside of my room. I opened the door to verify who that might be! But there was no one. This was repeating almost every day and I was growing suspicious that someone was playing pranks on me, such things not being uncommon in ashrams. Ashram managers sometimes resort to such tactics of using women, devotees, or fellow sadhus to drive away a newcomer who may be growing in popularity thereby threatening their position. So I thought it might be some such foul play and wanted to be careful. Without mentioning it, I watched the attitude of everyone in the ashram, but found no discrepancy in anybody's mind whatsoever. Then my attention turned to other possible angles. I eliminated the possibility of the sounds coming from the adjacent house. I decided to find out the truth by staying awake and alert during the nights, keeping my curious mind open to all possibilities. The sounds of *paayal* (anklets) were distinct and definitely not a hallucination.

One night, it may have been an hour after midnight, I saw a beautiful young village girl sitting on a bench beneath a tree outside my apartment-like room, right below my bedside window. I had never seen such a girl in that ashram before. Devotees visiting from neighboring areas were seen only during the daytime, and women were not permitted to roam around in the day, let alone at night. Then how was it that this girl was sitting like this in the garden, without any fear or without the knowledge of anyone in the ashram?

Even though my throat was choking from a bit of fear, I gathered some courage and in a hoarse voice asked her who she was. She glanced at me but did not answer, seeming to be in deep silence. Though I repeated my question two or three times, there was no answer. My peace had now gone to the winds. Noticing her unusual attire and suspecting some paranormal activity, I closed the door, sat on the bed, and doing *aachamana*, started vigorous *japa*. In the morning, I narrated this happening to Baba, but he was not ready to buy my story and responded with—"Can you not see that here in this ashram Maa's presence is immense? There are no impurities in the surroundings either, and that rules out existence of any such thing." His argument sounded logical too and such was his belief in these matters. Or he might have thought I was hallucinating due to the stress and strain of continuous *saadhana* of the past few days. I chose to remain tight-lipped, though with displeasure.

Now I could not expect him to help further on an issue incomprehensible to him. So taking back my file, I decided to meet the situation from a different angle and perspective. I requested Baba that he be at my disposal during the odd hours of the night when these odd incidences occurred. I asked if I might disturb him then, and he assured me that he would be at my call whenever such a need arose. After a few days, there was the repeat of the same sounds of anklets and vision of the girl. The matter now having turned to be a prestige issue, with accumulated courage, I called out to the girl from inside the room. She was out in the garden, when I asked demandingly "Who are you, and why are you here?" To my surprise, this time this so-called girl, spoke to me with a sense of familiarity, like a normal human being. She was young, wearing ornaments and makeup and dressed like a bride. She said, "Ram Ram Babaji!" When I heard these words, I started to sweat, sensing that this was a ghost. I had read and heard before about them, but here was a real encounter with one of them. I asked why she had become a spirit and she said, "A few years back, when this area was not much inhabited and developed, it used to be a little village with a narrow road running through. It was my wedding day, and I was being taken to the village of my in-laws immediately after the marriage ceremony. It was already a little dark, almost sunset time. There was an hour's journey left, and three or four bullock-carts full of our celebrating marriage party, were moving along. The man driving our cart was drunk. A motor vehicle was coming from the opposite direction, and the headlights of the vehicle frightened the bullocks which got agitated and started running amuck and went out of control. The cart in which we, the newly married couple were sitting, overturned and I, the bride, died on the spot. Due to lack of knowledge about death rituals and rites, neither my parents nor my in-laws took any care to absolve me of my situation. And so here I am, estranged and shuttling." She stopped for bit and I asked, "But, why you are here now, sitting in front of my room."

She replied, "We spirits get agitated too, due to worldly disturbance. I felt some solace when I passed this place recently, so since the past few days I have been visiting here regularly. The sound of the mantras that you chant gives some relief. Please don't drive me away, I won't harm anyone." Meanwhile a wind chime hanging in my room started making a pleasant sound due to a light breeze blowing in from outside. Though it was very soothing to me, that girl was unable to withstand it and she disappeared. I knew by hearsay that the sound of chimes keeps away such spirits. I understood now the reason for the usage, having seen it first-hand.

Though I was disappointed that the ghost left, but in talking to it my fear consciousness disappeared, and I had gained some knowledge about that spirit. The next morning when I met Baba, I did not initiate the topic bluntly like the previous time. Instead I asked him, "How old is this ashram?" He replied," May be more than thirty years." Next I asked, "How long have you been in this ashram?" He replied, "I have been here almost from the beginning." "Oh", I said, "And when was this main road laid?" Baba said, "About twenty years ago and before there used to be a small unpaved road. Since the place was quiet and peaceful, we selected it for our ashram." I asked, "I wonder if you remember an accident which took place here, I believe some people in a marriage party died." Now Baba unable to contain himself, moved to the edge of the chair, like a fan of Sachin Tendulkar when he was about to hit a double century! He exclaimed, "What! How do you know that?" I said, "The name of the young bride who died was some Raagini, from Mahu." Baba was now fully stumped. He had no choice but to hear my story. I told him all. He said, "Oh, she is the one who is frequenting nowadays. You did talk to that *preta* then". I affirmed and said there were still a lot of things yet unknown about her, but though the chime had frightened her, I hoped she would come back.

Baba requested me not to reveal this to the others, since the boys in the ashram, especially the Bengali would become scared and run away. Then he would be in trouble for want of servants. I told not to worry, that this was only the movie trailer, the real one was yet to come! I said, "Look here, Baba, if some *karma-khanda* (ritual) is required for appeasement in order to release her from her plight, then you should help me." Babaji said, "Definitely. I am willing." And he said, "If you are afraid, you can stay with me." I replied, "Not at all."

As a consequence of this incident, my whole attitude about *pretas*, astral bodies and spirits changed and an unknown confidence and courage filled me from within. That night I slept very well. All the facts that I had read about *preta*, spirit, and astral body came to memory one by one. I concluded that I must do whatever possible within my power to rid her of this state, which would make me happy too. The next day, as expected I heard the same jingling sound. This time without any perplexity, I called out to her by name. When she heard her name, I was able to see her happiness. With a jump she reached near the window, and did *pranaams* to me. She said, "After leaving the body, this is the first time I hear someone call me with such love. In the plane where I am now, such a thing is a miracle. If you can move me so much, I hope you can save me also from this *preta yoni*." I asked her if this was the first time that she was haunting this ashram. She replied, "Yes." I asked her why she didn't do so before. She said, "We, who are in astral bodies, cannot stay still in a place, even a spiritual one, if there is a lack of purity, or in front of people who do not have enough vital power. After many long years, you have come here and are doing *satvic mantra japa*. *Pranayama* that you are doing gives you strong vital force making you fearless. Unless *pranic shakti* is strong, one cannot become fearless. That is why I am able to remain in front of you for such a long time, and you are also able to talk to me normally without any fear. Until we *pretas* find ourselves such environments, we cannot remain static and have to keep on moving, and we cannot feel peace either. I am getting all that now." She started again pleading with me to do something to save her from that yoni where she had been stuck without any direction to go further. "Pease help me", she said in a pathetic voice. Now that my nerves had calmed down, and I had gained ground in understanding, here was a situation with potential to give insight of a hundred births, for a sincere spiritual *sadhaka*. Though to a person living the ordinary everyday life of superficial existence, this dealing with para-normal existence may not appear so useful, to me the value added is great. I searched for a solution in my memory bank of acquired knowledge, for something to elevate this soul to higher realms of existence. Then there came hazily to my memory, rituals performed in such situations by Kerala *Nambudiri brahmins*. Sometimes individual souls have their own set of karma too.

By now she had disappeared, and I didn't know why. For a few more days she did not appear, perhaps because I had failed to ask whether she had any specific desire needing fulfilment before release could happen. Now it did not seem like an extraordinary incident to me anymore. But with the sincere longing of a man who knew the way to help such a soul, I waited for her reappearance. And I decided that if that did not happen, I would still summon her in my own way.

The next morning, with the prelude already in place, I passed on to Baba all that had happened, and what was expected of me. He started flip-flopping now and I said, "Look, one is not supposed to expect or look for reasoning for every experience. We have our *shastras* as proofs we must believe in them. Though you don't see the sweetness in sugar or jaggery, you certainly experience it. No certificate is required from others for what you have personally experienced, though they may think it illogical. We cannot give demonstrations for everything to everyone." But, I did want to prove to Baba what was happening there.

There were no more encounters with the girl. Recalling her anguished voice, I felt that she had been trying to convey something more, but something was blocking and curtailing her attempts or perhaps threatening her. Otherwise she certainly would have appeared since she was getting so much solace. Or perhaps she was afraid that I might subdue and exploit her, like most other *tantrics* do with spirits. I have seen such people who turn millionaires as a result—glaring examples are to be found in Delhi, a city of intellectual idiots.

So I devised a program of my own. After a few days on an

ashtami, I asked Baba to be with me in my room at night, without revealing the purpose. In the meantime getting some sandalwood, I carved out a statue of the girl Raagini from it. Recollecting relevant details from memory, I made preparations for all the rituals. After midnight, I performed a small pooja in the name of Raagini, which caused her to appear on the bench under the tree near my bedroom window. I asked Baba to look at the bench where she was sitting, but he could see nothing, though he was able to hear the sound of the *paayal* or anklets. I requested her to grant a favor by revealing herself to him. She replied saying that he would not be able to see her, since he was still harboring worldly desires. Existence of such desires made one weak and unable to see entities like her. And if the entities did allow themselves to be seen, those powerful waves of desire would drag the entities back into this world. She especially did not want to return to our world from where she was now. Because seeing from her place, she now knew more about our world than we do, and she thought our world the worst one to be in, for a pure *atma*. But she said if I touched him or he touched me, she could be visible to Baba. Fortunately, Baba could hear her saying this. Touching my shoulder he looked at the bench, and now Raagini had become visible to him as well. His face changed, and he asked me to tell her to leave that place for ever.

I conveyed this to Raagini. She replied, "It is not a question of my leaving the place—somebody has to first release me from this yoni, and for that a favor needs to be done on my behalf." When I asked what that might be, she replied, "You must give a *bhandara*, a feeding of the poor, in my name and submit that karma to God. Then upon that merit, I will be able to shed this body. The *bhandara* must contain *Dal Baati Churma*. I promise that after that act, I will be liberated and leave this place." I agreed to this, promising to do all that on the approaching *amavasya* day.

When Baba saw all this, and heard her speak her like a normal human, he was left with no option but to obey. But a miser is ready to forgo his life, though not his penny when it comes to giving it. It took a lot of convincing to make Baba realize the retributions that would result from going back on his commitments as a *sanyasi*, who should view such situations as divine commands. Thus on the next *amavasya*, we did a good *bhandara* and made plans for a *pooja* at night. A small idol of a young girl was made out of *chandan* (sandalwood). *Dal Baati Churma* were prepared and other *pooja* items arranged. I performed the pooja in my bedroom itself. After the *aavaahan*, I spoke to the idol, "You must show me proof that you have accepted my *naivedyam*, and that you are leaving this place." Just at the time of offering *naivedyam,* we witnessed that the plate in which the *naivedyam* had been kept, shook a little. After *arathi*, the lamp that had been lit for pooja extinguished by itself. Such a thing happening is an indication of liberation to the departed soul. Baba was spellbound and now looked at me with altogether different eyes. He was now filled with renewed belief and faith in our *shastras* and *rishis*.

In Kerala, the *Nambudiri* Brahmins often perform such *poojas* and *kriyas* for the benefit of departed souls. I learnt to perform them from a relative in my native village during my college days, just out of curiosity. Now that knowledge had come in useful.

Afterwards, when news of this spread, some intellectuals who were ashram visitors and thought themselves kings of the *Babas*, who shall remain nameless, came forward and started scrutinizing me and upbraided Baba for permitting such irrational and absurd things to happen in the ashram. I assured them that there was no deception or cheating involved, that I had all particulars of the girl with me, that they were welcome to cross-check facts, and that I would entertain all questions. Of course, modern scientific process has no value for such things and does not accept fourth-dimensional existence. For science, knowledge is to be gained only from the visible three dimensions. In order to enter the fourth dimension you have to leave, or rather kick the ego that requires scientific validation. Spirituality will never conform to those norms, and science should lick its (spirituality's) feet. Science is going to take you to the ignominy of having to provide a DNA certificate to prove your parentage. This is what shameless perverts teach us as science. Scientific thinking, in the manner of a parasite destroying its own host, destroys the very mind in which it took birth. The mind can never reach the heart. If you forget to put the spirit in it, if you don't know what a heart is, you will never know the music of life. Then what would be the point of living here, even with all those amenities provided by science? Scientists have turned humans into testing grounds for their inventions. This has become a kind of slavery to greedy scientists, and not to science.

From Here To There And Back

It is not necessary that at every time, everything should happen according to the desires of a human being for him to develop faith in God. But if his desire bears in it a tinge of divinity, or if it is for the pervasive goodness of others, or if it is unblemished by any selfishness, then someday it will definitely materialize. If it does not, then one must be determined and add that missing element to the desire, so it can be granted. For that, one needs to wait with full patience and belief in the way of functioning of the law of nature, without tampering with the rules.

It took more than sixteen long years for me to complete the first part of my research works on Sri Vidya. Those days I used to be in Kurnool, in Andhra Pradesh. The work of "The Science and Essence" was complete, and I now started typing it up. The volume was more than 500 pages long and I could complete the first phase of the writing work in a few months. After the first writing work was completed, it took the form of a hard-bound book. I planned to go to Kashmir, but the secret intention in my mind was to really go to Gyanganj in Tibet. Ramesh arranged for the money and booked tickets to Varanasi starting from Secunderabad. I did not inform the families of either Ramesh or Satyanarayana about the likelihood of my proceeding from there to Gyanganj to submit the manuscript of the research work to the great Gurus of Gyanganj, only due to whose permission and blessing, I could complete the work. I felt that an element of grace was missing in my work, or some missing links were needed to make this work a reality.

I reached Varanasi, and stayed at the Sringeri Mutt in Kedar Ghat where Ramakrishnananda, the then manager of the Mutt was a good friend who would help and take care of me at every visit there. We used to sit at the Harishchandra Ghat every evening and chat, meditate, or have discussions on *saadhana*. Even though he was known to be short- tempered, his attitude towards me was always friendly, and even brotherly. So after pleasantries were exchanged, I shared with him the incomplete work of my dreams, and my aim of seeking the blessings of my Gurus and asked for this advice. His first move was to pick up the spiral-bound volume of "The Science and Essence of Srividya" and place it in front of the shrine of Maa Sharada, the presiding deity of that *mutt*, after which he performed a Saraswathi *pooja*. I stayed with him at the Kedar Ghat Mutt for a few days and then embarked on my journey to Tibet. It was difficult to get a ticket to Kolkata by train, and so I opted to fly up to Gauhati and from there, travel on to Gangtok by road. The journey to Gangtok was a most pleasant one, the entire route was scenic and almost unearthly beautiful, the natural kind which I have always preferred. Since I had no acquaintances there, I stayed in a room at the famous Hanuman Tok Mandir. Though I was trying to find the route to Tibet where Gyanganj, my place of interest was located, I failed to obtain any accurate, detailed information or leads. Since the weather was bad at the time, I decided to go to Arunachal Pradesh to find the way to reach Gyanganj. I informed Ramesh and others at Kurnool about this, telling them not to worry even if I was late in returning and that I was held up in Itanagar, the capital of Arunachal, because of bad weather. I had to stay there for a few days to arrange for my inner line permit to travel in that politically sensitive area.

When the weather improved, I decided to proceed alone towards Tibet, and by walk, as I had done previously. Keeping in mind the last few journeys' experiences, this time around I kept some eatables with me, like *murukku* and *pallipatty*, which sisters Sujatha and Hari had prepared for my journey. Usually for every journey they would prepare for me such food items to carry along. And as for the experiences I met with, I shall talk about those in a separate episode.

Again At My Father's Abode

I WAS AT THE Himalayas again, the abode of the Universal Father Shiva, who dwells here with his consort, Mother Parvati. It is the universal truth. Anyone wanting to feel their presence can do so here with a pure heart bereft of preconceptions. I felt exhilaration at reaching once again this part of the earth, where the gigantic mountains standing here give their message that one should lead the kind of life that will make one hold his head up high. They seem to say—be like us: egoless, spotless and pure, peaceful and full of the confidence that springs from strong foundations, else prepare to face the inevitable wearing away or erosion.

I recalled the days spent in these mountains during my previous sojourn to Gyanganj. And just like that time, this time too I walked. I walked, and walked all day long feeling no need for rest, nor breaking the monotony of solitude. The journey was a joy in itself. But before the onset of night, I would seek shelter in the form of a *vihara* or *gompa*, or some dwelling place for Buddhist monks. By the fourth day of travel all the food stuff I had brought as snacks, I had eaten. Now I had to depend only on whatever was served at the *vihara*. As a rule, anyone from the plains planning travel in the mountains must use only boiled water to the extent possible. Otherwise they should have mineralized water, since the water in the springs and rivers there is raw, not containing any minerals needed for the body's upkeep. As I was unaccustomed to the type of food there as well, on the sixth day stomach problems started plaguing me, with episodes of diarrhea more than a dozen times a day. It had now become difficult to walk. Somebody in the *vihara* gave me some native medicines similar to *Ayurvedic* herbs. I was forced to keep myself to the bed in the room where I stayed, my stomach not getting much relief. The next day one of the lamas came to my bedside and asked me to lay down in *shavaasana*. Then catching hold of both big toes of my feet, he pulled up my legs, then dropped them to the floor. He said, "You will be alright with this technique, no need for worry." To my wonder, I had recovered by evening!

My wandering in those Himalayan hills was all alone, on terrain with no proper roads, and with no aids like compass, guide, or map to help me. All I had was an intuition, and an unknown divine impulse guiding me through, as I moved along with just a prayer in my heart to my beloved Guruji, the impulse being the thirst to meet the great masters.

It was the eighth day of my trekking, and it was nearing sunset. A chilly cold wind blew, and the air seemed charged with a strange, supernatural feel. The Himalayan heights are always yielding mystic experiences. To my dismay, there was no sign of any village, *gompa* or *vihara*, in fact no sign of human inhabitation whatsoever. Adding to my lot, rain started pouring suddenly, and within a few minutes it changed to dense snowfall. I was finding myself in peril, with my body and clothes drenched completely. Fortunately, the manuscript I was carrying was well-packed in a plastic cover, so there was no fear of it getting ruined. The shoulder bag in which I was carrying my belongings had now become heavier from the weight of water. Nowhere near could I find any shelter from the snow. I perched inside a cleft in a small rock nearby, and from the shoulder bag pulled out the small plastic sheet which I always carried with me during my journeys. This time Ramakrishnanand had purchased it for me at Kashi. Covering my body and shoulder bag with it, I sat there for a long time. After an hour or so, the snowfall and rain ceased but darkness had now descended. I thought it would make sense to stay there the whole night, and face what may come to pass.

For me, that night is one to be remembered lifelong, as it gave me a lot of insights into the state of being alone. In fact, it is not unlike the tormented soul within everyone that travels alone for many lives together in different bodies, in the wilderness of ignorance. We only imagine that we have plenty of company. To have the solace of company means that one should know everything about one's companions, and they know everything about one too, and that it should all be supported by verifiable proofs. Actually, whatever we know about ourselves and of others, is just like talking in the night in a jungle: there is no reality to it. So for all practical purposes, that ignorance is also very much like a wilderness. We do not really know anything about our parents, wife, children, friends—whatever we claim to 'know' comes just from assumptions—there are no valid facts with corroboratory proofs. If at all we seem to have company, it is only of the Guru, the incarnation of the Almighty.

The night was getting darker and I shivered in the biting cold of the blustery wind. In drenched clothes and praying to my Guruji, I sat there doing my *japa* with intense focus for some time, and heaven knows how long I did so, for when I opened my eyes it was morning. I discovered that I had slept leaning on the rock itself, and now the sun was shining.

I searched for signs of inhabitation, and finding none I swung into action again. The clothes were yet to dry and I was feeling hungry too. I was thankful when I spotted a *vihara* at a distance. It took a while to reach there and I stayed there for the rest of the day to dry my clothes and have a good wash. They gave me some *roti* and curry, whatever was at their disposal, but it was very spicy. Perhaps in those colder regions of the upper Himalayas, hotter and spicier food is needed for survival. After taking a nice nap, one or two lamas, inmates of that *vihara,* sat with me asking about my mission to Gyanganj. I narrated my experiences of the previous Himalayan journey. Being locals they gave me some invaluable clues about the area too. So the very next morning, I continued on my journey.

By evening I had reached the foot of those hills where Gyanganj is situated. Just by being there I felt a sense of accomplishment. I had done it! I had finally reached my destination. I was overjoyed to see Bhruguram Paramahamsa at the main entrance of Gyanganj itself, as if he had been awaiting someone's arrival. Perhaps it was me? He received me with a beautiful smile and said, "Son, I am happy that you have completed a part of your research work. Now that the work is ready, you'd better take it to Mahatapa Baba and submit it at his holy feet."

The next day, Bhruguramji, accompanied by the same older *swami* with the Tamilian look, took me to the inner cave. The cave was filled with divine effulgence and fragrances. This was the first time I was coming so close to the holy feet of the great guru Mahatapa. With all reverence and an unknown fear, I placed the spiral-bound volume of "The Science and Essence of Srividya' near his feet. He was sitting in *siddhasana* posture on a rock, probably made of crystal. Though he never opened his eyes, yet we could all hear very well the humming of OM reverberating in the cave. This was the sign that the work submitted at his holy feet had received the supreme approval, as per the tradition of acceptance. Bhruguramji then asked me to pick up the manuscript and follow him. When we had reached just outside the cave, he turned to embrace me and said, "Son, after more than fifty years, this is the first time that we heard the sound of our Supreme Guru Mahatapa. His accepting your research work is a success by itself. May the whole universe be benefitted by your work". I had tears in my eyes. Bhruguramji asked me to rest there for a day with the same Tamilian *swamiji*. I agreed, and just as it had happened in the last visit, this time also the *swamiji* remained oblivious to my presence in his cave, showing no interest in talking to me, nor giving me anything to eat. Even though I tried my level best to talk to him about something, he ignored or avoided me, and God knows why!

Bhruguramji called upon me in the morning, and accompanying me to the main entrance to bid me farewell, permitted me to return. With *pranamas* to all gurus at Gyanganj, I embarked upon my return journey.

The Must Forget Faces

THE ART OF purposeful forgetting is a valuable one. If practiced well, it can free us from a lot of the dross material that we collect in life's journey. This may have been cast on us—perhaps by a neighbor or by an enemy, and sometimes carelessly, sometimes unknowingly, or sometimes on purpose. Almost everyone can recall from their lives, a few faces that have definitely irritated them, like thorns in the flesh. We must, through proper means, try to eliminate them from memory as early as possible, before it becomes a cause for concern. We have to forget them forever, or the blood pressure will go heights of seriousness. I do remember an incident, one of sorrow that had left a scar in my heart.

It was during the initial stage of the construction work of my Jammu ashram. One swami was in need of shelter, and I too was in need of a person able to oversee the work in my absence. Since both our want and necessity met this way, I requested him to stay there. I do not have the temperament to extract work from labourers, and I also had to travel here and there to arrange money for the work. I had met him during my stay in Rishikesh a few years ago, and he had been a good friend there. He readily agreed to my proposal. After accommodating him at the ashram site in a small kutia, which was just a thatched shed at that time, I left on a long trip for some other work. This was way back in the 90s, when cell phones were not available and not even invented. Thus there was a huge gap in communicating, but I had left in the innocent belief that there was no need for worry as he as a friend would be monitoring the work. It was in this interim that I had the chance to go to Kailash and my return from there, I was then assigned a task by one of my mentors at Vanavasi ashram etc. All this happened while I had almost no communications from the Jammu ashram for a long period of time.

I was staying for a few months in Haridwar after my return from Jaunsar Bawar[18] (Chakrata—Dehradun). One day I met some devotees from the same village on their monthly trip for *Sankranti Snaan* at Haridwar. Among them was one of my disciples from the village who was in charge of the construction. He insisted that I return to the village urgently, but he did not disclose any further details. He kept pressing me to return as early as possible. Of course the major portion of the construction work was over, with two temples dedicated to Shiva and Durga completed. On enquiry I was given to understand that the behavior of the *swami*, whom I had brought and kept there, had now changed, and he happened to be quite indifferent. Neither he nor the villagers were able to cope up with their respective expectations as a *sadhak* or as devotees. This could damage the spiritual ecology of the village to any irreparable extent. If we do not understand the writing on the wall, we may have to pay the price of losing the dedicated devotion of the villagers. Conceding to their legitimate arguments, I decided to go to the Jammu ashram. When I reached there, or so to say even before reaching there, the sadhu had learned of my return to the ashram, and he started a smear campaign against me with the help of a few of his cronies.. As I had expected this already, I did not entertain anything that might fuel his agony further. I understood that since he had been here for the past few months, taking pains to look after the ashram all by himself, it was only natural for a sense of insecurity to erupt in him after taste of the full freedom in every dealing that I had assigned to him. Sharing or forgoing

---

18 Details on Nadanandaji stay and work at Jaunsar Bawar is given in *Autobiography of an Avadhoota*—Volume 1

a right, power, or status after having tasted it is not an easy affair. So I wanted his presence there as in the normal way and as usual, which was not an issue for me or for the villagers. But that did not appeal to him and he started manifesting symptoms of dislike. He disliked my very presence there, often using rough words of acid towards me. And worse, he started polarizing the devotees of that small area. Some of the disciples in that village informed me of this fearfully, that this polarization was disturbing the peaceful coexistence they previously enjoyed. Since he continued trying to make divisions among the disciples, I had no option left but to request him to return to Haridwar. I told him politely that as the construction work was now over, his esteemed service was no more solicited, and extended gratitude to him for his help during that long period. He grew angry at this, registering strong resistance. Though I explained to him of the damage of goodwill being caused in the village which we as indebted sadhus to the village people are to uphold, but it failed to effect any understanding or mean anything to him. From fear of unwanted confrontations, I had to resort to some firm steps, and replaced the request to leave with a ceremonial send off. He decided on a *dharna* outside the gate of the ashram and tried to create some sympathy, but when he saw that he was not getting much traction, he left the place. But not without threatening drastic consequences of returning again and threatened me with his dishonorable lingo. Then he sat for a whole day and night just at the ashram gate, for which he was successful in generating a sympathy wave towards him from some of the villagers. Now I had to show sensitivity in answering and satisfying everyone, without damaging the goodwill for sadhus in the hearts of the devotees. I wanted to get rid of the mess, but diplomatically. Without a least knowledge of what a more serious trouble I was going to get into!

In between I made a trip to Rishikesh to meet one of my *swami* friends, who was staying in an *ashram* there. There I met with another *swami*, who was acquainted with the swami who was disturbing the peace in Jammu, and making an issue with me. In sweet but ensnaring words, that swami told me that the other swami was fearful of him, and they were not on good terms with each other. And hence if he came to stay with me, that other swami would not dare disturb me anymore. As I was in deep agony, his words were of high solace to me. Believing them, I took him to bosom. I too liked this idea, but never reflected on the consequences. To be frank, I was too naive to anticipate such politics, or any crookedness and manipulation in behavior. So to get rid of a devil, I decided to jump into the deep sea where worse sharks live. This new swami joined the Jammu ashram. Subsequently, the troublemaker swami left, to come back once more, but afterwards left permanently. I later learned that these two swamis had once stayed under one Guru, and so were really *gurubhais*. A few months went by in peace. But this new man who had come as a savior was also an efficient manipulator, and started picking contacts around very quickly. I thought that this socializing would help him handle the devotees well with his experience and knowledge. But the undercurrent was otherwise. He started extending his tentacles in another way. One day my sanyasi disciple Swami Omkaranand came with disturbing news that this new incumbent swami had started some kind of business in the ashram, but in the pretence of doing '*samaj seva*' or service to society. He was casting horoscopes of people from nearby villages, doing sorcery, selling *navaratna* gems as horoscope remedies, and giving medicines for unwanted purpose. The ashram had turned into a business establishment. Activities contrary to the basic motto of the ashram were being observed. At first when I noticed that he was often surrounded by many people, I thought this was because he was dispensing spiritual advice, or conducting *satsang*. But with close observation, I realized they were not participating in *satsang* but were his 'customers'. From old devotees and from villagers too, I came to know that this swami was earning a good amount from his side business. By now, there was a growing demand from those staunchly spiritual people who had helped establish and were supporting the ashram, to get rid of this swami. Ignoring their demand did not appear a sound idea for the welfare of the ashram. I was now a fix, not being the kind of person who can easily utter the word 'no' and get out of a situation pretending apology. This was going to be as painful as labour pains for me. So for days I rehearsed asking this swami to find himself a new market, and let the ashram remain a hermitage. Finally, after accumulating some courage, of course with the help of Omkaranand, I requested him to find some other suitable place to stay. When this came to light to the public, his clients were infuriated. These were his so called 'beneficiaries' who were getting horoscope read, fixing dates for marriages, or getting '*navaratna*' rings from him. This group supporting that swami rose up in revolt and behaved a little roughly with me. But the traditional support prevailed, and the swami had to leave the ashram for a distant place. Misinterpreting the message, the old devil came back to the village some days later, and even started frequenting often. Even though he dared not oppose me face to face, he was rearing enmity on the side, playing politics and the result was a little dangerous.

One day, it so happened that one of that swami's 'wellwisher' came to the ashram at evening pooja a*arathi* time. He was fully drunk, and started calling out abusive words at me, and tried to break the temple door and throw away the *pooja paatras*. At this some of the villagers assembled together and sent him back. The next day I called for the village *panchayat* to meet to discuss what was to be done next. Since the culprit who had used obscene words and damaged the temple belongings was a close relative of some of the committee members of the governing body of the temple, hence relationship tool an upper hand over justice.

This seemingly insignificant incident brought a virtual confrontation with some of the important entities of the setup. Finally, I decided to withdraw from the scene once and for all. This came as a shock to the devotees in my innermost circle, though they have remained rock solid in their devotion till today. These disciples were not in agreement with my decision to leave that ashram forever, I was adamant. Once again I called a *panchayat* meeting to inform them of my decision. Before leaving, I also wanted to have that person do a *prayaschitta pooja* to the deities for his *paapa*, so that his family or villagers were not affected from his sins. In a day or two they arranged for the *prayaschitta pooja*, and I arranged for its cost of more than seventy five lakhs, which I collected by 'begging' money from my disciples from all over India. Handing over everything to Omkarananda, I declared him my successor. I then left the ashram as if nothing had happened, just as I had entered the village one day long ago, with the same single shoulder bag, my *kappar*, and *kamandal* that I carried when I arrived there.

The Parasite Guruji

MUTUAL DEPENDENCY IS the rather secret law of nature. Every being in the whole of creation, not just of this world, is dependent on each other. For, the Almighty is divided into two parts as Uma and Maheswara, and there was delight in this dependency—nature and spirit as inverse and complementary to each other. We, the created, are unable to understand the order behind this arrangement. The difficulty is in our understanding, and not in the arrangement. Every being here exists along with the other beings, and none of them can survive alone, or try to eliminate or dominate the other. Especially in the life of a human being, this is a truth apparent. The four pillars of the *Vedic* concept of society, the four *ashrams* or stages of life, were designed to help humans evolve in mutual harmony till the attainment of the ultimate goal. In the process of evolution, those in a particular ashram at a particular point in time, should not make the blunder of asserting that their own stage or ashram is independent of the others. Just as give and take is a part of life, dependency is also a part of life. So the tendency to regard any other living being or any resource as irrelevant to oneself, is in fact self-destructive.

Once I was travelling from Guwahati to Delhi by train on a second class a/c ticket which one of my disciples had reserved for me. The train was about to leave the station. Two young militarymen who looked like officers, entered into the coupe where I was seated. They were carrying with them a lot of heavy luggage.

When they saw me, a *sanyasi* sitting in an a/c compartment, these guardians of citizens were unable to bear it. The founders of post-independent India rose to power by minting and selling the fake coin of equality, but how they defined that 'equality', they have never specified. But impostors are now rolling in money, money they received as favor from the government, and the country is reeling in distress from their incompetency and degeneracy. The militarymen glanced at me as if they had spotted some kind of extraordinary animal. While arranging their luggage one of these great Indian liabilities said, "Hey *baba*, this may not be your compartment. This is 2nd class AC compartment." "Oh!" I exclaimed and kept quiet, deciding to relish their expressions of agitated arrogance a little, and buried myself in the book in my hand. This infuriated them more. I thought these two might have thought me a helpless, wandering sadhu traveling without a ticket and with no knowledge of railway traveling class (1st, 2nd, general etc).

Now displaying their own lack of class and decency, one of them added, "*Baba,* you are not hearing me—I told you didn't I, to go to the general compartment." They had already taken their seats in front of me that had been allotted to them. My external appearance was not very impressive, as I was returning from a long journey of several months. Matted hair, beard, old worn out *kashaya* clothes, without a proper bath for days—all these made me naturally look almost like a beggar. If those had been the times of British rule with imposed dress codes, I surely would not have been eligible to travel looking the way I did. But now I was in free India, founded upon the yet-unrealized principles of equality by opportunistic leaders. The first officer was telling the other in coarse English, "Such baggers are polluting our country they like parasites and kamaying (earning) money. And if time and situation favors, stealing also." I replied in English, "I also have been blessed by God with a clean mouth and pure speech. I beg that you gentlemen take note of this. Yes, I may be a parasite, and perhaps a beggar or thief. But don't worry, I have a valid a/c ticket up to Delhi. And if at all there is an event of theft, you can trace me back to my ashram and this is my visiting card." I tendered them a new visiting card. Their faces grew pale with astonishment. They were thinking, "Oh, thes baba nows Englesh aalsu." By this time the ticket examiner entered into the compartment. The train was now moving and while handing over my ticket to him for checking, I asked the ticket examiner, "Sir, is there any law in the railways that a beggar like me is not allowed to travel in the a/c compartment even if he possess a valid ticket?" Before checking my ticket, the ticket collector touched my feet with reverence and did namaskar and asked, "What is the problem, Swamiji? Why you are shooting such a question?" I replied, "Nothing in particular of course. Just that these gentlemen in special clothing are intimidating me into vacating this compartment." I could very well see the furtive eyes on the pale and frozen faces of those military officers. The ticket examiner while checking the tickets admonished them to behave properly. After the TT reprimanded them, they were cringing.

The train had crossed the river Brahmaputra and a heavy, disturbing and mortuary-like silence hung in the coupe. I took out the book *'Ashtavakra Geeta'* in English, from my shoulder bag and started to read. When I ignored their very presence, the two military officers seemed very disturbed and wanting to make amends for otherwise the journey might end up in sorts of sandbag-carrying. One of them taking him the initiative, stood up and touched my feet and pleaded apology, "Maharajji, we have done a mistake. We should not have spoken to you like that." I said to them, "No problem brothers, it all happens when you assess a person based on his external appearance, or value someone on the quality of his clothing. You people with modern education have only superfluous vision of anybody." Now the other officer also stood up and started soliciting pardon for the mistake. A coffee vendor appeared and they ordered three cups of coffee and offered one to me, and the situation eased off from deterioration. As if nothing had happened, I started sipping the coffee. Then we started exchanging pleasantries, etc.

This has however become the trend in today's education, where they teach how to assess based on outward appearance. There is neither the time nor the patience to go a little further and dive a little deeper to gauge the reality. This is why people keep adding enemies in their lives. They presume themselves intelligent enough to assess others easily with just one look, and find it unnecessary to respect others' sentiments. This is the way others are assessed: with just a look, we are ready to jump to a conclusion about a person in front of us. It need not always be correct. The external appearance may be bad or odd, but before using hard words with anybody, we have to hear him out first. Analyze him or try to understand him first. Presumption always hurts.

I invoked Rishi Ashtavakra to drive home my points. The officers had now trained their ears towards me with newfound zeal. It happened thus with one *Maharshi* Ashtavakra a saint of great repute of his era, who once entered the court of the great King Janaka in an informal way. He was named thus because his body had eight (*ashta*) deformities. The scholars in the court, jealous of his repute dishonored him by laughing at his entry in the king's court. Ashtavakra also laughed uproariously in response. King Janaka wanted to know Ashtavakra's reason for laughing, because he understood the reason for the others' laughing, which was on account of his looks. Ashtavakra *Maharshi* said, "I had heard that Janaka's court was filled with enlightened ones. But here I see only butchers and cobblers by default. That is why I laughed." At hearing this, all were annoyed with Ashtavakra. Janaka asked him again to elaborate. Ashtavakra said, "Maharaja, butchers value the meat on a body, and cobblers value the skin. And I see the same happening here. Your people in court have given me external evaluation— looking at my body twisted and bent eight ways, my dirty clothes, my dry wrinkled skin etc. No one saw the wisdom hidden in me, is it not? None of you has even tried to see the wisdom in me. This is the reason why I laugh." Struck by this, Janaka accepted Ashtavakra as his Guru. And the other assembly dissolved.

I narrated this story to the military officers, which was an eye-opener to them. After this turnaround, they displayed more and more interest in hearing me throughout the journey. I also took this opportunity to plant the seeds of knowledge as much as possible, so they might sprout at the opportune time of rain after the drought. Till we reached Delhi, there was plenty of such *satsang* and to my wonder, they never allowed me to pay for my food etc., during the journey. Before reaching Delhi, I wanted to reimburse them for the expenses they had incurred on my behalf, and said, "Even though we have travelled together for two days and there was a lot of conversation, I still do not think or feel that the impression in your minds about *sadhus* has changed. You think of us parasites that suck and live lavishly off the money swindled from devotees and disciples. Heck, you make sure that we pay even for every drop of water we take, and sometimes several times more than its worth. The world takes more and gives less, but we . . . .we take less and give more."

"You people have no knowledge of the knowledge we have bartered for this life. When you do not know anything about a currency, you must not think of appraising it, shopping or dealing with it, or make allegations about its value. We give our service to the society for very little in return. Society owes a lot even to an insignificant *sadhu*, let alone the so-called *gurus*. You do not have any knowledge of our capacity to give to humanity. Try to understand what we *sadhus* are doing for humanity, and for the nation. You guard the borders of the nation, but we guard the minds of disciples and devotees, and of humanity itself. We never allow our devotees' minds to cross the border and go to the land of evil. We teach them this art of safety."

The train arrived at Delhi railway station and we were all ready to alight. At the platform, one of them took my Jammu Ashram's address, and we all separated to our own ways.

To my surprise one among the pair of military officer came up to my Jammu ashram in search of me a few months later. He had been transferred somewhere near the region. On the next *Guru Poornima,* I initiated him with *mantra deeksha,* and he became a disciple of the sincere kind who tried and gained deeper understanding in spirituality.

So my appeal hereby to the world is this: do not practice, nor encourage the habit of undermining the importance of spirituality in human life. Do not misjudge spiritual people from their simple looks, or misinterpret religious symbols either. The attitude of irreverence to spirituality can cause irreparable damage to the whole of humanity and any hasty decision from such an attitude is a sin equal to negation of life itself. So do not entertain such anti-life attitudes, and withdraw support to them. If anyone wants to see the world happy, this is the real service to humanity anyone can do.

Bhagavadajjuka[19]—The story of a prostitute and a Sanyasi

THERE REMAIN STILL some wounds in my mind, the results of unfounded hostility still green in memory. I tried medicines of sorts to dry and heal them, but the inflictors of those wounds were adamant in making them ooze. Once, when the memories went back and touched that same corner of the mind, I could see very well that the wound was yet to dry up, and needed intense care.

I was in Haridwar, staying in an *ashram*, young then in my thirties. I was busy in routines of different aspects of *saadhana* like *purascharan*. The studies in *Vedanta* were also progressing well. After dinner I would walk along the banks of the Ganga daily, (in most ashrams in Haridwar etc. the dinner or evening *bhiksha* is served between four and six pm), as a habit. Sometimes I walked with like-minded *sadhus*, and sometimes alone. I liked to pause and sit at a particular *ghat*, simply brooding on my thoughts etc. On one such walk, I saw a girl in her teens sitting at the same *ghat*. She was looking into space, with soiled and gloomy face, tears in her eyes. I thought first that she was perhaps a devotee of

---

19 The chapter contains a story which resembles a street drama hence Avadhoota Nadananda names this Bhagavadajjuka, after the doctrine of a great saint of historical times, Bodhayana.

Ma Ganga, like Meera. Often one can see such scenes of drama in drawings of comic books, and I thought this too might be one such case. But the indications didn't match. Since such a scene has also been the prelude to many a suicide attempt, a compassion of unknown origin sprang in my heart. After my mind had exhausted itself from finding alternative explanations, gathering some courage, I went near and asked the reason for the crying, weeping, shaking and all. At first she shot at me a lot of arrows of suspicion, of course by glance. Then I perceived a ray of trust. She told me her cinema-like story: she hailed from some village in interior Uttarakhand, had studied up to high school, possessed an eye-catching body, came in search of a job of dignity, but society had cast her into prostitution. She stayed on the other side of the Ganga with a distant relative, an old lady who had also been in the same profession previously. The girl told me she was disgusted with her place in life, and she wanted to end it all by jumping into the Ganga. But the memory of her ailing parents, for whom she was lone breadwinner and support, was dragging her back from such an action, and yet the other side was hell.

I have always been a sentimental fool and hearing her story, became very upset. It is strange indeed in this world that people are never ready to share even an iota of their happiness with others, but unhesitatingly make you the lone successor to not only their sins, sorrow, pains, sufferings, sometimes even of their ancestors, in a single will without a power of attorney! People would have definitely ridiculed me if they had seen me talking with that girl for long. But at first sight itself, an affinity towards her had developed in my mind. We used to meet daily at the same time, at the same ghat. My boat of *saadhana* was heading for shallow waters, a bit disturbed, earning me stigma points among friends. Even then I remained true to my conscience, for the inclination towards that girl was not at all carnal. The shared pain transformed into affection, forming a crystal in my mind. Even at that time I was unable to make a meaning from this, since my faculties of comprehensive understanding were immature and unripe, I was almost a child at that time. Somewhere from some literature I had read in the past, came up the phrase—'an unknown feeling of pain in heart towards someone is called love'. Love always happens between hearts willing to share happiness. Not even God will share anybody's pain, or promise to rid of it completely. Let no one live under the illusion that one day God will descend to share their sins, pains, and misdeeds. But if we show acceptance of our situation, God always helps us reduce our pains, and also helps multiply our happiness if we share it. Thus I was wondering with painful confusion if that's where I was heading to. I had nothing to do with that poor girl. Though I had heard her story many times, there was no sympathy but a sweet unfamiliar pain in my mind. I requested some shopkeepers I knew to employ the girl as a sales girl in their shop, but none did.

Our relationship grew deeper as days passed. We both felt restless if we failed to meet an evening. But I never had any urge to find what her feelings towards me were. My mind was almost disturbed out of bounds though, and finally I decided to do something favorable for her and relieve my mind of its turbulence, in case the so-called '*yoga bhrashtatha*' happens.

By chance someone introduced me to a *sanyasini* of repute who was also head of a *mahila ashram*, exclusively for women. An idea clicked in my mind and I narrated to that *matadhipathi*, in moving detail, the pathetic story of that girl. But that *sanyasini* remained impassive. So I did another *saptaaha* (long narration) of the same story, and she melted a little, changing from unmoving to reluctant. A ray of hope had appeared. She was still hesitant to take in a prostitute into her ashram as inmate. The next day I went to meet the *matadhipathi sanyasini* again with a more updated version of the issue, and after long discussions and arguments, my efforts finally paid off. I had convinced her to give the girl a new lease of life but her condition was that the girl be initiated into *sanyasa* prior and that she lead a life of strict discipline thereafter.

Now the ball was in my court. It was my turn to persuade that teenage girl. She of enticing body who had traveled a long way on the highway of exploited sensuality in a fancy car, where she had not been able to find a single drop of what she had really wanted:

to walk on the footpaths between country fields, bare-footed too. That was the meaning of the situation developing around us. The next day when I met her on the *ghat*, I openly told her to leave the 'pig sty' and enter in a new life of 'bhagava (fortunate, blessed).' She was not ready to accept it as her logic was very different. She said, "Look *swamiji*, I am a *patita* (fallen woman). I don't want to pollute that *pavitra* (purity) ashram and its inmates with my negativity. Don't ask me to do this, it is impossible." I tried to convince her by telling her, "*Punya*, and all other concepts of *dvandva* or duality, arise only from the play of the mind. Though you may consider your body *apavitra* or impure, your *atma* or soul is not. The *atma*, or the *chaitanya* is ever pure and *shuddha*. Now if you insist that you have erred, you then have to do something to wash off that before your lifespan is exhausted and you have to move on. And even if you do not believe in rebirth, but want to see the face of peace, not wishing to live the same pig-sty kind of life, then this is the best option given by Ma Ganga, because she too is a woman knowing a woman's heart best. So clean up your sins with a positive mind, doing *japa* and lead a strict disciplined life. You will be saved from *narakas*. *Paschathaapam (repentance)* is the greatest form of *praayaschittam (atonement)*. Do repent on the deeds, or *karmas* done so far. Bathe in the holy Ganga with repentance, say goodbye to the world of exploitation and come with me to that *ashram*.'

It was about to be dusk. She was in silence for some time and disappeared into the darkness. That day I sat there for a few hours. I took it too much to heart, thinking about the failure of my mission and role as a savior in giving a new life. There were tears in my eyes from the sincere yearning of my heart that she be able to lead a life of dignity for the rest of her life. The possessiveness was such that any bystander would take it as love only. This dawned in my mind only after the problem had been solved and the intoxication come down. Yet there was the undercurrent of positive thought in my mind in wanting to save that poor girl from the darker side of life.

The next morning while I was bathing in the Ganga, I spotted the girl at a distance away. She had appeared, out of routine in the morning, and came and sat near me on the ghat, waiting for me to complete my bath. But I felt a little irritated at her presence and without paying much notice to her, I started moving towards the road. I heard a sound from behind, the sacred word I wanted to hear from her mouth—the certificate of recognition of my efforts—"*Bhayya*, (brother) just wait. I am here to obey your orders. Please take me to the *ashram* where I can get that safe and secure life. *Ganga mata ki kasam*, I will never look back, as you said, or even remember the dark life I have lived so far." I was moved when she called me '*Bhayya*'. Since I've always been a sentimental fool, I wept taking her hands into mine. We both walked towards that ashram and as per the *mathadipati*'s conditions, I entrusted her in her hands. I rejoiced as one of my missions had ended in success.

After a few years, once after I had settled at the Jammu ashram, during one of my visits to Haridwar, I met her in *kashaya*. She was standing on the banks of Ganga with one of her *guru behens*. Approaching her, I looked to her face and asked, "Do you remember me?" It took a minute or so for her to recollect me. "Oh, Bhayya", she cried out, but this time out of happiness. After so many years, Ganga *mata* had given us the chance to meet again. She said, "*Bhayya*, you, only you are the reason for this new *avatar* of mine. You have saved my life."

Once again I had tears in my eyes. But this time the tears were of joy, or *aanandaashru*. *Ganga mayya ki jai*.

Experience Oneness

It is a cloudy winter morning and a cold wind flows gently down the Himalayan glaciers. Here the Ganga flows quietly, her waters crystal clear and her gait, *gajagamini*-like, slow. The sound of *omkar* reverberates from a bell ringing in a distant temple. The calm and serene atmosphere around is as if time itself is in deep meditation. There is the chanting sound of *mantras* from the neighbouring *ashram*. The elevating smell of the smoke from the just-concluded evening *havan* (offering in the holy fire) wafts around and cold wind ceases blowing for a moment. Yes, this is Uttarakashi, where I am now, the abode and confluence of great minds. Of sincere, serious and dedicated seekers (*sadhakas*) of all branches of the Vedic stream, Vedanta, Tantra, Bhakti etc. Uttarakashi is as well known among *sanyasis* like Kashi and Rishikesh are. Kashi is the seat of learning. It is natural after learning to have to practice it, and the word '*uttara*' means 'after', 'further' etc. So Uttara kashi is the place to go after the learning is done. If Kashi is the seat of learning, then Uttara Kashi is the abode of experience. The ecology and topography here itself is such that it is very conducive for contemplation. Contemplation in the initial stages can be very difficult. To recognize, comprehend, and establish what has been learnt and to practice meditation requires some effort. The calm, peaceful, and serene atmosphere in Uttarakashi attracts serious *sadhakas* to the lap of the Himalayas. Everywhere one sees ashrams of sorts, Veda *mantras*, *satsangs*, and chanting are heard, and Mother Ganga dances in ecstasy at this, her waves of purity blessing the shores.

I remember well those days when I was staying at Kailash Ashram in Ujjaily, on the outskirts of the town, a few kilometers towards Gangotri. Most of the *sadhu-sanyasis* staying there, subsist on the *bhiksha* (daily dose of food) provided by the various *annakshetras*. They move in groups, called mandalis for collecting *bhiksha* and it is an eye-purifying visual on the roads during morning times—groups of *kashaya*-clad *sadhus* parading to Kali Kambaliwala, Punjab, Sindh or Dandi ashrams. After collecting their daily due of food, they either proceed to the banks of Ganga, or any ghat, to sit there and partake of the food. Or otherwise, a few would take their food (*roti, dal, rice, sabji*) to their rooms, and enhance the taste of the dal a little by seasoning, or pouring on a little ghee and consume. As I was in Kailash ashram, I used to take my morning and evening food at the ashram itself. Very rarely did I go for *bhiksha*.

Swami Umanandji was the 'Kothari' (caretaker) of the ashram—a nice man who taught me to chant the *Shiva Mahimna Stotram*, the official prayer of *sanyasis*, a unique experience worth mentioning. I was not familiar with this prayer then, since my circle of *saadhana* was mostly centered around *Devi*. It was not like I had any hate for it or anything, it was just that the situation had never risen that I might pursue it seriously. The '*Mahimna stotram*' is considered equal to *Rudri* and is part of the strict routine as evening prayer in all *sanyas* ashrams in Northern India, and now in other places as well they have started emulating this practice. In the evening after the concluding *arati* all the inmates of the ashram sit together to do the *Mahimna Paath* in a mesmerizing rhythm. So naturally in Kailash Ashram, Uttarakashi, which is a purely *sanyasi*-oriented place, it was inevitable. All the other sadhus took it for granted, that I being well-lettered, garbed in kashaya, handsome to look at, would surely know it. Nobody ever cared to confirm this either. When others chanted in full rapture, I used to keep quiet closing my eyes, and pretended to chant, by moving my lips. But I was not able to escape for long. I felt too embarrassed to tell anybody that I didn't know how to chant it, and the ego, refused to acknowledge anyone as guru too. At last one day I came under the radar-like eyes of a *swamiji*, who observed in me the black hole. He summoned me to his room, got me to vomit out the truth, and gave a good scold, typical of a reputed *vedantin*. I left hanging my head in shame and on my way out, stumbled upon Swami Umanandji, the Kothari of that ashram. When he asked for the reason, I told him what had happened. He patted me on my back, and with hand around my shoulders, took me to his room where he handed me a book with the Shiv Mahimna Stotram in it. He asked me to follow his tune and rhythm of chanting, and asked me to repeat twice what he had recited. He took out a good one hour of his time on a cold night to teach me with much affection. I returned to my room with wounded ego and a resolve and determination sprang from the innermost realms of my being. A voice within was saying—"Why do you worry, you can memorize it overnight." At first I thought I was hallucinating, but it was a voice of confidence. I tossed and turned on my bed for some time, then got up and decided to try for a bit, till I memorized one or two verses. I was on shaky grounds initially, but an unknown faith had revived me and I continued, memorizing the verses one by one. I did not feel sleepy, did not glance at my watch even once through the night, and no one will believe it was five in the morning, but I was already on top of Everest. So the lunchtime came, and I saw the *swamiji*, who had bruised my ego. He also was a Malayali, a well-known *Vedanti* of that time who commanded great respect even among advanced scholars, and had an ashram at Amarkantak. He stared at me as if I were a worm. I just drank that venom and kept quiet. To avoid any further friction, I went to my room with the staunch decision to learn it and did a few more readings. It was evening and time for the *Mahimna*, and everyone sat down to chant. I sat in the last row. The chanting was going on smoothly. In the *Mahimna stotra*, there are a few such verses, and places and lines, where if you are not careful, you will keep on chanting the same thing. So all of a sudden right in the middle everyone made a mistake and lost the link. And to my surprise even the radar-like *swamiji* too. But mine was the lone voice that was chanting on without any interruptions, like I was the oldest and most expert chanter there, with a sweeter voice grace of my Mother. It was from me that all others got the missing link to continue and complete the chanting. But the *swamiji* was staring at me open-jawed in astonishment. Now he invited (the previous day he had summoned) me to his room. He shook his head, his eyes full of amazement and complimented me for chanting with utmost care and beauty without the help of the book. And he wanted to know how I had accomplished this feat overnight. I told him that it was just his blessings in disguise that a whole night's practice had made me memorize it. *Swamiji* said, "You Malayalis are very dangerous. Until you are hurt, you will do nothing. But if somebody touches your 'ego,' you Malayalis become fierce. Come and sit by me." I sat near him, and he blessed me and started telling me the deep meaning of each and every verse. Of course he was an invincible authority on the scriptures and when Umanandji came to call both of us for *bhiksha*, *swamiji* was still lost, deep in the Samadhi of explanation, and I lost in the *Samadhi* of listening, to complete his *vyakhya* interpretation of the *stotram*. Once he finished, I thanked him with *pranaams* and said, "Swamiji, you have certainly proved that Malayali *sanyasis* are determined. I retaliated by memorizing the stotram overnight. And you have completed the discourse in one sitting." I knew that he was also from Kerala. (Usually sanyasis never disclose their *poorvashram* name or place or date of birth, as it is irrelevant to others). The point I want to drive home here is: our mind is made up of so many faculties of learning, storing, reproducing, retrieving, and updating (sixteen such are counted in shodasi vidyas in *tantra*). So it is to be remembered that the capturer of them all is the memory. Whether we in our life keep clean any other faculty or not, we must try to keep this faculty as young as that of a child. If not, there is no use, whatever high position you have, your life will be just a waste.

Another memorable incident also occurred in Uttarakashi that left me inconclusive of certain basics of spirituality. Though I had come across many kinds and categories of sadhaks, some even established at the top, one among them perplexed yet appealed to me. Whenever I crossed through the marketplace to purchase something, or went for *bhiksha*, or for a walk, I would see a middle-aged *swamiji* sitting under a tree at a particular place near Kailash ashram, by the Ganga. He never changed the spot, always in a different mood of his own altogether. Though he was clad in rags, his stunningly bright eyes were characteristic of a great soul. Whenever I passed by him, I use to pay a courtesy glance. One day by chance or by destiny, I observed a big wound filled with oozing pus on his left leg, just near the knee. He sat looking at that wound with a smile on his face, as if he were in ecstasy. I felt that I should go and do *seva* to that saint and so I went to the market and purchased some cotton, soframycin powder, a small bottle of Dettol, and some bandages and walked up to him. As usual he was sitting looking at the wound and smiling. I sat near him, but he ignored me as if I was not there. I just did my *namaskars* to that saint and touched his feet with a prayer to allow me to clean and dress his wound. When I touched his feet, he pulled his leg back with a jerk, and to my shock one or two worms fell down. Immediately the *swamiji* shouted, "What you have done, you fool!" He started crying loudly as if some of his near and dear ones had died. I was wondering what had happened. He scolded me, "You fool—you have thrown them away! They were happily having their food in that wound. You sinner! Think twice before you act." With utmost care and affection, he took the small worms in his hands and placed them back on the wound and smiled again. He sat in silence for some time and looked at me as if asking me to get lost. Slowly I stood up and walked away, and threw the medicines and bandages with a prayer to Ganga Mata. The medicine plunged into the water but not my worry that I had disturbed that great *avadhoota* saint in his ecstatic moments, and I hoped he would not curse me. Everything happened due to my lack of proper understanding at that point of my saadhana, about the various states of the saints and their attitudes towards this world. There were a lot of questions in my mind about the veracity of such *saadhana* and states etc.

My mind had fooled me and I was not satisfied with my own understanding. Then the radar-vision *swamiji* came to mind and I approached him with reverence, for he is a master on his own accord, and narrated to him the incident.

"Nadanadaji," with love and concern he started explaining, "it is very good that you have attempted service with good faith and regard. But you must remember one thing while serving sadhus. Their attitude towards the body is entirely different from that of worldly people. Common people in the world of sensual satisfaction, want to cure the body in the hope of extracting from it more enjoyment of any type, till the last breath is reached. But when sadhus attempt a cure, it is only to keep the body in order, so that it helps them as a vehicle to reach deeper and wider in accessing the subtler areas of self-knowledge. There is no point in spending money on a junk car. Another thing to know is that just enduring a pain in the body is not going to take you to enlightenment—this is not a norm or standard that we should accept or propagate. I interrupted to ask how it was then that in the Chandogya Upanishad, it is stated that, *Samvarga Vidya* is the greatest state of attainment, which was imparted to King Janasruti by sage Raikva who appears as a cart driver. That sage too was like this *mahatma*, with inflamed sores all over his body, and he is considered one of the greatest *avadhootas* of the Upanishads, and how was he different from this one. Swamiji was now in his element, and started explaining. "Look," he said, "the actual state of mind of the avadhoota, and that of another person merely practicing or reenacting his behavior after hearing about it, are different. This mahatma might have heard that story, and it probably made a deep impression on his psychology, and so he adopted it in his life. It is an isolated kind of thinking. If such things become standard procedure or behavior for attainment of enlightenment, then everyone would be nursing wounds, and will all creatures with wounds become realized? It is all right that you went in good faith to serve an ailing soul. His mindset did not permit that service, and there ends that story. Whether he is supposed to suffer, whether it was a state of greatness etc. are all useless considerations till we get clear supporting data about him. So, why do you take it too much to the heart and are so gloomy? So goes the saying, 'Serve the needy.' Before serving we must first establish that the needs are genuine, and aimed towards seeking of knowledge. Seva in order to feed your ego or helping sensual gratification is not service. Without proper understanding of this, you will be diverting the source of help in the wrong direction. Helping the undeserving is another irrevocable sin. If this mahatma is choosing to endure all this as a *saadhana*, let him carry on. This is allowed in our scriptures, and we should not interfere in his choice of *saadhana*. If he solicits help, we can certainly attend to it within our capacity."

The clouds had become dense, and the wind ceased to blow. All of a sudden it started to rain. The heavy downpour gave relief to the clouds. And my heart felt the same way, like the clouds. It lasted only a few minutes and the sky cleared. There were no clouds anymore. I felt the freshness of nature around me, and a renewal inside me as well! Sometimes when a new *sadhak* comes across such extreme behaviors, he might mistake it for an advanced state of attainment. However, it need not necessarily be so. One can still choose to adopt such an attitude as an isolated practice, but the attitude need not necessarily subdue the mind. Take care that you not develop ego, basking in the name and fame that might result from such behavior. It is a rule that any calculated, premeditated suppression and endurance of suffering only takes one into the opposite indulgence. It will not help in purifying the karmic residues. That is why it can be seen that some *sanyasis* become wealthy later, due to the ego's payoff of their sufferings in the first stage of *saadhana*.

Mud On My Face

IN MY LONG life as a sanyasi, one of the enlightenments I got was that a sanyasi should be very cautious in their behavior and reactions. Especially a sanyasi leading a life of service to society, should be very deliberate and conscious at each and every step. Otherwise he will end up wasting his time in answering, and clarifying questions and doubts of the ignorant, immature, and irrelevant people. They are the ones always looking for some insufficiency in you, so they can defame the whole system and establish themselves as nearer to godhood. They intend to hurt with razor-sharp thoughts, words and deeds.

During one of my stays at my Jammu ashram, I unexpectedly fell sick due to some unattended cardiac problems. This was my second episode of a cardiac arrest. It was a cold December night and chilly wind was blowing. I, along with Madanlal, Sharmaji, and Omprakashji were in a car going to the railway station. I had to catch the train to Mumbai, as per my schedule, and they were coming along to see me off. On the way in the car I experienced severe throbbing chest pain. They took me directly to a doctor who admitted me in a private hospital in Pathankot, a city in Punjab. I was put under sedation, and other medicines were also administered. By morning I felt some ease. The next day some of my disciples and devotees from the village learned about this, and came to the hospital to visit and wish me a speedy recovery. As the attack this time was much severe than the previous one, the doctor advised hospitalization for nine days. I was discharged on the tenth day with instructions to be in bed rest for at least one month. I was carried back to the *ashram*, but left alone to fend for myself. I was weak, and so debilitated that I was even unable to walk up to the bathroom by myself etc. One of my disciples, a middle-aged lady, volunteered to take care of my needs in spite of responsibilities to her large family. Her husband used to come and stay in my room to care for me, during the nights. Days passed with medicines, rest and after a month or so, I felt better. Now I could move on my own and take care of my personal needs. I thanked that couple and requested them to now take leave and attend to their household, and that I would take care of myself. But they declined, as I was still weak. One day, a few other disciples and devotees gathered together and assembled around me to discuss my health. They were all praising the lady who had served me for the last one month.

Some people cannot bear to hear another person being praised, this seems to be a rule of humankind. One of the ladies, an old woman sitting among them, became agitated and furious, and started accusing the lady, saying, "Are you not ashamed of taking a young man (me) to the bathroom, and giving him a bath etc. You should have felt that this was inappropriate. Why did you do this? In this village there are many young boys and men. None of them came forward to do any *seva* like this? I have doubts about your character." I first thought it was a slip of the tongue. There was an uncomfortable silence in the room for a few minutes. I was shocked to hear this, and never expected such a thing. It had been in good faith, and the whole family was present. And the villagers sitting near were glancing at each other. But none had any clue about what to say in reply, or the courage to come forward in the lady's support, such was the height of ignorance of these people, who I had been wishing and dreaming to make prosperous in all fields of life!

The gem-like lady, I would call her so, who had been in my seva, exhibited such valor and acumen in such a situation. Without losing her faith and devotion in me, she replied without even an iota of shock and perplexity, "Look *mataji*, you have much respect and status among us. This type of short-sighted behavior is unbecoming of you. And in dragging someone through mud this way, you will only lose the high regard that you currently have. It is a Guruji that I serve. After someone is accepted as guru, the status of that relationship becomes much higher than any other worldly relationship. It's not just me, no one else in my family has viewed our Guru at par with an ordinary relative; He is viewed only at par with God himself! Though he may exist in a male body, my Guruji is verily '*Amma*' (the Mother Goddess) to me. Your talk is about my serving him for just these few days—why, if such a necessity arises, we will place our entire live at his feet, at his disposal. I feel sorry for you, that you are unable to view the truth of him with your eyes. To me, getting to do *seva* to my Guruji is just like offering pooja to God, and no one under these skies has any business poking their nose in it. We took up this task voluntarily, and consider ourselves fortunate that Guruji even permitted us." After this speech, there was a deep hush all around. Most of the people sitting around listening showed deep appreciation at the fearless, timely, and apt response of the lady with the golden heart who had served me. The baseless allegation caused me a lot of distress, even a little anger, but I did not say anything.

But the next day onwards the rumor mills were filled with stories about the incident, and allegations being made all over the village about relations between me and that lady. It is surprising that in this world every kind of person finds a sponsor. It is naive to think that only good actions are being sponsored. In post-independent India, in fact it is much more of the anti-social, anti-human, anti-national, and immoral kind of thinking that has been sponsored, rather than any genuine case of rights violations. The old lady doing the slandering also had some sponsors, in the form of new religious preachers, who were looking to establish hold upon these innocent people. These preachers were in reality anti-Vedic—preaching against our established and well tested system of spirituality, and against the Gods and the Brahmins. I was a thorn in the flesh to them. They drew the greedy lady into their network and trained her to launch the insult campaign that was actually targeted at me and my way of preaching. At first I was unaware of this angle but later gleaned it from the feedback I received. But it was really unfortunate that some kind-hearted people were hurt in the incident, due to some other people's deficiency of seeing things in correct perspective and their lack of patience in cross-checking details. It is the very nature of some people to take decisions and jump to conclusions, or form opinions on situations, surroundings, visuals, etc., without first evaluating the power of their own intelligence. We are so arrogant in our own abilities to reason, and believe that there is nothing beyond those capacities of ours. This is the main reason for all the conflicts that prevail in today's society. So it is necessary that we develop the art of cross-checking the available data and information. Information processing is called *viveka* or discrimination and if you have *viveka,* it will keep you in peace. Otherwise a lot of time is wasted in dealing with allegations and counter allegations, and nothing constructive comes of it though it is sure to give you never-ending pain. I then told the lady who had been in my *seva,* "Stay here for a few more days. Let what may happen, your husband knows the truth well. You need not go to your home now. Let them continue their propaganda. When they are tired they will stop it." That lady, her husband, and I stayed for a few more days together.

When my health had improved, my disciples insisted on convening a *satsang*. They wanted to clear the air feeling that the village was becoming divided from the behind-the-scene activities of the anti-religious elements. The campaign of these cunning elements was to instigate, persuade, and attract increasing numbers to adopt that new religion. Almost all my devotees in the village and surrounding areas attended the satsang, where I gave a fitting reply to all those who had criticized me and that old lady too managed to attend the satsang without any sense of guilt. I told them to remove the black glasses obscuring their vision, which they had received in donation from the anti-Vedic elements, who had hoped these good people would end up following them in spite their higher social order. I told them not to fall for the divisive tactics disguised as *bhakti,* for one day the division may become so much that you will not live even with your parents anymore, let alone with the outside world. After two days I placed before them plenty of proof that all this was a plot. I admonished them that if they became greedy for some short-lived benefit, one day they would lose all originality, such would be the brainwashing. (I heard later, after I had left Ramnagar, these people had purchased land and even built a *satsang* hall.) After listening to my talk, the old woman who had started the smear campaign, finally recognized the true colors of the people behind this. She stood up in the middle of the satsang, and asked pardon for her wrong doings. I accepted it, but not without mentioning that the incident was a warning bell for all of them.

For the past one thousand years, and especially after the so-called independence from British rule, the whole world has realized the power of sacrifice (or *tyaaga*) upon which our Indian way of life is established. Some of them do not want Indians to think for themselves. Now if most Indians will start reflecting and thinking carefully, then those who have so far made a living by prostituting themselves, will begin to face difficult times. So such people have conspired to defame the social order which is the strength of India. Since Indian social order is dominated mainly by temples and *ashrams*, they have targeted these entities. They exploit the human weakness called poverty to their benefit. It was by chance or by choice that I too happened to face that bite. It was only due to the dedicated devotion of the lady who served me, that a big plot was foiled. It also served as a test of devotion for the followers, and even till date she remains one of my highly reliable *shish as* (disciples).

Oneness As Fire And Heat

ONE CANNOT PREDICT what is kept in the womb of 'time.' Time brings anyone and anything together and can separate them quickly too, but this is not through irrational whim, wish or will, but by law, unlike most imagine. We may flout laws but not time. We live our lives like the proverbial logs in a stream that come together and separate according to the speed of flow, as per their karma. There is a secret lying buried within the same saying: if there is a wish to permanently be with some of those logs, the persons met at particular times in our existence who have helped in promoting, enlightening and guiding us towards final liberation, then that is possible too—to be together forever. Everything is predestined and happens as per the plans of destiny. This eternal truth of the inherent spirituality is something which everyone must remember in all dealings.

I was staying at Siddhi Vinayak Mandir in Chowl, a remote village in Maharashtra. I was in search of two youngsters who I had met in my dreams and came to this village with Keshav. The two of them, Mohi and Raju were found here and initiated by me into *Shakti saadhana*. As I had promised Keshav earlier, I had also initiated him too earlier into the order of *sanyas samskar* at Omkareswar on *Guru Poornima* day. This new *sanyasi baba*, now known as Vidyanand, stayed back in Chowl for a week or so to get familiar with the preliminaries of sanyasi life, and left me to continue further *parivrajaka* life. The two other youngsters started their intense *saadhana* under my guidance.

One day Mohi invited me to his house for *bhiksha*. I noticed that in his personal household *pooja* room, he had installed only *Maa*. Some inspiration sprang from within that made me tell him that *Shiva* and *Shakti* are inseparable entities. Without *Shakti*, *Shiva* cannot exist and function, and in the complementary way, without *Shiva*, *Shakti* cannot manifest. He told me that he did not have an authentic *Shivalingam* to fill in the gap and that he would install *Shiva* too along with *maa* when he met with the situation that would prompt that happening. I don't know what inspired me, but I placed my hands inside my *kappar* and a *Shivalinga* manifested in it. I gave that *Shivalingam* to Mohi. Everybody took it as a miracle, and even today it is enshrined and worshipped in Mohi's *mandir* dedicated to *maa*. So with mother, the father too was installed. In the meantime we made plans to construct a hut for our saadhana in the nearby village of Vave. It was in a secluded place, surrounded by forest and hills, and a few furlongs away from the road. The hut was erected and even though Mohi was running a jewellery shop in those days, he spent the maximum time possible with me there, immersed in *japa*. But Raju, the other young man was unwell, and was admitted in hospital. After he was discharged, he stayed back at home to continue his *saadhana* to the extent possible. Another youth named Mangesh had now joined us too, who also owned a jewellery store in Srivardhan, a few hours' journey from Chowl. There was a lot of disturbance in *saadhana* due to the forest insects, especially during the *homams* at night. They would came in swarms and fall down into the *homa agni*. So we decided to shift back to the Siddhi Vinayaka Mandir. As Raju's house was near that temple, he also joined us in *saadhana*, and spent the maximum time possible with me there. That *mandir's* 'guru' (priest and owner) Ravi and his family, and his sister took responsibility of my everyday needs.

In the meantime I was affected by the condition of 'slipped disk' and doctors put me in traction. For that I had to be shifted to a house nearby belonging to Dasarath and family, relatives of Ravi. For a month or so I underwent much suffering and the treatment available there was not enough to give relief, so I left for the Jammu ashram along with Raju who continued his *saadhana* there. (From then Raju was always with me, serving and taking care of my needs for more than fifteen years, till he left me at Kurnool, to be with his ailing parents at Chowl in their last days).

After few months stay at the Jammu ashram, I returned to Chowl and stayed in Mohi's pooja room itself. During those days, Mohi and his friends arranged a very big *Ganesha yaagam* at Mukhari Ganapathi Mandir in the village, which was well attended and appreciated. It was a record that I chanted mantras for the *yaagam* for more than twelve hours nonstop. I had the good company of the youth at Chowl, all Mohi's and Raju's friends, and a few of them took *mantra deeksha* too.

Everything was going well. Even though I occasionally visited the Jammu ashram or Samalkha as needed, after a few days stay there I would return to Chowl to stay with Mohi and Raju. The bond with the youngsters was deepening with time, and my dependency on them was increasing without my notice. It may have been because of the fact that bonds have to be broken when the time comes, 'time' started playing tricks. For no apparent reasons, a few misunderstanding cropped up between Mohi and me. We fell apart overnight. Though he was only ten years younger than me in physical age, I was always with him as guru. He admitted to this, on his return to me after ten years. During this period Raju used to come and stay with me at Jammu ashram, or Samalkha or Kurnool, and he served me more than a son serves his father, when I fell seriously ill. After a long gap of ten years, Mohi returned to me and by this time he was married and blessed with a son and daughter. Raju was with me at the time of his arrival when I was bedridden due to cardiac problems. Mohi was accompanied with his guru bhais Mangesh, Bawa, Praveen and Anil. Mohi requested me to return to Chowl at least once, and I too was inclined to visit the village again. After one or two months, Bawa and Mohi came with a car to take me there. A grand reception awaited at Mukhari Ganapathi Mandir, arranged by Mohi and his friends, and I was taken to Mohi's residence where a *mandir* had been constructed by him, in the form of a procession. Raju returned with me to Kurnool and stayed back for my seva. Their *saadhana* went well, and I decided to give the *poornabhishekam* to Mohi on a Guru Poornima day. This displeased a few of my other so-called senior disciples at Hyderabad. Mohi's *saadhana* had yielded results and I could see the difference, so the decision was correct and timely from my view point as a Guru. Spiritual *saadhana* is not a government job to get 'promotions' according to seniority. The one able to brings out result from *saadhana* will get to advance to the following steps automatically, as it is said "*yogena yogamaapnuyaat* (from the practice of yoga comes the eligibility)." Even though Raju 'pretended' to understand his Guruji well, and always spoke highly about me to my other disciples, he may have felt a bit hurt at my decision to offer *poornabhishekam* to Mohi. It seemed like Raju may have been under a wrong impression and been mentally preparing himself for it, without my permission. Raju's dedication to me as guru and his seva was certainly faultless, and I was even ready to hand over my *kutia* and other assets to him as reward for his long and faithful guru *seva*, and maintenance of my '*samadhi*' mandir. But now he left me, and I am sure he was never able to read or realize the affection I had for him since I am not very demonstrative. Even though he left me in the false pretext of taking care of his ailing parents, the undercurrent of his leaving was nothing other than his 'dislike towards Mohi' and his gains in *saadhana*. Raju returned to his village on his own accord, with some envy in mind, but even at this moment I love him and have the same feeling, deeming him 'my own,' which should not be present in a *sanyasi*. At Kurnool before he left, my spiritual brother Abhayanandji and my sanyasi disciple Omkaranand tried in vain to convince him that he was taking a wrong step by leaving Guruji. He went ahead though, leaving a painful scar in my heart. It may be that 'Mother Nature' never relished my '*mamata*' (mother's love) towards him.

    Cruel time plays tricks in human life now and then, when one tries to make a permanent connection on worldly terms. It is only the relationship based upon spiritual purpose and pursuit that continues through births. Such a relationship between guru and disciple is not created for worldly benefit and continues to exist forever, however weak, fruitless, tasteless it might seem sometimes. No other relationship however good—be it wife, husband, mother, father, or son that we may happen to get in any birth, will continue with us in the following births. But the connection with the guru however bad it might seem at the time, will definitely continue and we will always be in contact with him. This is the wonderful arrangement of the Almighty for the protection of its most loved creation called the human. This is because God is human-like, and not because humans are god-like. But his own replica called the human does not have the time to feel the intensity of this love that the lord has in his bosom for us. At the very moment one recognizes this pure devotion for him in our heart, it will pour out in gratitude. This incident was also one among them.

Anantham, Atmabandham

I JUST RECEIVED A call from my spiritual brother Swami Abhayananda Saraswathi. I had e-mailed him a few chapters of the just completed episodes for the first reading and his feedback. Some 45 minutes later, he called me up on the phone to say, "It looks fine, please continue the writing work. Do not stop, the flow is fine. Only a few spelling and grammar mistakes. I will correct it and return it to you." I was wondering at this. Of course he is the best friend and brother to me in the spiritual path, but he is a bitter critic too. Like everybody, he had his own perspective and logic for everything, and we used to discuss a variety of matters with each other. As I have my own perspective too, we would quarrel too due to our unyielding natures. After exchanging a few words on the difference of opinion, he would sometimes compromise with me, his mind, being so pure and calm, unlike mine. I have a different methodology, but he is a little conventional and conservative with modern perspective. Yet I have always had a soft corner for him, as we have known each other since days of yore: from Shivanand ashram in Rishikesh. Till date, our long affectionate relationship has lasted more than thirty years. We used to go on pilgrimage of sorts, we used to stay together, share pleasures and pains, and exchange select and choicest *gaalis* (insults) too. A never-ending relation prevails between us till today, and I pray and hope that it remain as evergreen till the Ganga flows. Especially in the recent past, when I was suffering agony with the 'burning feet syndrome' for a few months at Kurnool, he stayed with me for a long time till I recovered.

I remember one trip, when we were heading towards Rishikesh from Khedighat (a beautiful *saadhana*-oriented spot on the banks of the Narmada, Madhya Pradesh). We also considered going to Thiruvannamalai later, an abode of knowledge where inspirations flow involuntarily and easily. Since we are both mostly inclined towards the *gyana marga*, we share the same core thinking, saadhana etc. Thus we picked this place to stay for a month or so, as a spiritual retreat. After a few days' stay at 'Koyal Ghati' (Rishikesh) in an ashram, we left for Haridwar to catch the train to Delhi, and from there on to Madras or Chennai, as it is known nowadays. We hopped onto a shared-ride van from Rishikesh to Haridwar. On the way to Raiwala, a few drunkards in *kashayam* boarded our vehicle. As they had all filled themselves up to their necks with country arrack (liquor) of 5th grade (brewed especially for them with the good intention of reducing the population of poor India) they began shouting and quarrelling. A little later they started breaching the limits. The driver too was fed up and saying he would drive the automobile to the police station. But devils listen to none but the cane! I was a bit anxious. By the time of reaching Saptasarovar, we were all fed up and Abhayanand getting very angry and infuriated, caught hold of one of the drunkards and delivered a well-aimed blow. He then kicked them all out of the auto, and asked the auto driver to proceed to the railway station.

So with such friction-filled travel, we found ourselves at last at the feet of Arunachala, and due to communications exchanged earlier with them, we were able to get accommodation at the Sri Ramana Ashram for a few days. We were provided with a room which we shared, and planned to stay there for a month or so. Early every morning we used to go on '*Sri pradikshina*' (a radius of 14 km around the Arunachala hills) which is the main item of *saadhana* prescribed for whoever comes to Thiruvannamalai in the pursuit of grace for knowledge and by extension for liberation.

Thiruvannamalai represents the mountainous fire of truth or knowledge that manifested upon the solid surface meeting point of two aspects: one the deep-rooted values of life, and second the unscaled and unscalable heights of worldly achievements in the ever expanding sky of possibilities. There was an ego clash between these two aspects—the creative aspect or the height of worldly achievements (Brahma), and the aspect of sustenance—the base-root of the deeper values of life (Vishnu). Both clashed for supremacy on the surface field of actions and activities. Lord Shiva manifested as a mountainous fire of knowledge in order to teach them a lesson, and confer on them the realization that for peaceful coexistence, both aspects of creation must meet at the plane of connecting activities, and reciprocate and complement each other. Knowledge does not favor even the most towering empirical achievement, no matter how useful it be or high its magnitude, if it does not ally with the deep-rooted values of life, and if others' existence is not accepted at par with one's own. So knowledge manifested as fire between them, and ordered them to prove their worth and claim by challenging each to reach the peak or depth on either side.

Brahma took the form of a *hamsa* or swan and started scaling the heights of (towards the head of Shiva) achievements but he failed. Feeling frustrated and dejected after a very long journey, he, Brahma the advocate of worldly achievers, brought with him some fallen, dried out leaves and flower, of no use to anyone anymore, to prove his case and claim the prize. On the other end, the believer in the deepest of life values, Lord Vishnu took the form of a monstrous pig, Varaha, and started digging downwards. He started fathoming the deepest root of his faith, but he too met with the same plight. He was sincere in his search though, and realization dawned upon him when he understood the futility of fathoming the depth of knowledge, and recognized that knowledge, Shiva, is verily the lone eternal truth. Thus end the ego clash in a uniting note, with no necessity for lengthy arguments or voluminous books, and by its own accord. Such is the glory and meaning of Arunachala, the embodiment of knowledge fire, so says the Geeta as '*gyanagni dagdha karmanam*'.

The great saint Ramana, true to his title of Maharishi, was a vast reservoir of subtle knowledge in its undiluted natural glory. He is one of the most recognized saints of our time, non-controversial, silent and revolutionary. His declarations are all irrefutably exact up to each letter. One of Abhaya's long- time friends, Rudrappa, who had also been an inmate of Shivananda Ashram, and was now doing his *saadhana* in Arunachala, joined us for the daily *giri pradikshina*. As he was passionately devoted to the Lord of Arunachala, after leaving Shivananda Ashram Rudrappa settled in Tiruvannamalai for *saadhana*. Rudrappa and I never enjoyed each other's company as we were sort of like strong repelling poles. Whether he was self-assuming, assertive, or egoistic I cannot tell, but he behaved like a realized soul. Abhayanand and Rudrappa used to have discussions on a few Vedantic topics, which I never dared to get involved in, or even cared for either. Thus passed our time during the stay in Arunachala, highly enjoyable and elevating nevertheless!

The only fellow who was more upsetting besides Rudrappa was my own tummy. My mind was irritated with Rudrappa, and my tummy with the Tamilians' tamarind-laden food, made only with tamarind and chilly. I used to have bad-smelling burps but even then I could not hold my tongue in check, so tempting was the taste. Whenever he, the stomach, played the tune, Swami Abhayanand would get angry and start giving me sermons like— "You are fascinated with South Indian food, and you keep eating more and more. That is why the indigestion." Sometimes he would be revolted and say, "It is difficult to stay with you in the same room, I am leaving." He took away his bedroll and spread it on the floor of the kitchen in the apartment where we stayed. I felt very bad about that, as the kitchen was just used as a storage room, having never been cleaned in a long time. I knew that because of me Abhayanand was getting disturbed in his *saadhana*. The next day onwards I started *upavas*— fasting for few days. But on the second day Abhayanandji came near me with a sense of guilt, and spoke solicitously, "Maharaji, sorry for the hurt that I inflicted upon you by my behavior yesterday, I beg your pardon, please don't do *upavas*. Take this." He had brought some native bananas and *dal vadas* for me. He insisted on my taking them. Our eyes brimmed with tears. A moment of love, an occasion to remember even today with evergreen emotions.

The stay continued. Abhayanand, a book worm, used to go to the *ashram* library and made use of it to reflect and contemplate. My routine was, or rather my preference, was to sit at the *samadhi mandir* of Maharshi Ramana[20]. One day my eyes suddenly went to the cloth Abhayanand was wearing which appeared of very good quality and appealed to me. Feeling a strange temptation to own it, I asked him to give it to me. As it was old he declined, but I kept insisting that I needed it. (Even today I have no idea why I was after him for that piece of cloth). Abhayanand left without saying anything. On return I noticed that the cloth was not on his body. I thought he might have thrown it away. But the next day he brought it to me, well washed and well ironed by a washerman. I never used that cloth, and took it back to Jammu where it still sits in the small almirah in my *ashram* room. Something was bothering me about this—what was the reason behind asking for his old cloth and keeping it in the almirah? But even today, I have the mandatory practice that whenever he visits me, I offer him a pair of clothes which he happily accepts, thanks to his good heart.

We were returning from Thiruvannamalai after the one month stay. Reaching Delhi, we continued straightaway to the *ashram* by train which was very late and reached Chaki Bank (Pathankot) at night. We hired an auto-rickshaw to reach Ramnagar village where the *ashram* is situated. There were four people in the vehicle—the both of us, and the driver, and another man picked up along the way. He, the stranger, was carrying a small dog and was fully drunk. After traveling a few kilometers when we reached in front of a Nagaraja Mandir, the driver said, "Baba, we have arrived at your ashram." They both insisted that we get down from the auto. This was at around 2-3 am at night in an unknown

---

20 Ramana Maharshi was an Indian sage and liberated master who lived in Thiruvannamalai or Arunachala hills of South India.

village. So Abhayanand shouted at him to keep moving. After a few kilometers, the driver again came up with an excuse that the headlight of the auto was not working. Abhayanand promptly took out his flashlight, which the driver didn't expect. Then with no option, he continued. I could easily see that *swamiji* was looking for something in his bag. In a minute, he took out a small knife and showing it to me, confided to me in Malayalam, "If these people bother us any more, this will be enough." He was very courageous and never afraid of anything or anybody, rock-solid in his views on the *shastras*. I myself am not so knowledgeable in Vedanta or shastra, except for the *shaakteya saadhana* which I have been following since childhood. He insisted that I study some of the shastra texts as his beloved guru Sri Swami Ramanandiji Maharaj also would recommend. But somehow attending a class or memorizing anything, was almost impossible for me.

I have observed it happening, especially since the past few incidents, that whenever I fell seriously ill, Abhayanandji was always by my side to take care of me with love and his trademark scolding! His physical presence and psychological support have several times brought me back to normalcy. In him, I have seen a real friend, a brother and much, much more. Yes, our relationship continues to grow deeper.

Being In Awareness

Once I was at Khedi Ghat, a small hamlet just by the banks of River Narmada, I lived in an ashram called Virakta Kutia. That is how it was known among *sadhus*, because they admitted only sadhus who do not handle money for any reason or purpose. This ashram has an interesting story.

The founder of Virakta Kutia was one *avadhootha*, who never wore any clothing other than a loincloth or *kaupina* throughout his life, like Maharshi Ramana of Arunachala, although their states are different. The *avadhoota* was the only son of a rich landlord, but right from childhood he had enormous physical power, being able to effortlessly lift weights much heavier than the average human could. In the normal world if someone sees such potential in a child, they will try to exploit it, but his parents who had some scriptural knowledge through *satsang*, wanted to investigate the reasons for it. They consulted many doctors but no one was able to give them a convincing explanation. In the meanwhile a *sadhu* of considerable attainment came to their house one day, asking for *bhiksha*. After hosting him, the parents asked the *sadhu* about the abnormal phenomenon they were observing in their son. The *mahatma* said that the boy was a *yaksha* (a demigod) who by some misdeed had to become a human being, and that was the explanation for the physical power. They brought the boy in front of the *sadhu*, who confirmed this with some *kriyas*. The parents wanted to know if there was any redemption for this, so they could help free him. The sadhu said that it was possible if he did some work of benefit to sadhus.

At hearing this, the fifteen-year old boy then left home, and came wandering to Khedi Ghat. Bathing there in the Narmada, he received some inspiration and decided to stay there, taking shelter under a banyan tree. He stopped wearing conventional clothing, remaining only in *kaupina*. Once every morning he would go to the nearby village called Bharwah which had a bazaar and eat whatever he received as *bhiksha*. He would return to remain under the shadow of the tree. One day an idea struck him about making a *kutia*, but the place was low-lying, and would get waterlogged at the time of rains. So even without being aware of it, he started lifting huge boulders from the Narmada, and within one week he gathered more than fifty tonnes of rock this way. Using these and soil, he put up a high raised platform, upon which he started building a makeshift room-like structure. And all this had been happening even without him being aware of what he was doing. But by providence, after completion of the room, one *parikramavasi sadhu* arrived there and said that he was in search of a place to stay during *chaturmaasya* (rainy season). The *avadhoota* offered the kutia to that *parikramavasi* with joy, and he himself continued staying under the banyan tree. But this small action did wonders to the *avadhoota*. Due to the merit he acquired from submitting his *kutia* to that *parikramavasi* Maa Narmada blessed him with enlightenment. Till then no passerby had ever wondered how such a *kutia* could have been built single-handedly by one man within so short a time. Then everybody came to know about him and later his devotees built him this *ashram* etc. Thus the *yaksha* actually, in the body of a human, absolved himself of his sins due to the meritorious deed, done unknowingly, in the name of *sadhus*. The building stands today as testimony to the event in the year 1950.

The Narmada area itself is a *siddha bhoomi*, and adding to that the ashram is a *siddha sthaana*, and hence a doubly beneficial place for effortless *saadhana*. So I chose this place for my 14th *purascharan* of the *shodashi mantra* of Srividya. It is a beautiful place near Omkareshwar, on the North bank of Narmada, with a few rooms equipped with basic needs for the stay of *sadhus* and *sanyasis* to do their *saadhana*, the food being arranged by the *ashram* administration. I stayed at the small *kutia*, made by the *yaksha* incarnate *avadhoota*, and it was vacant after his *samaadhi*. It was renovated recently and is maintained by his devotees. There is a *smashaana* (cremation ground) near the *kutia* that is being used by the villagers.

While I was staying there, an unconventional *sadhu* calling himself a swami was also staying nearby at the *smashaana* grounds with his pet monkey. I was enjoying my *japa purascharan* with an exhilaration I had never experienced before. My spiritual brother, Swami Abhayanand, was also staying in the main ashram, which is a little further down from this kutia, and where I needed to go for my daily *bhiksha*. Days passed smoothly without any involvement with, or disturbance from others. I kept myself submerged in *japa saadhana*. Except for the irritation from the occasional visits of a few villagers, an ideal and quiet atmosphere prevailed.

However just as *Satya Yuga* cannot remain forever, and the testing or *Kali Yuga* time descends, there was disturbance due to a *swami* staying in a *kutia* of his own nearby. He had arrived from Uttarkashi, having been expelled from there, after serving as a *kothari* for a long time in a famous *ashram*. Since the last few years he was staying in his *kutia* here for his *saadhana*. He too was a *tantrik* but part-time, who unfortunately involved himself in petty issues like cases of childlessness, love affairs, and mostly *satta* (gambling). Like international politics and inter-state politics, there is inter-*ashram* politics too, the reasons which will always be some tale-bearing, greedy villagers with vested interests. But the victims are always the *sadhakas* staying there whose peace, alas, is destroyed.

As already mentioned, this place has certain specially charged powers (both *siddha bhoomi*, *siddha sthaana*). So anything that is said, done, given, thought, and practiced at this spot has added, and quick results. The people who settle here in the garb of *sadhus* exploit this aspect with black magic to who they favor. So the *sadhu* in this scenario gave a *tantric* mantra to one of his devotees, using which the fellow began earning large sums through gambling, which is a scourge in that area. When money comes in, in unethical ways it will also be spent in unrighteous ways. The devotee's character, and that of his family began deteriorating. The children, a young boy and girl adopted unwholesome habits, the wife took to drinks, all because the money had not been earned in a righteous manner. Nevertheless the *sadhu* was getting his share of money.

One day the devotee by chance came to me and told all the stories. I told him, "Look, you are already doing *japa* of a black magic mantra of *tamasic* nature. If you value peace more and not money, I will give you the solution. Your previous mantra will not work to create peace." The man now had realized the value and price of peace, so he said, "*Swamiji*, you just pull me out of this hell. I am ready to forego my money. I would rather be a laborer, but I need peace." I gave some *saatvic* mantra and in one week he had regained his mental poise and will power. When you decide to walk on the path of righteousness, destiny will also come to help you. I stumbled upon a mill owner, who was in search of a good man for the post of manager. I suggested this fellow to him, and he was appointed and was satisfied too.

Afterwards he stopped visiting the part-time *tantrik sadhu*, who had introduced him to the *tamasic* mantra. Any *tamasic* mantra if unaccompanied by japa etc. will harm the guru, so the *ṣadhu* now started facing troubles of all sorts. I was not aware of this turn around. As his *tamasic* mantra was blocked by *saatvic* mantra, he who was now doing *saatvic* mantra was kept safe by the power of the new mantra. But the guru came under the grind. He did some detective work and came to know all that had happened from others, though not from the parties concerned. So he assigned the blame for his downfall upon me. He started a smear campaign against me, trying all the tricks under his sleeves to get me out of there. He had been using that black-listed mantra very well to his advantage, and now that it was blocked and its retrieval only a remote possibility, the deity started harassing him. But he himself was unable to come face to face with me, and had been fumbling for days. Finally, on the verge of breaking down, he approached me early one morning while I was on my way to the river to bathe. This tantric stood right in the middle of the path and began abusing me. I patiently asked for the reasons and if I had caused him harm in some way. But he was too agitated to even hear me.

Hearing his furious, high-octave voice, Abhayananda came running out from the main ashram, to see what was going on. He understood the real and the one-pointed agenda of the tantrik in keeping me out of Khedi Ghat, for he smelt a danger to his network of gambling dens. The tantrik had just lost a good contact too who might cause even more damage if he went out and spilled his secrets.

Abhayanandji decided to get involved, and discussed the issue with the swami and villagers, which I disliked. I told Abhayanand to stay away, as it may disturb the serenity we had both attained, but he was not ready to hear me since the swami in the quarrel had been known to us for long. Somehow with his tact and diplomacy, Abhayanand solved the problem, and the clouds of *ashanti* cleared. But the peculiarity of these clouds of *ashanti* is that when they rain down, the earth instead of getting wet goes dry. So the after effect of being a party to the situation was that my mental equilibrium was disturbed, or rather lost. I had to toil hard to regain it.

A *Naga sadhu* staying in a nearby *kutia* owned a *mala* made of copper, in beads shaped like small skulls. This resembled the *mala* which my Guruji had given me during my stay with her in the Mookambika forest. I gave the *mala* later to Mohi, my disciple in Maharashtra, for whom I did *poornabhishekam* in Srividya. That mala with 54 such skull-shaped beads, became a fascination in my mind. I requested the *Naga sadhu* to give it to me, but he refused to part with it. I started pestering Abhayanand to help me make it mine by any means. He knows my basic nature, that if I set my heart on something, even out of a small fascination, I would somehow manage to get it. This skull-like *mala* of copper, strongly resembled the *mala* which my Amma had given me and it had somehow aroused in me, the thoughts of the past, making me nostalgic. And there was no chance of my abandoning this chase, for after so long I had come across this unique thing. Abhayanand applied his tactics very diplomatically, and managed to bargain for the *mala*, paying two hundred rupees for it. I was so happy to have that *mala* in my hand.

In spite of these undesirable encounters, the days went by very smoothly at Khedi Ghat, with proper saadhana, discussions, and long walks on the banks of Narmada. Abhayanand used to visit Omkareshwar, not far from there, to meet his Guruji occasionally. My *japa purascharan* was almost nearing completion, but this time there was nobody to sponsor a *havan*. But that was immaterial since that ashram too did not permit such rituals which were against an *avadhoota*-hood. Nor was common feeding done there. So doing *japa* without break, with full devotion and faith was sufficient. Abhayanand made the suggestion that since I was unable to do havan in the concluding phase, ten percent more *japa* could be done in addition. He knows such rules of scriptures which was always helpful to me. I was never particular in following all such rules, but he insisted on them, sometimes even quarreling with me, if I failed to follow the orders of the scriptures. Of course, such a scolding from a dear friend was only for my betterment in successful *saadhana*. I completed my *purascharan* and by then Abhayanand had to go to Rishikesh for some contingencies. So with my company gone, I lost interest in being there and decided to move to Indore, where I could do something about my research work that was stagnating. I would be staying there with a baba at Anandmayi Ashram, to continue my research work in Srividya. Abhayanand also left for Rishikesh.

The baba at the Indore ashram welcomed me happily and arranged for my long stay. The accommodation had a bedroom, with an attached bathroom, a pooja room, and a living room. I started the work on '*chiti yantra*'. A *yantra* was drawn on a 6×6 feet wide sheet of copper costing more than five thousand rupees. Baba arranged for the amount through some of his devotees, and I started applying myself by doing japa and practicing certain rituals based on the *chiti* mantra. All night long I would do *saadhana* and a lot of *japa*, accompanied by continuous reading, analyzing, meditating, and thinking. There would also be discussions on the practical aspects of experiencing the 'awareness' of 'being.' In the daytime I slept. Every morning I walked for some time in the beautiful garden in that ashram.

One day I spotted a small, beautiful butterfly with wonderful designs on its wings lying dead on the ground. I felt the thrust of an unknown pain in my heart and holding its tiny body in my hand, I started moving towards my room. On the way I saw Baba and one of his disciples (a doctor by profession) sitting on the verandah in front of Anandmayi Maa's *mandir*. I went up to them, and as if prompted by some power within, asked the doctor, "Sir, could you certify whether this beautiful butterfly is actually dead or some aspects of its existence are still there, and if could be revived?" He looked at it, then touching it said, "Yes, it is dead in all aspects. But tell me Swamiji, what you are going to do with this dead butterfly? Or, what you were you wanting to know or looking to prove?" Baba was also very curiously looking at my face to hear my reply. I told the doctor, "See, it may appear to be dead, but our scriptures mention many other aspects of existence, of a being. At the instant of dying, only the main aspect called *prana* leaves the body immediately. The many other aspects still remain and take more time to leave the body. I feel that sub-*pranic* aspects similar to subatomic particles should definitely be in its body. It is only from these that nature arranges for the next body of that soul. An analogy is how we do not change the body for every piece of clothing we have. We change the cloth as per the body's needs. So in a biological existence, out of the sixteen elements, only one element, the life force prana, gets depleted from the allotted quota. The others remain in dormancy. So if we might be able to identify them we can infuse *prana* or vital breath from outside." I was going on talking like a mad guy. The doctor and the baba looked puzzled yet fascinated. But the doctor hooked me by saying, "Can you identify them? Do you know anything constructive?" By reflex, I said, "Yes! Though I have not demonstrated it yet, I have confidence in the words of the scriptures, they never say anything misleading. I do have reliable knowledge, though not experience."

Then the doctor said, "You should demonstrate it now to the extent possible."

Now I came to awareness, and wondered why such a situation had arisen abruptly. I thought to myself that it should not be a miracle but just a scientifically established process and that some voice from inside me would help prove the truth of my belief. There was some conviction from nowhere. I said, "Give me a day's time. I need some data in this regard, with which I may be able to understand this truth. Surely, tomorrow morning on your visit to the ashram, I will show you a miracle. This butterfly should fly." He said, "That is impossible. Dead things never come back to life again." I argued, "Your science can declare this one as dead, because your science has its own parameters, and by that its own limits, which are more destructive than constructive. Your system is not an inclusive system of knowledge like the Vedas."

"We, the Shakti sadhakas, are taught to not consider death as the end, but only as a phase in evolution, because manifestation does not happen in phases. We don't believe that one is dead until some other factors are also not met. So *shraadha* etc. is done even after one has passed away. That atom or *paramaanu* might definitely have been existing equally in both dead and live things, which we call 'Amma'. With the strength of the *sanghtana- vighatana* (creation-dissolution) theory, I will bring it back to life. Meet me in my room tomorrow morning." We parted, bidding each other farewell.

Now it had become an unexpected and self-invited challenge to me—to establish that the science of spirit is superior to the science of matter. I went to the market with *brahmachari* Kanaiah and bought a small glass box with a hole on its top. Placing the dead butterfly in it, I kept the box in my *pooja* room. Right after that, it seemed as if my whole being was almost possessed with the thoughts of reviving that butterfly with a second birth. After the doctor left, and I came back to the room, I had flash-like inspirations about some *mantras, kriyas,* and rituals from long ago—like accessing forgotten government files. I strung them all into some logical sequence and order. The inspiration to do all this came spontaneously, with virtually no effort, and I started applying them. (I cannot divulge details here for this is not the context.) All night long I kept sending vibrations of sankalpas and j*apa mantras* through the hole in the glass box where the butterfly was kept. I believe in the scriptures and in my *guru mandala* which never liked to see me fail. I do not know how the night passed, but I was still immersed in my world when early in the morning the doctor and *baba* came to my *pooja* room. I could easily see the doubt on the face of the doctor. The baba of course believed in *mantrashakti* too. But the application was an unattempted one. The scriptures say—'*mantraanam achintya shaktihi*' (immense are the powers within *mantras*). When both of them had sat comfortably in the pooja room, I opened the glass box and with prayers to my Guruji, I clapped just once. Lo! The butterfly moved its wings and took off in the room but fell down to the floor after a sortie, like a failed Indian satellite. I picked it up and checked, and the *pranashakti* was indeed out of it.

The doctor and *baba* congratulated me at this wonderful success in bringing the butterfly back to life through the methods prescribed by *mantra shastra*. It was amazingly encouraging and the feat accomplished without any proper guidance, exact knowledge or preparation. But the little creature had lived only for a few minutes. They wanted to know the reason why it did not live longer. Even though I too felt sad at its death, I could understand the reason behind this. Though it was an incident of small success, it had taken away a lot of the accumulated powers from within me. Thanks to God that I had a little in reserve due to the successful *saadhana* and *purascharana* done in the past few months at Khedi Ghat. This creation is not a one-man play—all the three energies work in synchronization for every single creature to survive in this cosmos. Any one of those three, if it moves away from the establishment, will lead to doom. I informed them that it was due to the results of the long *saadhana* I had done immediately before coming here, that the elemental force of creation or *srishtishakti* (*brahmashakti* or the ability to create) had awakened a little within me, and that of course by chance, not by choice. It can happen in anyone if they do intense and systematic *saadhana*, and I am not an exception. Creation cannot live without a sustainer; creativity cannot exist on its own accord. So to behold the created, and so that it be able to travel till its destination is reached, a sustainer or the Vishnu is a must. In my case through oversight, and out of over enthusiasm, I had forgotten to bifurcate the available source of energy before the attempt was made. Immediately after the creative process is completed, the sustaining energy must become available to take care of the created. But once the cat is out, you cannot amend your *sankalpa*, it is not permitted.

This is where I missed the link, while I was satisfied with the result, I was also ashamed at violating the established code of nature. But I am glad that I had first-hand experience of the veracity of the *mantra shastras*. They are equally effective, applicable, and relevant even today, depending upon the thoroughness with which we acquire this knowledge from a competent authority. Our failures cannot be attributed to the scriptures. In spirituality this is a point which has to be remembered with caution. Otherwise one will end insulting the *rishis*, incurring their retribution. So since *sthithishakti* (Vishnu *shakti* or the authority to protect and sustain) was not with me and not taken care of, I failed at keeping the butterfly alive a little longer. They were also satisfied with the explanation I gave, and left me with a pat.

But I was remorseful that I had gone against the laws of nature, as I was not supposed to attempt such things. I felt I had wasted my earnings on pitfalls. Expecting, attempting, or developing interest in such things is a big downfall for any *sadhak* who starts walking this path with the single-pointed desire of gaining enlightenment. But solace! I had only tried to prove the power of *mantrashakti*, even in this age of nihilists, and at the time of so-called development in the science of destruction. Hopefully some wavering *sadhak* with meaningless modern education drifting in the middle will be encouraged by this out-of-routine attempt. To succeed in our efforts at ushering in a new era of spiritual science, such things are sometimes necessary. I beg pardon from my Guru Mandala for violating the laws of nature, and our scriptures.

Beware, They Are Watching

Once after a long pilgrimage, I returned to Haridwar, and with a hope to get accommodation in any of the ashrams I reached Saptasarovar, but it was in vain. In those days as I had vowed to wear just a piece of gunny bag, none of the ashrams were ready to open doors for me. I decided to stay either on the ghat of Ganga or on the verandah of any of the ashrams. I opted to stay on the verandah of Virakta Kutia as I felt it would be a safe and secure place than on the ghat. In the nights there used to be the menace of stray dogs and night time Romeos. The fishermen especially used to be at the *ghats*, even though fishing is prohibited in the Ganga in that area. If I stayed at the *ghats*, I would definitely be tempted to oppose them and there would definitely be a quarrel. So I thought it better to avoid a scene there.

It was winter at its peak. I had with me just one blanket to save my body from that biting cold. Spreading a cloth on the verandah, and covering my body with the blanket, I tried to sleep in that harsh winter. Once night, perhaps at midnight, a *swamiji* came near me and covered my body with another *kambal* (shawl). I had not been able to sleep and was partially awake, so I could easily identify him. I had known him earlier from my stay in Gangotri. He was a reputed scholar in Vedanta, and well-known for his selfless service to visiting *sadhus* in Gangotri. He had lived in the Himalayas either in Gangotri or in Uttarkashi for years, not even coming down to the plains. But however strong one may be in mind or body, it is only nature that has the final say. The facilities for *sadhaks* in Gangotri in those days were just the bare minimum. They often fell victim to malnutrition first. Now, after a long stay, he might have felt the inevitable changes in health and life, so he was back in Haridwar and staying at Virakta Kutia during the winter time. I remembered well his help during my *purascharan* on Srividya mantra at Gangotri, about which I have narrated in volume 1 of my autobiography.

The next morning I thanked him for his generosity and told him that I didn't need an extra kambal and could withstand the cold with just one blanket. I was thinking of returning it to him but he disagreed and said the cold was going to intensify and one blanket would not suffice. He asked me to keep it as reserve, and I did so. Slowly our relationship grew deeper. I wondered at his scholarship and deep contemplation of philosophy. Of course as usual, we would have difference of opinion on the spiritual subjects, but somewhere in the core of my mind I liked him and considered him a good friend. He too was a free bird in his own way of life like I was. I did not attach myself to any *mandali* in Saptasarovar leaving myself to be free in my day to day life. The normal custom in Haridwar is that whenever a newcomer arrives they enroll him into some *mandali* depending on the ashram authorities. But I never liked his short temper and arguing nature. He tried to impose new 'school of thoughts,' which had no support of the scriptures, and I was not ready to buy his thoughts as they were.

The sense of free life is often misinterpreted by waywards. Such people in the garb of *sadhus* can create problems, and do damage to the credibility and reputation of *sadhus* and if they have no control in their behavior, they can prove worse than a devil. So it is mostly recommended that either a *sadhu* be in the company of his group (*mandali*) or keep totally away from '*samsara*' and live in a lonely place without interacting with anyone. And predictably problems also came up with this *swamiji* friend as he was free with everyone. He used to go to a particular ashram for his daily *bhiksha*. In spite of all his normal behavior, I noticed in him an oddity that at times he would be lost in unknown thoughts. I watched this for a few days and enquired about this from others as well, but failed to make out anything clearly. One day when I accompanied him to the ashram for *bhiksha*, I noticed a girl in her teens there, the daughter of the cook in that ashram. He was abnormally intimate in dealing with her. I smelt something rotten. I was hesitating to say something about it, seeing a good *sadhu* with good education going astray, which could be seen as a disgrace among the society of *sadhus*. So finally the cat came out of the bag that she had fallen in love with that *swamiji*. She moved around him during his *bhiksha* and whenever she met him, she would follow him and talked about this or that. Of course he tried in vain to avoid her, and the people around started gossiping, adding their own *masalas* and started teasing him. When I delved a little deeper, I learned that due to his intelligence, scholarliness, and modern education he was lured and persuaded to adopt the girl's cult, one with luxurious incentives coming from a moneyed and politically powerful modern religion. A few of his friends similarly baptized recently, had become *mahants* (chief priest) of some places of worship in Punjab. One day I suggested to him that it would be better for him if he left the situation at least for some time, so the rumor mill could die. But he was reluctant to do so, preferring to stay back and then instead of facing the situation he started confronting it. He allowed it to be blown out of proportion by the rumor mongers. A few days passed and the situation had degraded so much that a private matter was now public drama, with a lot of actors surfacing now in the form of commercial interests, and cult and inter-ashram politics. A fierce competition between these forces ensued, each tearing down the other. The issue now became a headache for the other *sadhus* as well and they started regarding the swamiji differently, and avoiding him.

One day news was in the air that the swami had disappeared from Saptasarovar. Nobody knows till date where he has gone! Fruitless talk again started in the society of *sadhus*, a few of them saying he perhaps left for the Himalayas, and a few casting suspicion. A story of his suicide too started spreading in that area, and a few thought he might have been murdered. Anyhow, though years have passed, nothing about his existence is clear. But a good sadhak went astray because of a little worldliness. Maya weaves very enticing nets where flies may get caught, but elephants can tear through them.

There is a popular saying among the *sadhu* fraternity: "*kilay me raho, sui dhaaga nahi rakhna, maang ke khaao.*" Translated, it means: live in the fortress of sadhus; never try to patch up or mend a friendship or relationship broken for any reason; if you make any definite source for your daily needs like bhiksha etc. live life on a day-to-day basis and don't store. These are well-tested dictums recommended by conventional saints. The one thing I understood from this episode is that a sadhu must stay alert in the modified ways of today's world. We *sadhus* along with being *sadhakas* or spiritual seekers for ourselves, also bear the responsibility of spreading the message of the Upanishads as expounded by Bhagavadpada Adi Shankaracharya. Historical evidence shows what stupendous work he did to reestablish the true meaning of the Upanishads. However the forces that misinterpreted the Upanishads then at that time, have still not died. Armies of them still exist, some even in the form of alternative schools of thought. They plant misgivings and play havoc, and some modern educated *sadhaks* too fall into their traps. Such defilers and polluters have always lived in society, be it the present time or the Vedic period. Though society has thousands of eyes that can easily see the surface of an issue, they are unable to see the clever plotting behind the curtain. The destructive elements train people in society to view issues only in a certain light, depending on the tint of the glasses that these elements are providing. The unfortunate result is that many actions of *sadhus* will now be analyzed or criticized by unsuspecting people according to the feedback and prewritten scripts provided to them by the subversive elements. So it is really a herculean task for a *sadhu* to save himself from the pits dug by these elements, before they start accomplishing their *rishi runa* of telling the world the reality of the Upanishads.

A Bittersweet Experience

Looking back, I realize that the wounds in my heart are yet to heal from the dearth of proper responsive devotion so far. The difficulty with love which transforms only later into devotion, is that it knows only one language, it cannot learn any other tongue. And that means you can deal with it only if you know its language. It cannot answer to you in the language of your choice and will be like a mute child.

From childhood to my age now, I have struggled and suffered a lot. And other than my Guruji's great gift to me—the inclination and opportunity to serve others and live for them, I gathered no material gain in life other than the treasure of experiences, some good and some bad, but all of them full of meaning. If I chose to weigh them, I would say the bitter ones will be heavier than the sweet. The farewell message of departing *atmas* or souls, to the living *atmas*, has been to not be under the illusion that this world is the sweetest one. Human life is a payback trip. When I contemplate on my struggles, it is easy to understand that this could only have been due to the effect of my karmas and by extension, those of the others. We might have perhaps done wrong to those people who are now settling scores with us in this birth or *janma*. No *jeeva* has the capacity to predict anything about the *gati* or path of karma. So perfect are His rules.

One thing I know for certain, that even with all the bitter experiences, I have enjoyed this life as a sweet one, as a grace or *prasadam* offered to me by my Guruji.

Whenever I felt I was falling, there would be my Guruji to give me a helping hand. She would have never ever permitted me to fall. Whenever there were tears in my eyes, her loving hands would appearing on my face to wipe them. Whenever I was a bad mood, I could hear her laughter to cheer me up. Before my clothes wore out, I was provided with new ones. Whenever I was hungry, there would appear the good food I deserved. Before I had to worry about shelter, she opened up new mansions for me to stay. Whenever I fell ill, she appeared in the form of a doctor with stethoscope, carrying packs of suitable medicine, sometime even barefooted. She seemed to declare those beautiful words "*yogakshemam vahaamyaham*," (I carry the burden of your needs) if you remember me with passionate love.

When she is with me every step of the way, why should I even pause to consider if my life has been a successful or accomplished one? During the critical days of my *saadhana* in Himalayas and elsewhere, she was with me like a shadow. Sometimes just behind me protecting, and sometimes in front guiding like a beacon light to show the path. Everywhere, at every moment, and in every event . . . my Guruji was with me, is with me, and will be with me.

Though we may recount only the memorable and significant events of achievement in our lives, it is important however to remember that our scriptures have attached more importance to the simple events that demonstrate the depth of love. One day I had a sudden desire to eat dates (*khajoor*). I asked one of my disciples if they were available in the house where I was staying. She replied, "Yes, I'm sure they must be in the kitchen's pantry, I shall get them for you," But something else came up, and we both disconnected with that thought. Yet even till the evening my disciple could not get around to finding the dates for me, perhaps it had slipped her memory. The same evening another disciple came to meet me with his family, and I saw a packet in his hand. It is the usual practice with my disciples that they bring fruit, flowers, or something useful to me when they grace me with a visit, as busy as the world is today. They offered me the packet, and to my wonderment, when I opened it, I found it contained dates. Believe me, I burst into tears for entertaining such a desire. It was only after this happened that the first disciple was able to now suddenly remember her commitment!

What should I glean from this incident? I do know one thing: that since at every moment my Guruji is with me, she also knows of my *ichha* or desire to eat a particular thing. And although it had not been served in time, surely it was Amma who had planted the impulse in the second disciple's mind to pick up that thing I was craving. This is not to be counted as a miracle. The guru is *paramatma*. Nothing is impossible for a guru. Even the smallest *ichha* of this ignorant child of Amma is fulfilled by her through her *ichhashakti*. But the lesson here for a *sadhaka* is to not always keep trying to engage divinity in fulfilling worldly needs. Those are possible to be fulfilled with the help of mortals. One should aspire for the higher aspects of human life, possible only through the absolute grace of divinity.

Knowing my guru as *sarvantharyami* (Inner ruler of everything), that I did not need to ask to fulfill my needs, I used to keep away my *ichha* from myself. Yet being a human, the mind sometimes does pop up with certain *ichhas* which can lead to bitter encounters. There may then dissatisfaction or overindulgence, negative reactions, side effects and undesirable outcomes. When the *ichha* or rather itch is not treated or fulfilled with proper effort or means, object or, method, then there is bound to be disappointment, depression or anger. So beware of the mechanism of scratching that itch. '*Asha hi paramo dukham, nairashyam paramo sukham*' (desire is misery greatest, desireless state is utmost bliss), there are such sayings in the scriptures. The cause of all miseries are *trishna*, *moham*, *ichha* (desire, thirst, longing, illusion). Bear in mind that here nairashyam or *niraasha* does not mean disappointment as is commonly understood, but it is the condition of being *asha rahita*—or a level of detachment, a stage of no needs. If you talk about having a certain outlook, attitude, or way of dealing with day-to-day needs, that implies existence of *ichha*. You should be satisfied with what you are, with what you get, with what you eat . . . That was my disposition during my Himalayan life, during my intense *saadhana*.

A Dream Comes True

During one of my visits to Sri Sailam, I went to Atmakur, a small *kasba* in Kurnool district. I remember it was in the year of 2003. I used to stay in Atmakur with one of my senior disciples Dr. Satyanarayana who practices there. Both he and his wife were ardent disciples and were doing vigorous *saadhana* in Srividya. They were doing their *shodashi japa* during that visit. His wife's sister Uma (from Vishakapatnam) had also been initiated by me during their visit to Jammu ashram during one Guru Poornima.

I was very much depressed in those days, because of not being able to find even a single sponsor to publish the manuscript work of four books on Srividya. They were lying around in the way Maharshi Shuka lay in his mother's womb for sixteen years! Wherever I went, I would carry the manuscripts along, to try to find a sponsor or publisher, like scholars during those days of kings. Yet the lucky soul, the would-be publisher eluded my search or say my fishing! But yes, the dawn finally did come. I was introduced to one Gollapudi Gowrishankar, Uma's husband, during my visit. Being in pessimistic mood from all my efforts seemingly coming to point blank, I was planning to return from Atmakur within a day or two to Srisailam, and then to Hyderabad to go to Delhi. The doctor enquired about the reasons for my low spirits or emotional breakdown, and I narrated my mental agony. But in reality it requires a sympathetic heart to grasp the state of a mind that had been tirelessly swimming trying to find a log of wood with no success. After leafing through the manuscript, Gowrishankar spoke the beautiful words that my ears had been longing to hear: "This will be done". He would take care of publishing one of the books. He asked me to meet him in Kovvur where he worked as a manager in Andhra Bank, and said that we would finalize the matter of the publication of the book.

The following week I reached Kovvur, a small town with good infrastructure near Rajahmundry and also known as Goshpada Kshetra (footprint of divine cow Kamadhenu). The river Godavari divides the two districts East Godavari and West Godavari. Occasionally I used to go to have a bath at the Godavari Ghats. Accommodation was arranged at Gowrishankar's residence. Looking at the final manuscripts of the books, Secrets of Sri Chakra, Raja Rajeswari Kalpa, and Matruka Yantra Rahasya, Gowrishankar opted to print Secrets of Sri Chakra, a small book, and the first of its kind. It is a research paper and thesis resulting from my contemplative study on Sri Chakra. Gowrishankar arranged for some money to start the printing works. The first contribution amount was donated by one Subba Rao (son of Gollapudi Maruthi Rao and Gowrishankar's elder brother) of Chennai. The desktop publishing work started at the Lakshmi Ganapati press in Kovvur. Since I had now also received some contributions from disciples in North as well as South India, the printing of Raja Rajeswari Kalpa (the ritual part of Srividya—in Sanskrit) also started. Dorbala Prabhakar Sharma and Bhamidipathi Ram Gopal helped me proofread the Sanskrit.

By now of course, I was feeling quite a bit relieved from these new and unexpected developments, and was very happy that the publications were finally a reality on the horizon of my destiny. I will not say this is the first book written and published by me. In my *poorvashram* too I used to write and translate some plays, some still remain unpublished. My first book Mruthyuradhya was published by the prestigious publishing house National Book Stall of Kerala, with the financial assistance of my uncle. A few other books and play, translated from the English and Bengali originals were also published with the help of School of Drama, Kerala.

It was during these days that the all Graceful Mother blessed Gowishankar to be initiated into the great Srividya through me. Even though he was busy with his bank work, he used to take out some free time daily to help me in proofreading and press-related work. For more than one memorable year I stayed with that family. Along with the pre-publication work, we were also able to arrange Lalitha Sahasranama *paarayanas* in many houses and also conducted many *poojas* on Sri Vidya in Kovvur town. In between, it often so happened that I had to travel to Samalkha and Jammu ashram in order to arrange for some money needed for printing work. By now a good number of my disciples from different parts of the country like Jammu, Panipat, Hyderabad, and Kurnool, started showing interest and cooperated financially to print and publish these books.

Once the printing was over, plans were made to release the books in a grand and graceful function at Shivaji Spoorthy Kendra at Srisailam. Although it was not a very big event, it was by no means a small one either. This event was at the Shivaji Spoorthi Kendram on an Ugadi day in 2003. Gollapudi Maruthi Rao, a well-known writer and cine artist from Chennai was the chief guest. Sridevi Sajit (Kerala), Prof. V. Sarala (Hyderabad) and almost all of my disciples from across the country attended the book-release event. Two books and one CD (on Srichakra pooja) were also released on that day. Being Ugadi day (Telugu New Year day), there was a heavy crowd in and around Srisailam. A few choultries were booked in advance for the accommodation of the participants, and Dr. Padmanabha Acharlu (Organising Secretary) of Shivaji Spoorthi Kendram, generously permitted us to use the hall and rooms for accommodation and function.

There were no words to express my feelings on that day, when the dream came true. Dr. Satyanarayana of Atmakur introduced Gowrishankar (his brother-in-law) who had been the instrumental force for the entire works right from the printing to publishing, and in the book-release function. My *poorvashram* older brother, sister, brother's daughter, sister's son, my sister-in-law etc. also attended this prestigious function.

That was the first time I happened to taste Ugadi *pachadi* which is prepared specially for Ugadi celebrations in AP. It was brought from K. Satyanarayana's house at Kurnool and reminded me of my life, with all its flavours—a little bitter, a little sweet, a little sour etc. I thanked all who worked to send this *pachadi* and for distributing it to everybody who attended the function. Thus the occasion became both bitter and sweet. In my thanksgiving speech after the book release I tried my best to convey my soul-stirring feelings to all associated in turning my dreams into reality. But I was not satisfied in doing so, because such was the emotional recharge, such was the love and dedication of each and every one, in making it happen. After the release of books I stayed for one more day in Srisailam, and left for Kovvur with Uma. The books were taken by M/s. Giri Trading Co. of Chennai for distribution. Gowrishankar personally went to Chennai and made arrangements for the distribution of the books and signed an agreement with the company.

A Joke Of Six Lakhs

On Guru Poornima[21] day in 2009, my friend Gollapudi Maruthi Rao, perhaps after seeing a few of my scribblings here and there, once planted in me an inspiration and made a request too, asking in one of his lectures, "As you have the talent and knowledge, why don't you pen down your memories?" He stressed further, "That may be in the form of an autobiography. If you so grace it, it will be and remain a source of immense inspiration to the coming generations." Any unapplied talent provided by nature eats away into our confidence level. A yearning to scribble erupted many times in me, but mostly people would pour water upon it, to make sure it wouldn't arise again. But it is the law of nature that anything suppressed comes out with double the force, and sometimes in double volumes! Remember! Maruthi Raoji had only fanned the flames, for I had always been pondering with weak hesitation at how it would be possible for me to pen an autobiography. I had of course, read several autobiographies of many well-placed celebrities, titans, sages, saints, towering personalities, temple figures etc. Whether they were really true or not, they sold like hot cakes. I know very well that I am a simple man though not a simpleton, but was I a person to venture an

---

21 Guru Poornima is an Indian festival dedicated to spiritual masters and is celebrated on a full moon day in the month of Ashada according to the Vedic calendar, sometime during July-August.

autobiography...? But when inspiration comes from a sincere and dedicated source, that itself takes care of everything. That's what happened to me after hearing the sincere and inspiring words of Maruthi Raoji, and the disease spread to my so- called inner circle disciples too. The pressure started mounting, and the writer in me woke up from the *Samadhi*. And now it is with doubled force that my nature is slowly but surely guiding me to write down my experiences as *sadhaka*, *sanyasi*, friend, beggar, stranger, luminary, disciple, guru etc. etc.

Just within a week's time, necessary points were conceived and the embryo started gaining mass and I started writing. Or rather my fingers with some impetus, started playing on the dead typewriter keys turning those buried experiences into live words, like a painter. Sitting in the upstairs room of Ramesh's residence at Vishnu Township, I started typing directly on one old typewriter. True to my conscience, the only *sakshi* or witness to my writing was my Guruji, and I always sensed her presence in the room. Though I had conceived a lot of writing in my *poorvashram* life, I had not delivered much and had not written anything except for one or two stray experiences. It was a good thing that it did not happen, otherwise it would have much hurt many hearts for lack of sophistication in expression. At that time, the faculties of expression were still developing, and reached fruition later through guru and guru's grace. So untimely expression can actually nullify the purpose of a work. That is where the guru steps in. She did not permit it to happen, and the *poorvashram* and its fellows were spared. Then again, what does an *avadhoota* have to do with the *poorvashram* at all! What is there to be said that's new? The whole world is verily stinking and sinking in that, and irrecoverably too. How and why should one try to describe an untasted and rotten mango? So skipping this en masse, I started writing about experiences starting from those all-graceful golden days after my leaving home and the desire-rich *ashrama* (stage of life), moving to the knowledge-rich universe of *sanyas ashram*. It was the story of a search with full of hurdles, pain, and bitterness. But not at all a wasted life, being based upon the solid and eternal principles of our Vedic *rishis* who laid down their lives with joy for the welfare of the whole of humanity. In the record time of just thirty-five days I completed the writing of the first part of my autobiography which is titled 'The pyre of the destined'. When I completed writing an episode in the book, I would ring the bell calling to my room either Sujatha, Hari or Swetha, and ask them to read aloud the just-typed episode, listening to it as if I were a third person. And the sweet ripples created in my being would plunge me in ecstasy, tears in my eyes at hearing my own say.

After the thirty-five days of writing the first part, I came to live in Brindavan Nagar at Satyanarayana's residence, where I stayed for four years. Sitting in my room there, I started re-writing (the second writing) the matter. One Nagaraju (of Sri Ram Typing Institute) would come every day at night to help me with the typing and that was completed in a very short time too. I used to send a few episodes to D. Sitaramaiah in Hyderabad for first reading, who sent his comments daily over the phone. Maruthi Rao also sent comments through e-mail. The comments from both were very encouraging, boosting my mental strength and the inner faith that this could be published.

But I had to deal again the same devil of hunting a sponsor or publisher. As I was a new entrant, none of the famous and well-established publishers were ready to take on the risk of publishing my autobiography (where the name sells, not the stuff). Finally I decided that Abhaya Varada, the savior will take care of the printing and publishing. Just passing the buck onto an imaginary entity would not solve the problem, in order to raise money, it is we humans who have to 'roll out the *papad*' or put in the arduous work. So, though the prospects of arranging money for printing the book looked bleak, yet fishing for them continued.

In the meantime, some of my distressed disciples in Kurnool read the manuscript too, and though they were generous in offering their comments, were not generous with their money purses. Prof. Varma took a copy of the manuscript to his father Sudarshan Varma at Ananthapur who began translating the book into Telugu. Prof. Krishna (a friend of Sudarshan Varma) also tried his hand at rewriting the idioms from the English version. But I was not satisfied with the rewritten version, since in the process much of the originality was lost, and the work had turned into an abridged form. So I humbly declined his changes and decided to publish the original version. Sudarshan Varma also completed the translation work in record time. He told me he had an experience of the presence of my Guruji (Avadhoota Tara Mayee) during his translation work.

Once the translation work was over and the Telugu manuscript came into my hands, Duvvuri Narasa Raju (my disciple and General Secretary of Ashraya Trust) offered to take over the responsibility of getting it printed through his friend, Balaji Naidu of Conquer (Hyderabad), without a second thought and even without any idea of how he was going to finance it. But anyway the Telugu version 'Nirdeshita Gamyam', publishing work started at Hyderabad and at whose impulse, Tara knows! Later, the total costs of printing etc. and hosting the book release function were borne by the dedicated souls, Kurakula Satyanarayana and Maram Ramesh Babu.

On Makara Sankranti (Harvest festival) day in 2011, an elegant function was organized for the release of 'Nirdeshita Gamyam'. A few recognized dignitaries in the field of literature and *samskara* were invited, and a grand function organized to accomplish the release, wherein Harikishore Kumar (Vice-president of Ashraya Trust) took the onus of convening the programme. Dignitaries like Chokappu Narayan Swami, Chakilam Vijayalakshmi, Bhaskar Madanpalli, Mamidala Krishna Murthi, Ashytavadhani,... etc attended and released the Telugu version. I was very emotional at the function and during my speech on the book, I burst into tears several times. Mohi and Raju had a difficult time bringing me back to normalcy whenever I was in tears. Even though my disciples pressurized me to give the books for distribution, I decided otherwise. I wanted them to be given free to readers. (The bad experience with the previous book distribution through Giri Traders had very much disturbed me, as they had not paid any proper amount).

Up next was the task to publish the original version 'The pyre of the Destined' at the earliest possible date, and for me a herculean one. Balaji Naidu, the printer's rough estimations of the printing cost would be too high. Devulapalli Ravikumar, another of my disciples in Hyderabad, came forward to sponsor the publication and committed to payment of the costs. Publishing work of the book started at Hyderabad, while I was staying with Devulapalli Ravikumar at West Maredpalli in Hyderabad. All along with this was the liability of an ailing body and overtaxed mind, since I was suffering in those days from the inherited cardiac problem that was the boon of my *poorvashram*. But for Sujatha who was like Maa Tara's twin I must say, in taking care of my needs during the proofreading of the book, it would have been very difficult. Once the pages were typeset, Balaji Naidu calculated afresh the cost of paper and printing, binding charges etc. and it turned out that the amount exceeded what we had anticipated. Now Ravikumar was showing signs of developing cold feet, stepping back from his commitment as the amount was now looking too large and beyond his capacity. On the other side, Balaji Naidu was not ready to compromise on the quality of paper/printing etc. either and was stuck at adopting the international standard for the book's body.

    I was in a disturbed mood, and upset with myself at having done this blunder of writing a book. Though it was no *papa* or sin to do so, it had become a huge source of tension for me and my disciples. There must have been some hidden impetus though—because even a second proofreading was happening. Kalyan Chaitanya, another disciple in Hyderabad was helping me regarding that. One day I was brooding about the money, that I did not have even a single penny and nothing in hand to pay for the advance to Balaji Naidu, the printer. In that fitful mood of anger and stress I scolded Ravi, and it may have been due to that he also was in an irritated mood. Kalyan then arrived as usual to help me correct the proof. Ravi closed the door in anger and would not allow him to enter and meet me. Kalyan felt insulted and so did I. I called Kalyan back and pacified him. Even with all these tensions, I stayed back at his residence till the proofreading was over.

    I resumed the search of somebody to sponsor the expenses

of printing the book. One Nagishetty of Atmakur came to the rescue. He was willing to furnish the entire amount for the printing charges, as well as for the book release function. He is a businessman dealing in red chilies, having shops in Atmakur and Vijayawada. Providence at last lead the amount to be handed over to Maram Ramesh and I now had some relief from the tensions. The printing work of 'The pyre of the destined' was complete and a date fixed for the release of the book.

There was a grand function organized at Vishnu Township on the day of my birthday (Vaishaka Poornima) of 2011. Mananeeya Surya Narayana Rao, a senior pracharak of Sangh was the chief guest for the book release event. My spiritual brother Swami Abhayananda, Dr. Vijaya Sarathi (Chief Editor of Jagruthi), MDY Ram Murthy, and Dr. Padmanabha Acharlu (Org. secretary of Shivaji Spoorthi Kendram) were the speakers. T. Harikishore Kumar of Bangalore and Swapna Akhil took up the responsibility of anchoring and the programme was conducted very well. I was very happy and charged with a lot of emotions that day. My health condition was very unstable due to episodes of severe heart problems. Even with the overcast weather on account of my health, I could remote-control the event to the satisfaction of all.

A few months went by with this sense of a dream accomplished, but then there came a bolt from the blue. One day, even as I lay on the sick bed or you could call it death bed as well, the same great generous Nagishetty, the person who had spent the good amount of six lakhs for printing, publishing and arranging the book release function, came to visit me. Most matter-of-factly, with no remorse, repentance, or sense of guilt whatsoever, and in simple words he asked me to return the amount. I was shell-shocked, and felt as if my bed were sinking into the ground.

After Abhaya Varada had given him the due receipts acknowledging his donations for printing this book, and his contribution also recognized duly through acknowledgements in the book as well as on the podium etc., if after all these he was now asking for the refund of his contribution, was not that a cruel joke? Previously too he had donated some amounts at every event. He was a calm and composed person, who had good faith in his Guruji. I took it in good humour, I thought, after all what had happened to him? His version was different. He told me that he had already informed Ramesh to whom he had handed over the money, that his donation amount was only the interest portion of the total handed over. Somewhere there had been a serious communication gap, perhaps the strange combination of Nagishetty not knowing Hindi, all talks and money transactions taking place through Sujatha or Ramesh, and me not knowing Telugu while everyone else did. But Nagishetty was single-pointedly insisting that he should get the amount back. I discussed this with some of the disciples, but all of them told me that once the receipt is given by Abhaya Varada, and his name printed in the book as sponsor I should not feel obliged to return the amount. So, no one was in favor of paying it back.

But my perspective on this issue was different. I took it otherwise: that Nagishetty helped me when I was badly in need of money. Now he may be in need of it, and that is why he's asking it back. So, even with the objections from all quarters against this empirical wisdom, I decided to re-pay the amount with all dignity and treat it as a loan. I asked Ramesh to borrow some money from moneylenders on my behalf and return the amount to Nagishetty and Ramesh, as an obedient disciple, borrowed three lakhs from somebody and did so. Even now I owe Nagishetty the balance of three lakhs, which I will be prepared to repay as soon as I get a source to generate that amount.

I never had a personal bank balance, my days counted upon *aakasha vritti*. Which means not even a 'day-to-day basis', but on a 'moment-to-moment' basis. Living with *aakasha vritti* means living free and unattached like a bird of the skies, depending solely on God-gifted alms. One thing occurred to my mind: that I had perhaps done a mistake or *paapa* by writing the autobiography. Did I do it because of the push of ego wanting to project myself as a good *sadhaka*, or perhaps it was from the ego stemming from a journey spanning the Himalayas with unique experiences, or maybe the ego wanted to portray me as a 'special' guru? We had all suffered stress and strain during the making of this book and I curse myself sometimes that I put my disciples into situations for money matters, for printing of my books, in addition to my day-to-day expenses for food, accommodation, travel, medicine, etc. I prayed and prayed to my Guruji again and again, several times with tears in my eyes, to not allow me to be so foolhardy as to write books or go around to my disciples 'begging' for sponsoring the works for publication. Even now, as I am typing this second part of my autobiography, 'Roaring Silence,' I feel guilty and a bit anxious too, whether I am not getting ready to repeat the same saga. But the consciousness empowers the emotional factor and convinces me: "No, pen down the experiences you had, in experiential life as a guru, which will definitely be useful to the coming generations." So, the work is in progress . . . .

A Runa Paid Off

WHEN SOMEONE ACCEPTS a favour from another, the former will be indebted to the latter, until the debt is repaid this way or that way, in this birth or the following ones. The salt that was eaten must be coughed off by any means. So if you have enjoyed the favours of others, in any way in any form, and at any time, remember the dictum: you cannot escape from paying it back. Either pay it back in the same life in the manner received, or offer the same type, kind, quantum, or quality of favour to a needy person. It is possible that one may have used the favour as capital and earned some profit, but lost the capital later—then one must be ready to pay it back in some other form. Only then will the one who accepted the favour be relieved of the debt, in the books of the Almighty. The law of '*karma*' is a very intricate web, and no one can claim to have understood it without any doubts, without consulting the scriptures, or through the long-time hearing of satsang with those who have crossed the barriers of worldly attachment.

During one of the medical camps conducted in a very backward village near Kurnool town, the doctors came across a person suffering from paralysis for three or four years. A Muslim by birth, he had been doing petty jobs and manual labour to earn his bread and had been happy and contented with his small family and a few friends, until misfortune hit him with paralysis from waist down. Unable to move around, he had become dependent upon his wife even to attend the calls of nature and was cursing his fate. But even after several rounds with many doctors, who had tried minor surgery, medication and physiotherapy, Lady Luck did not smile on the poor guy and the doors of fortune seemed closed for him.

Our team of doctors also visited him and tried to do the best of whatever they could. They came forward with a plan of treatment in some so-far unexplored direction. First, they started treating the bedsores on his back. They approached me to discuss the possibilities of rehabilitating him back to normal. I told them, "If you are prepared to take care of his day-to-day treatments with deep dedication like the ordeals of daily visitation and dressing of wounds, arranging for physiotherapy, and all such other needs which may be become necessary, then you go ahead. As far as finance is concerned it will not be a problem. I will take care of the money matters personally." They agreed, and arranged for physiotherapy after discussing with some senior doctors in town, and regular ambulance was arranged through a service organization (of course, with payment for driver, petrol charges), and everyday one young doctor from Ashraya (a service wing raised by our devotees to meet such contingencies) team with his two friends took him to the centre for his exercises with the most modern machines. On our behest, an average of ten thousand rupees every month was spent for this purpose: for the ambulance driver, petrol charges, charges of the doctor at the physiotherapy center, medicines and even for nutritious food for the patient.

After many months of hard and dedicated service of the young doctors, there were some signs of hope of recovery seen in the patient's body. After about six months, the doctors updated that he was now far improved from the crippling stage, and if we could provide him with calipers for supporting his legs, there might be a possibility for him to walk. Right from day one that our team started his treatment, I had a positive feeling that by the grace of the Almighty he would recover one day to lead a normal life. And it had become a dream for me to see him that way.

The act of *pooja* is nothing but a means of developing the factors of mind, called one-pointed dedication and unfailing attention even to insignificant aspects involved in any action. I wanted to make the few boys, especially involved in the medical profession understand the power of dedication and surrender, and wanted to instill in them the sense of service. This had come as a God-given opportunity. The boys too took it with the right attitude.

If we want to transform whatever action or *seva* we do in our daily life into *pooja*, we must cultivate the attitude that the recipient of the *seva* is the omnipotent Lord himself comes in disguise to test us. And this will put us in utmost vigilance. So, actions done with full vigilance never fail, and that is *pooja*.

Finally I had managed to arrange for the money from some disciples working in America for the purpose. Those two disciples as a habit used to keep aside one dollar daily without fail, and on my birthday they would submit it to me for utilizing in any such service activities. A few of the other disciples also contributed for this particular rehabilitation purpose. Almost ninety thousand were spent for the cause, all shouldered by such dedicated souls.

On Guru Poornima day, as the *guru pooja* was in progress the young doctor with his two friends came to me carrying a laptop in their hand. They showed me the photographs of that patient, walking in his courtyard with the support of a walker. His face was shining with the satisfaction of returning to life. As my Guru Poornima message to disciples I appealed—"This is what I expect from all of you: do seva and get results like this young doctor and his friends, the immense sense of satisfaction of having done justice to their learning and life. I am proud of them." Everybody was happy with the incident and they congratulated the doctor and his friends.

On day one, actually I had a memory flashback of my college days, when I too had faced such a paralysis from neck to feet and lay on my bed as good as a dead body. An *Ayurvedic* doctor and my sister's son, then an *Ayurveda* medical student, started treatment with *panchakarma* procedure, which is much more difficult to administer than allopathic. With the utmost care, love and dedication, I came back to normalcy in six months. But to my wonder, the *Ayurvedic* doctor who had treated me never accepted even a single *paisa* as fees or even for the costly medicines that had been prepared for my treatment. Every morning he used to come from as far as fifteen miles away to treat me. When my family and I insisted that he take payment, he replied, "It was from this house that I had my preliminary training as *Ayurveda* doctor. Your uncle (who was a famous *Ayurveda vaidya*) was the guru who taught me and I am not supposed to take any pecuniary benefits from my guru's house."

When I first heard about this case of paralysis, that incident from my college days prompted me to act—due to the favour received from that *vaidya*, there was a *runa* or debt credited on my head. Even though I had forgotten this incident in the pace of life, my Guruji never forgets. Amma had calculated and absolved me of my *runa*, making me an instrument to arrange *seva*, of course with the co-operation of a few disciples, for a person badly in need of treatment. When this was accomplished, that moment I felt a sigh of relief from within. To whom I should say thanks, to my destiny? To my Guruji? To my disciples? To the doctor who treated me? But each and every one must say thanks to Him, the Almighty, for we are all just students in his school called world, where he teaches us the basics of being and living this existence, in the inimitable style of His own.

This is not just to remind my people around, but to hold near to their heart this: do not take a 'runa' by accepting services from anybody. Learn to live within our righteous resources, and if at all any occasion arises to accept any service from anybody, make it a strong point to repay it with a sense of gratitude, as early as possible, either back to him or to anybody badly in need. This way you will be lighter to the core, when you leave this mortal existence.

Activated Inabilities

WHETHER ONE ACCEPTS it or not, my locus operandi or '*karma kshetra*' is Kurnool and the mediums of my operations, or the conduits through which I demonstrate my knowledge, are members of the Maram clan. If the others who were and are associated, connected or related with me, have any case about this, I would say to them that they have missed the bus.

I had been staying in Kurnool for the last eight years. During my stay in Kovvur, Kurakula Satyanarayan used to repeatedly insist that I must come and settle in Kurnool, but I would hesitate—once bitten, twice shy, I suppose. I was busy with the printing work of my first book on Srividya. Before going to stay in Kovvur, I had once visited Satyanarayan who knew a little Hindi as he had lived Hyderabad a few years with his parents. But Hari, wife of Ramesh, was totally unfamiliar with languages other than Telugu. Even though the other family members had all been initiated by me, and even their other two brothers, Sekhar and Murali in Atmakur as well as their children, the fish Sujatha was still eluding my catch, reluctant to take initiation in any school of thought from me. I knew she was at the fulcrum point, holding lots of elements together with her presence, this being from the quality of her saadhana done in previous births. So while waiting for the time to ripen, she engaged herself in *seva* that worked in her favour. Finally due to this, the resistance of the karma was eliminated and she now started expressing signs of interest. So on a good *muhurtam*

I insisted on her taking initiation and subsequently she too was admitted in the fold of Srividya *saadhana*. Of course, even before my arrival they were acquainted with *Lalitha Sahasranama, Shirdi Sai saadhana* etc. Now the family clan known as Maram family, are close-knit, spread and established well, with several offshoots like a giant banyan tree and that which accommodates *sadhus*. My intuition was that they are all well-blessed souls of commendable past karmas. Nowadays it is very difficult to gather such a large group of souls together into one such big family, all one-pointed in their understanding and getting along well together. I have forty-three of their family members as initiated disciples. This is a feat by itself and a record to have such a large number of disciples in one family, with a single guru and in one path. It is totally the result of the grace of Maa upon them. That such a large family including great grandchildren, does not live together for business reasons, but in unity with mutual love and harmony, is exemplary.

So there was a flow of reciprocal evolvement between the Maram family and I, and it was running smoothly at their residence, with occasional small get-togethers in the mornings and evenings. There would be daily discussions on *saadhana* or such related activities, which then turned into daily morning *satsang* at their house itself. At other times I was busy with my reading or writing on my forthcoming book on Srividya, a research paper on the vibrations of *bindu*. Slowly more and more people began visiting me and the *satsang* gained momentum.

I noticed a perceivable change in my lifestyle, as I was not allowed to do even my daily chores of washing my clothes, cleaning my room, or to remain on one-time bhiksha only etc., as they had taken up that work because of the deep devotion towards me. I was slowly becoming lazy and was like a bookworm eating away the words, only writing or thinking on my research or spending time with visitors for long periods. I tried to convince them several times to let me do such petty work on my own, but they would not permit me, and both sisters Sujatha and Hari took care of my needs to the minutest of details.

In the following months, I could perceive very well the changes and shift in their life too: the enhanced dealing patterns with the outside world, the depth and sweetness of love in their children, and their complete focus on service as the goal of their lives, both materialistic and spiritual. Their daily *saadhana* went very well, and the perspective towards a guru had also grown strong roots, especially more so in the case of Sujatha. She had been reluctant to take initiation in the beginning, and her metamorphosis into a motherly caring disciple was phenomenal and as in the true dictionary meaning of disciple: someone who believes and helps to spread the doctrine of another. But there was another problem in front of me, as they were now starting to treat me as a grandfather rather than guru. I was losing my identity as their guru and had become like an eldest family member, for they were dragging and involving me in each and every matter.

Here one day when I was pondering on whether I was doing right or wrong, I recalled Swami Ramanandaji of Omkareshwar, who had once got into a similar situation. He too has an army of *sanyasi* disciples, and battalions of householder disciples and admirers from all over the world. As for his credentials as a *virakta*, he had dozens of ashrams of his own, assemblies of hundreds of scholars who were recognized men of wisdom, and his impartiality and equal vision were all unquestioned in the world of spirituality. In spite of all these, he was once alleged to be luxurious, rolling in money, partial, more inclined and more concerned towards the welfare of some specific devotees or sanyasi disciples etc. As Swami Abhayanand was also his disciple, he knows about this better than I do. So one day, when they all had reached the point of frustration, one of them breaching all the guru-sishya protocols, alleged right at his face that he had been confined and tamed by a circle of people who were restricting him, and that was irritating others.

Swamiji did not have an answer immediately, but it hurt him for him being misunderstood. That evening itself we had met while walking and he dropped that pearl of wisdom onto me, which I cherish to wear now. Seeing his gloomy face which I had never before seen, I asked about the reason, and Swamiji said in his inimitable style, "Everything in this world gets its six relations without fail: opposite, reverse, friendly, neutral, substitute and itself.

There are six kinds of rules, customs and codes of conduct in this plane of existence.

1. The rule of the shastra which you want to attain.
2. Totally opposite thinking of what you want to attain.
3. Substitute thinking, a rule which makes you tempted to attain instead of the real goal.
4. Duplicate thinking, rules just to misguide the sadhak.
5. Rule of the helping, friendly aspects, which may be helpful in attaining your goal.
6. Neutral elements which neither help nor deny.

Only when you recognize, understand, and win over them will you establish yourself in the ultimate truth. Till then, one of these aspects will keep disturbing your understanding.... whether it is true or that is true, the world is true, we are doing exactly what is wanted... like this there may be so many branching of thoughts, which will not allow you to remain in peace.

Swamiji! These ignorant people make lots of rules of their own liking for *sadhus* and want to impose them upon us. And they expect that *sadhakas* should follow them, which has nothing to do with the scriptural requirements for a sincere *sadhak*. It is just a ploy of placing you in doubt so you will keep thinking of these matters and you will be wasting time, and they get away with what they want. Our main aim is how we can keep our thoughts intact, and continue to reach closer to our goal. Even though we live in this world, devotees provide us with our needs; it will not bind us unless we use it for the purpose other than mentioned, and not keep our goal in mind. A reformer cannot afford to have close intimacy with him whom he seeks to reform. It was not without compunction that I devised these pretexts. When it (comprehensive ability) began to grow in magnitude every day, our definition of it (knowledge, self, world) has also been ever-widening."

So the point here is that when a *sadhak* settles himself in a peaceful place for his meditation with the sincere help of dedicated devotees, they become the eye of storm for passersby, one-time acquaintances, time-pass devotees, etc. These people then start to exercise rights upon us using '*shastras*' that they formulated just to keep sadhus from influencing the common people. This is so that the weakness, and selfish interests of profit-minded pawn brokers, greedy financiers, and merchants can be protected. Some mean-minded and characterless drunkards, perverts, and immoral people helped them for a few pennies. After independence, these people who are anti-Indian, who had been the source of carnal satisfaction to the British invaders (Buddhists, Jains) all got together and started becoming converts, claiming equality with chaste Indians. So many school of thoughts have been deliberately spread among innocent people just to reduce the number of people becoming *sadhus*, to confuse the new initiates, and to stop people from serving the *sadhus*, the objective being their slow elimination. This was the main aim of the anti-Vedic religion. Unless the bull is castrated it will not be useful to a farmer for ploughing his land. Similarly the prostitutes, greedy merchants, exploiters, ritualistic pundits and anti-social elements can survive only if people are kept away from the influence of *sadhus*. So all such harrying and tormenting tactics find sponsors among any one of those elements. If we pay heed to them, it will only be a loss for the continuation of our mission to produce dedicated devotees and disciples. And we will be hurting the very principle of a surrendered *sadhak*. So we should not permit the emotional blackmailing, if you are able to offer the real stuff to give to anyone."

To avoid the growth of the affection bonds, I used to travel to Kashi or Panipat (Samalkha) or Indore to stay there for a month or so, but on return would find the condition was same. Once when I analyzed myself thoroughly and true to heart, I realized that my inner being wanted to do some solid things for this family group, which might be out of reach of my abilities or understanding. But something prompted me from within to do something so that the sense of service in them could be preserved, protected and developed as an example for the generations to come. Sometimes I felt like I was caged there, and even some other disciples in Kurnool sarcastically pasted a label on my forehead as 'Maram family's Guruji'. Finally I decided that if I had a solid and result-oriented thing to offer and if only a few were equipped to face the necessary hardships, I could then concentrate only just upon them. If even one among them gained perceivable results, it would be the gain of the whole clan, which is what the *shastras* also say. So I developed a deaf ear.

But their logic and perspective too is different, that they are doing their '*guru seva*', which is '*sishya dharma*'. If I buy their logic for some time, in reply will I be able to tell that I have done justice to the '*guru dharma*', what I was supposed to do?

Hungry For Affection

HUNGER IS BLIND to age, religion, caste, creed, and gender. Everybody is hungry for either this or that. Some crave for food, some others are after love, some chase after money, a few fight for fame, possession or status. But the name of the game is always the same hunger, the only force that drives this universe. The food satisfying each type of hunger has to be sourced, prepared, and eaten in a particular, established way. But a human does not use this logic, and tries to bend the rule of nature as per his whims. This then leads him to defeat in his pursuit, and deprives him of what he deserves, and he starts to feel depressed, losing interest in his actions. Eventually hopelessness sets in, and a sense of doom. In order to get anything, should not that thing exist in the first place? If what you are seeking does not exist in this world, or is not of this world, where are you going to get it from? Can anyone drink water from a mirage? Can a barren woman bear a son who becomes a hero and king of the land?

The hunger in the case of children however is different. A child only experiences the needs and necessities for survival—their hunger for food is only from that, and not the result of desire. So they can be called innocent and pure. When someone's needs are met or when we are able to fulfill their desire, we may feel happiness and they may be our dearest ones.

Meeting a need is duty, done with love. Fulfilling a desire is interest, done with *kama (desire/lust)*, not duty. I have been staying in Kurnool for the past eight years. All these years and without fail, my disciples have assembled together to celebrate my birthday in a grand manner, and almost all participate religiously with a sense of duty and devotion. They manage to find and steal a day's time away from the hands of materialism and their busy life schedules, and spend it with spirituality. A variety of programs are organized to make the day special. One year they had as usual decided to organize a Srividya *navavarana pooja* at Satyanarayana's residence, where I was staying like a bird in a cosy nest. Preparation was all underway, but hearing some unknown call from within, I felt that I should do something meaningful this time for my satisfaction. I told my disciples that instead of a big gathering and pooja etc., it would be better if we arranged some *annadaanam* or feeding of the poor, or give some educational assistance to the needy children around. My inclination always is to do some kind of *seva* for the needy, and my entire teachings too are based on the principle of *seva* itself as the highest *saadhana*. They agreed to conduct the pooja programme on a small scale at the home where I was staying, and to visiting a boys orphanage nearby that morning and distributing some clothes, books etc. I added, "Since we are doing the *seva* of distributing clothes etc, why don't we also organize lunch for them, and let us also dine along with the children." They agreed and made arrangements for procuring the needed clothes, notebooks, sweets etc., in addition to the lunch.

I involved myself in the arrangements too and told my disciples to also take ice cream in cups to distribute to the children. All of us including Satyanarayan, Sujatha, Ramesh, Hari, Ratnamaiah, Murali, Sekhar with his family from Atmakur, and a few others went to the orphanage where the staff had assembled the children together. I noticed the small children looking at me with perplexed curiosity. This may have been because it is not uncommon for *sadhus* to be unfortunately introduced to children as beggars or child-catchers. So they were eager to know why I was there and what I wanted from them. As I was totally a *nirakshar bhattacharya* (unlettered) in Telugu, the local language, Ratnamaiah had to briefly introduce me to them all. The children recited a few slokas from the Bhagawat Gita and one of them also sang a patriotic song in Telugu. The disciples who had accompanied me much appreciated all this and also played with the children for some time.

In the meantime, the sound of the bell announcing lunchtime was heard. We all sat down to lunch together, seating ourselves in rows without making any discrimination between the inmates there. After saying a few *mantras*, they started enjoying the 'Rayalaseema dishes' that had been specially prepared for that occasion. I was in a very joyful mood. With one of my disciples translating for me, I asked one of the boys how he had enjoyed the lunch. Seeing the happy and radiant faces of those children at that moment was really one of the most fulfilling experiences of my lifetime. Even today when I see small children relishing their midday lunches in our new-found establishment, the memory of that day comes back to me. We had all forgotten about the ice cream, and as they were almost finishing the meal, I declared that they were going to be served with ice cream. When the children heard this, they were so thrilled they screamed out in joy. For me it was not merely the sound of happiness but verily the well-chanted verses of the Vedas themselves. The ice cream was soon served and everybody began enjoying it. Among them was one little boy who walked up to me and told me in his childish voice, "Swami, I have not eaten ice cream before, today I am eating for the first time, it is so tasty." He was totally in the clouds, and I could see the rapture on his face. It was difficult for me to control my tears for some time. For a moment I recalled a scene during a visit to an expensive restaurant along with the family of one of my disciples. They were well-to-do, and the family consisted of husband, wife and their five-year old son. Usually I avoid such parties in hotels, but this family was very close to me and it was the birthday of the disciple. Just at the end of the meal, as was their ritual, they ordered ice cream. It must have of course been costly, perhaps of a hundred or hundred fifty rupees each. We were enjoying it and in the meantime the boy after just tasted it once or twice, left it on the table saying, "Mummy, ee ice cream em baaga ledu." (Mummy, I don't like this icecream.) I was very troubled at this, but kept quiet.

Now here at the orphanage I could sense the contrast in the attitude and approach and the contradictions in the world: the extravagance in the rich man's son throwing away the ice cream, and the deep enjoyment of a poor boy of the same age relishing ice cream, unmindful of quality. Though the ice cream we had taken to feed the children may only have cost around ten or fifteen rupees per cup, the happiness generated in the hearts of these children was far beyond any value. So one can conclusively say, and it is the conventional wisdom too, that if there is any single thing under the sky which money cannot get for us, it is affection. Everybody is always hungry, and hungers for the all-elusive affection. One cannot purchase love or affection with any amount of money. You may be rich, poor, or middle-class but to have the idea of purchasing affection is like living in a fool's paradise.

In the evening, all of us sat together in the hall for *Lalitha Sahasranama archana* with flowers. Just after the completion of *archana* and *arathi*, they gifted me with clothes, some money, and other useful items as tokens of their love and affection. *Payasam* (Sweet rice) which had been offered to 'Amma' as *naivedyam*, was distributed to all as *prasadam*. I was about to climb the steps to go upstairs to my room, when I saw the maid servant at the home standing near the steps. She shyly handed me a small napkin wrapped in paper, and eleven rupees and said, "*Mei ek gareeb hoon, aap ke janmadin keliye meine yah tofha laya. Sweekar karen.*" (I'm not very well-to-do, so I could only get a small gift for your birthday, please accept it), I gladly accepted it from her, feeling that its value was higher than anything else I had received that day. Once again there were tears in my eyes, as I remembered the story of the widow who offered humble *amalaki* fruits as *bhiksha* to Adi Shankara. Even today, I treasure that small napkin and keep it in my almirah. My thought is it's not the great *acharyas*, gurus, or *vaidika pundits* who sustain the real *dharma* -- but the unassuming and innocent folk, the real pillars of sustainable love in this world due to whom this creation is flowing smoothly in spite of all the mountain of flaws.

When I look back, I remember very well the days I lived in the abject agony of loveless relationships, and with the suppressions of legitimate needs as a child. And I am of the opinion that little children are always hungry, not for food but for real affection and love. These I failed to get, or had not the intelligence to feel when they passed over me, and never especially in childhood. This is what prompts me to train and educate children to recognize, understand and enjoy genuine love, and also pass it on to others in the same way and with the same quality they had received it. That is my life's mission. Children are our future. If we injure them, and debase human emotions, character and knowledge, what does that really imply for us? Don't forget that our future births will begin through entering the wombs of the coming generations, and that we will need to keep taking such births till we attain the final liberation. If we spoil our children's characters out of laziness, ignorance, or fanciful theories, we will only be preparing them to become the worst possible parents.

Bringing up a child is a full-time job requiring the utmost care, love, and attention. One may remember this.

Guruji with Meru

Planting Destiny

Food for the Soul

A Simple Master

Language of Love

Connection through lifetimes

Oneness through lifetimes

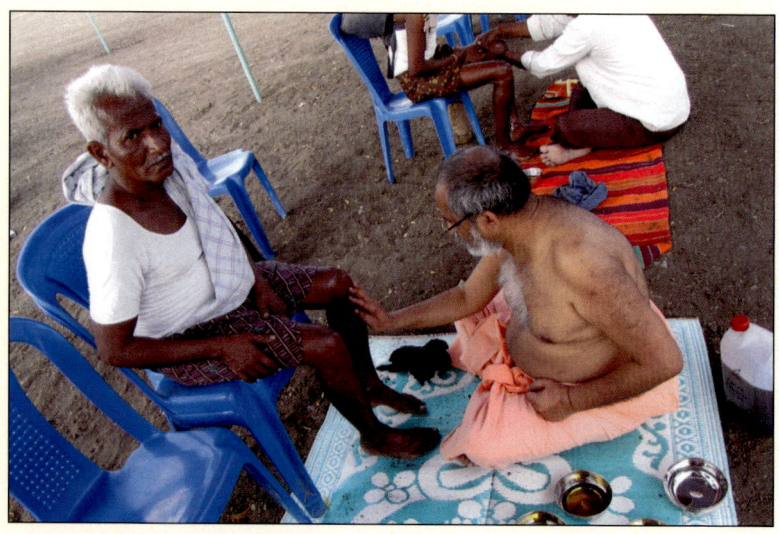

The hands that serve unconditionally

Feeding Oneness

The fire of Awareness

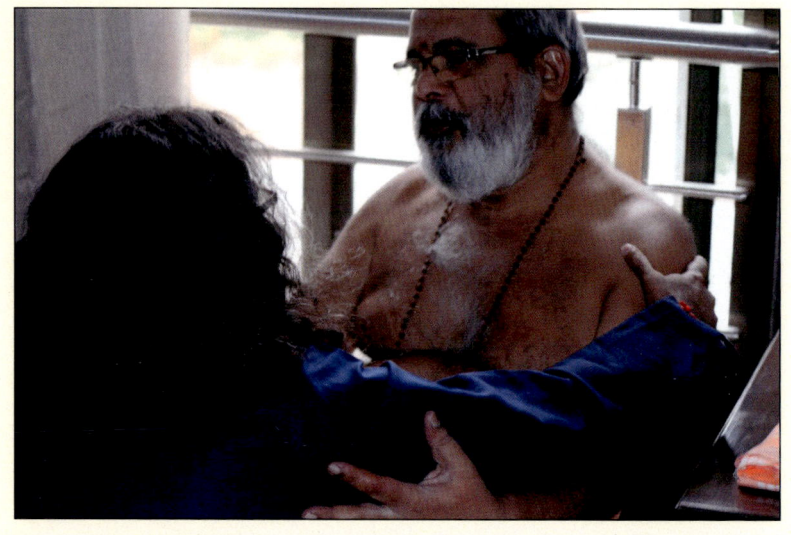

I am always with You

Guru Mandala puja

Unbridled Ecstasy

The wait of Lifetimes

Conferring Brahmarishi title to Mohanji

Guru Tara Mayee appearing

Curry Leaf Inspirations

In the South Indian culinary tradition, in almost every household there is the use of curry leaves (leaves of the plant *Murraya koenigii*), also known sometimes as sweet neem. It has the unique character of enhancing the aroma of the dish it has been added to, and also disinfects the food preparation from microbes. These days, curry leaf is an ingredient in a lot of medicines that are exported to western countries. In India, it is deemed an insignificant thing as it is readily available and in plenty, but without it the basic taste of the food is totally different. However the destiny of curry leaves has become such that before commencing eating, to first pick out and discard these leaves as a first duty. Sadly it is even considered good culture these days to do so in spite of its proven benefit in digestive disorders. I remember from childhood, that my mother or older sister prepared a drink consisting of buttermilk mixed with curry leaf paste and *hing* (asafoetida), when any of the children complained of uneasiness from indigestion or gas formation. When people put aside the curry leaf from the curry, *sambar* etc. while eating, they mistakenly think that its utility is over, it is now useless having done its job of transferring its fragrance into the food items.

Brooding over my role as a guru among disciples and devotees, I feel that my life too has not had more worth than curry leaves, and in fact my experience in this regard has only confirmed this conjecture. I am habituated by default to think about and work for the welfare of my disciples, not just for their spiritual development but in the mundane aspects of their lives too. I do not consider mundane development as something alien and separate to spiritual development. For wholeness and completeness in mundane life, it should contain the aspects of spirituality. And for spiritual life to be whole it, should contain the elements of a mundane life. They cannot be considered as separate entities, and should go hand in hand as reciprocal and complementary factors. They are not all at odd with each other. But spiritual welfare is paramount.

Since it has always been my aspiration that my disciples be blessed with good fortune, that tendency to look out for it has been in me right from my inception into the field of social work. I took to social work by choice, not fall into it by chance. It is my passion and dream to see everyone in the world sail life smoothly, effortlessly weathering any troubles in business, personal, social, or religious spheres. But in the eyes of some devotees and friends, this is an 'over-involvement' as a guru, which I am not supposed to do. But my understanding and logic, in the light of my beloved Guruji's teachings, is quite different. My life being society-oriented, it is only natural that those who are more in proximity with me in the sense of helping, aiding or associating with me in my mission, they will be bound to receive more grace, attention and interaction. This is just like how it is with body parts, it has to be even and equal. Everyone who associates themselves with any spiritual entity should remember this. In the *Gita*, Lord Krishna says, '*samoham sarva bhooteshu na me dvesyoti na priyah, ye bhajanti tu maam bhaktya mayi te tesu capy aham*'. (I envy no one, nor am I partial to anyone. I am equal to all. But whoever renders service unto Me in devotion is a friend, is in Me, and I am also a friend to him). If a bystander expects that my relationship with him will be the same as with someone who is a partner in my mission, then that is not possible. It is only in attitude that we consider every being as equal, though in the realm of karma not all are equal. Whoever serves Him with their work is really nearer to Him. The resources to carry out the mission are generated from here itself. Whoever submits themselves at my disposal to partner in my mission will receive the grace in that proportion. And also, if I take any personal favor from any of my disciples for my food, accommodation, clothes etc. that is treated as a *runa* (debt), and grace is bound to happen there as well. Everyone has to repay it in some way, because in this world everything is for a price. The words of Isha Upanishad come to mind: '*kurvan eveha karmani jijivishe shatam samaah*' (doing karma with detached perspective, the fruits will not stick to you in even a lifespan of a hundred years). A man himself is in debt, can in no way serve others or work for others. Only work done in selfless service alone can give us purity of heart. Work done for wages does not gives merit. As long as there is life in this body, it is not possible to depend on bhiksha alone, since I am in the field of social activities. I need resources, and good and generous hearts to back my doings. I cannot pluck money from a tree, not even God could do that. You have to learn to meet whatever you need, from the resources at our disposal. I need decent clothes, travel expenses and some other little things also required to carry on my day-to-day dealings. Carrying a magic wand for this purpose is a myth. All my needs will not be based on bhiksha alone and occasionally there may arise the need to ask the wealthy for assistance. They do offer it, but some of them do it with an 'application' in their minds like: 'I am giving this to Guruji, so he is now obliged to see to my needs too, and he must utilize his *tapashakti* (accumulated energy)'. I usually oblige to such feelings in my disciples and that may need me to involve myself in their lives if I discover them moving in the wrong path. I have to then direct them to the proper path according to the *dharma shastras*. It may not always be possible for them to follow but with my repeated 'involvements', I make sure that they do. They may get irritated and frustrated sometimes, but when they see positive results, they then appreciate Guruji and repent for the irritation too.

I have related my many visits to Andhra Pradesh for about twenty years. There was a family known to me, introduced by their father himself who was staying in Sri Sailam. At one time I was serving as a dedicated *sevak* in Vanavasi Kalyan Ashram. This was among the Jaunsari tribes of Dehradun district in then Uttar Pradesh, now known as Uttarakhand and the credit goes to Respected Bhaskar Rao Kalambi, who brought me into this social service organization that works for the betterment of tribals all across India in educational, medical, and self-employment aspects. While working there, I developed cardiac problems and was advised to undergo balloon angioplasty surgery and to go to Puttaparthi for superior treatment.

The family in Andhra Pradesh mentioned above helped me a lot in addition to one Prabhakar of Vanavasi Kalyan Ashram stationed at Hyderabad. After the successful treatment at Sri Satya Sai Baba's super specialty hospital in Puttaparthi, I was asked to rest for a month or so, and this family requested me to stay with them during the resting period. As they were a childless couple, they were both able to utilize their time away from office work, taking leave in alternative weeks. I stayed with them as one of their family members. They poured unconditional and unquestioning love upon me. It is only natural for a common man to want to do something for their devotion to grow. I too felt that I must do some *pooja* or *japam* for them for their conjugal life which was happy but vacant, and prayed to 'Amma' sincerely and wholeheartedly several times, to bless them with a child. It materialized just after a few years, after taking some boosting steps. Some *Ayurvedic* medicines were prescribed and prepared by my *poorvashram* nephew, a practicing *Ayurveda* doctor in Bangalore, and a *havan* also was prescribed and conducted by me in their house for that purpose. Finally, they were showered with the grace of the Almighty in the form of a baby boy. Of course they became very happy and I too felt relieved at the success of my mission, that I was able to effect some happiness in their life.

Years passed, and their devotion in me and their faith in God also strengthened. They used to visit me whenever a function was conducted by me, and I too stayed with them for a day or two sometimes when I visited Hyderabad. They too were initiated in Srividya by me, and they were doing good *saadhana*. They had purchased their own house, and received promotions in their jobs and were a well-to-do and happy entity as a family. I never thought of claiming any credit for all this, but this book being a life story, all my life incidents carry messages. So I will not be doing justice if I fail to mention it from fear of allegations of appropriation. But I know for sure that I was just an instrument in awakening their dormant *prarabdha* by inspiring and initiating them to do something, and encouraging them to repose faith in God. In all such cases, I never say 'because of me,' since I know well that it is the Mother, my *Devi* who I worship devoutly, who takes care of the needs of my disciples, provided they do their *saadhana* with devotion, belief, and surrender. I do work as an advocate if I find them genuine at heart. In this case too, the same thing had happened, due to their *saadhana*, and abundant faith and devotion to guru and Amma.

Later when I had settled in Kurnool, I busied myself with social service activities like *satsangs, samoohika saadhanas,* conducting *akhanda Sai nama japas,* and of course the rehabilitation programs for disadvantaged children, without concern for my rapidly deteriorating health. I was in need of more and more funds for building construction, or publication of my books, or such other needs to help the deserving. During one of such program, I asked this family too to donate some amount to the building funds. They not only gladly agreed but also committed a good amount in lakhs, and told me that my next trip to Hyderabad, I should visit them and that they would make arrangements for the money. Subsequently I was in Hyderabad for a medical check-up and was staying with another disciple, who took me to their house one evening, and I hoped to collect the committed amount. They welcomed us happily, serving us delicious dosas and coffee. When I brought to their attention the purpose of my visit to their home and reminded them of their commitment, they said, "Swamiji, it was a joke". (Another joke of lakhs!) I felt the earth moving away under my feet. The next day, this promised amount was going to go towards the advance payment for a flat in the city that was to be the liaison office of the trust. I managed to collect a few lakhs from some other disciples but it was not sufficient for the complete advance payment. As a result of this cruel joke, I failed to purchase the proposed flat for the liaison office and returned with my other disciples, without any comment on the issue. I thought to myself that I was not in a position to understand others or their capacities, and that was the reason for this happening. Or maybe at that time they were not in a position to spare such a big amount, so I told myself to forget this issue, and compromise with the disappointment.

Upon return to the home of the devotees where I was staying, as I was eating my lunch, I noticed the boy sitting next to me throwing away all the curry leaves on his plate. When I asked him why he was doing so, he replied with a smile, "Guruji!" Because its use is now over." What he meant by that I don't know, but it struck me otherwise. It seemed like the predicament I had found myself in, resulting from my naiveté. It was the very story of the curry leaves. One makes use of them for their fragrance, then throws them out unceremoniously when the purpose has been served. Everyday this cruel joke is inflicted upon curry leaves!

This type of incident could happen with anyone under the sky, but my request and appeal to everyone who reads this, is to never hurt anyone like this. When payback time comes, it will be very difficult to bear because in *Kali Yuga*, the interest rate is rather high.

Faceless Crowd Aimless Mob

I AM CAUGHT IN this crowd of faceless creatures, not people. They who have lost their faces in anticipation of nonexistent ones. I am in search of my face amongst them.

This crowd is like a herd of cattle, goaded on by the craze for money and the hunger for power. It does not move of its own choice but pushed forward, moving stream-like. In fact the crowd doesn't even know where it's heading to, yet it continues to flow aimlessly. It is being controlled, and its flow monitored. The police controlling the crowd will not permit any lingering or reflecting to think about the direction of movement. Day in and day out, and at every moment, we who are the crowd, are being similarly pushed through a journey that is uninformed, undefined and aimless. This is the order of life, happening right since the birth of this universe. That is why it has been called *samsara*—the word that means 'wandering through'. But why and what for? None but the guru has the answer to this. Everyone from behind is pushing the fellow in front, like in the story of *Ganesh Prasad*.

There is a story about a Ganesh temple in a village. As everyone knows, the elephant-headed god Ganesh has a broken tusk. The tusk of the idol in this temple was of premium size—it was so wide that one could put a hand inside. Some devotees believed that there was something special about this, so they would stick their hands inside the tusk of this Ganesh, and pretend to taste it as if Ganesh had graced them with *prasadam*. One day it so happened that after the early morning *pooja*, the *poojari* or priest inserted his hand inside the tusk as was the custom now, and suddenly started dancing like never before. Some people asked for the reason, and the *poojari* told them sarcastically that he had got a special *Ganesh Prasad* of divine taste that day. Believing his words, everyone there took turns at putting their hands inside and started dancing too. A sadhu who had just arrived there asked why so many people were dancing around, and a bystander told him about the *Ganesh Prasad*. The *sadhu* went near the tusk inspected it, and to his astonishment discovered a big scorpion inside. Whoever had put his hand inside had been stung, and it was out of the pain that they were all jumping, and not really dancing! But no one had stopped the others from putting their hands inside, and even encouraged them to do so. It was the *sadhu* who revealed the truth and stopped the drama.

It is the same case with the crowd: the constant pushing and urging to follow the crowd. Everybody is living by the command, and for the command of the crowd. People refuse to apply themselves, sometimes are not allowed to do so.

I was in Kovvur, in Andhra Pradesh in those days, fully involved and immersed in the work for the publication of my first set of books on Srividya. I was introduced to Datt and Madhavi, a couple who were friends with Gowrishankar and his family. This *Brahmin* couple, in their formative years had not received any systematic exposure to *Vedic* practice as recommended by the scriptures, but did good irregular saadhana by reciting *sahasranamas* etc. (I label this type of *saadhana* irregular, since it is preceded by initiation. In our Vedic system, one may do such things by watching others and feeling inspired and motivated by them, or due to some previous samskaras. Later when a competent authority finding it worthy or correct, can regularize the same thing by initiating one into the same *saadhana*. But it cannot lead to any fruit if there is no belief in the *guru-sishya* process. So in a sense one is negating a part of the *Veda's* teaching). By virtue of them being *Brahmins*, those natural tendencies had manifested in them, but they had not been properly initiated into any established stream of *saadhana*. Gowrishankar and his wife Uma insisted that I initiate them into the beginning steps of Srividya *saadhana*. Both were working, he as an accountant in a small shop and she as a kindergarten teacher. As a married couple, they had been childless for many years, and as the whole world does, they too approached me with this issue, and asked for a remedy. Seeing that they were genuine devotees of Maa, I initiated them into the rituals of Balatripurasundari. They performed the *saadhana* with the entire team.

They visited Kovvur for every religious program, and would visit me almost every day at Gowrishankar's residence to help me with the proof reading. When I completed my work, I left Kovvur and settled in Kurnool with the intention of leading a retired life, bidding farewell to the activities which I did previously. (But it never did happen at Kurnool, for in Hindi *kar*—means do, and *nool*—means endless thread!) So the direction of my activities was now diverted more towards service, serving people in whatever they needed—educational, medical etc. and with the aim of reducing the, what seems like an ever-increasing gap between the haves and the have-nots. But to achieve that I had the herculean task of convincing the 'haves' that whatever riches they owned were actually due to the blessing of God, and if they wanted to continue to be in His good books, they must help and serve the 'have- nots'. Otherwise soon both they, the 'haves' and the 'have-nots' will be without hope. In view of this mission, apart from my own daily *saadhanas*, I used to conduct common people-oriented events like *samoohika saadhana* like *lakshaarchana, akhanda Sainama japas, satsangs* etc. in Kurnool. This kept me even busier than before. Retired life had taken on an entire new meaning! Hardly could I find any rest, even though a separate and well-equipped room had been built for me at Vishnu Township by Ramesh. And in reality, it would never have been possible for me too, to live a life of retirement. Of course, as my disciples and friends say, it may be because of my over-involvement in their life other than their *saadhana*. Anyway, let it be as it is, because I love to be theirs, whether they like to be mine or not.

In the meantime, one day Uma called to tell me that Datt and Madhavi were not on good terms with their family members in

Kovvur, and as they had both lost their jobs, were finding it very difficult to meet ends. They needed my help in finding jobs or settle elsewhere than Kovvur. Even without a second thought, I discussed the matter with Ramesh, who runs an automobile spare parts shop in Kurnool, and he agreed readily to appoint Datt in his shop as accountant. The family then shifted to Kurnool, with Ramesh arranging a rented house for their stay, and Datt joining his shop as an accountant. One of my acquaintances, who happened to be the head of a private school offered to appoint Madhavi too as a teacher in her school. Thus they settled in Kurnool. I used to drop by their residence occasionally and they also frequented the functions arranged by Abhaya Varada. Years passed thus and the relationship with the couple deepened not only with me, but also with the family members of Satyam and Ramesh. All hearts mingled together, and Datt and Madhavi were treated as their own family members.

Then it seemed as if an evil spell struck us. I remember it was on the happy day of the marriage engagement of Swetha (daughter of Ramesh) at Siddhaganj in Vishnu Township wherein I stayed. Kalyan Chaitanya from Hyderabad, was also with me that day. As my health also was not up to the mark, Kalyan had been staying with me as a helping hand for a few days. We had been up the previous night working for the arrangements, for decoration etc., and in the morning just a few hours before the engagement event, we received a call that Datt had incurred a severe heart attack and was being taken to hospital. Feeling distressed at the news, I went inside my room and sat in front of 'Amma,' the presiding deity Maha Tripurasundari of Siddhaganj. I took a coconut and with a prayer to save his life, I broke the coconut in front of 'Amma.' Kalyan Chaitanya was standing nearby watching me. In a few minutes, I began to feel severe chest pain and fell to the floor unconscious. My body was shivering and had turned blackish, from lack of breath. In few minutes the pain reduced, and I was able to sit up. I told Kalyan and Sujatha that this heart problem was just one more added to the pool of borrowed, thrust, sent, and inflicted diseases in me. (Many times I have ventured shouldering such things from emotion, but lately, almost all the benefitting recipients have turned hostile to me) I asked Sujatha to call Madhavi and check on Datt. To their wonder, Datt had regained consciousness and was now out of danger. With shivering body and dry throat and feeling extreme weakness, I sat in my chair and watched the engagement ceremony of Swetha with Ravikanth (son of one acquaintance-turned relative, Nageswar Rao). Once the function ended at around 11 am, without caring even for some breakfast or lunch, I rushed to the hospital with Sujatha. Seeing my pale face and staggering steps, my driver Basha told me, "Guruji, you must rest for some time. We will inform you of Datt's health." But due to the sense of kinship, I was not satisfied. Reached the hospital, I met the concerned doctor with Ratnamaiah (Sujatha's father) to discuss on Datt's problem. An angiogram was decided upon, and after a few treatments he was discharged from the hospital after a week or so. The entire hospital expenses were met by Ramesh. I told Ramesh that I felt a moral responsibility to that couple since I had brought them over from Kovvur to Kurnool, so we should do the utmost we could. He did so, considering it *guru seva* unto me. He even paid Datt's salary, rent etc. during the off-duty days at his automobile office.

But after regaining his health, and contrary to our and particularly my expectations, I observed in the couple a considerable change in attitude. They were now well-established in *panchadasi saadhana*, and Madhavi had been continuing it. Sometimes especially when misfortune knocks at the door, people tend to think it seems, with two heads. The original one they keep aside, and think with the borrowed one, which always creates problems for them and anyone involved or dealing with them. So, it becomes a source of miseries and the same thing happened here as well. Datt re-joined duty after one or two months, but was not regular, sincere or even interested in doing the job as before. Initially we thought it may be due to the impact of the medications and so made accommodations for it. But as days passed, we realized that it was not as we had presumed. It was due to 'sense of inevitableness' that had crept into them. One day Datt came to the office and told Ramesh that he would work only if the remuneration was increased. He seemed to be in a 'shouting mood'. Ramesh called me immediately and asked what he should do. I told Ramesh to give him a warm send-off, and let him not suffer doing the job there anymore.

They spoiled the relationship, just for a few pennies. Datt left the job, and has never shown his face to me till now.

I look at the mirror now, and it seems to speak to me saying -"Oh! Here he comes again, it's the face of that depressed guy who often comes to meet me after someone teaches him a lesson in thanklessness. And now he is going to decorate himself in front of me, to get ready for the next lesson." The mirror asked me to laugh once so I recharge and bring back the color to my face. I tried and failed. I am not able to laugh. The laughs have become the 'copy and paste' kind. I copy others' laughs and paste it on my face.

So if anyone wants to see me laugh, they have to be happy and laugh first, so I can copy-paste it on my face. But to be truly happy and be able to laugh that genuine laugh, you must first serve my brothers and sisters. Nowadays, it is your smile that you will see me wearing on my face. So tell me now, don't you want to be happy?

Forget It—It Is Your Mistake

I HAD BEEN SUFFERING from dysfunction of the left ventricle of my heart for two years, and because of improper blood circulation also developed the burning feet syndrome. My doctors wondered how I was even alive! But it is not me who is living, it is my Guruji Avadhoota Tara Mayee who lives within me, and as me. So I have no fear of death. My Guruji never dies and as she is within me, I too am immortal. But my prolonged illness created a lot of heartache for my disciples. They prayed to Amma again and again for my health. They did *poojas, paats, havans,* even *daanams* for my well-being. But the sufferings were only mine, inevitable for this existence. When the sufferings will be over, this body will also pack off this mortal coil.

A trust was formed by my disciples to do some *seva* for the disadvantaged section of society. By my impulse, the trust received a piece of land as donation to construct a building to house the activities, and a good amount to commence the work. Since the funds at hand were insufficient for a permanent building, it was decided to put up a thatched shed to launch the *seva* activities. Ugadi (the new year of Telugu people) was near. Two experienced and well-disciplined people joined as organizing secretaries of Ashraya trust and Abhaya Varada[22]. As they had been in the field of social ser-

---

22 Ashraya Trust and Abhaya Varada are charitable organizations run by the disciples of Avadhoota Nadananda.

vice activities for a long time, they were assets to our team. We all planned for a unique kind of *seva*. Bhaktas doing walking pilgrimages are often provided with food, water and medicines by many service-minded organizations along the routes, but we thought of doing something different. We planned on offering medicated oil massages to the tired legs of Shiva *bhaktas* walking for weeks, so that their legs could be refreshed to walk out the remaining distance without any distress. I prepared about thirty liters of an Ayurvedic oil, the technique of which I had learned in childhood from one of my uncles, an *Ayurveda vaidya*. In addition to the snacks, tea, water and fruit, this was going to be an altogether different kind of *seva*. One of my disciples donated twenty thousand oranges, the first harvest from his orchard. A truck full of bananas, one lakh biscuits etc. were arranged to be given along with the massage as well as a few allopathic and homeopathic medicines. Some doctors too made themselves available, ready to do *seva*.

A vacant piece of land by the road side was selected to pitch the tents, and the enthusiastic land-owner made available a borewell within one day to meet the water needed for the use. Students from the local engineering college (young men and women) co-operated whole-heartedly for the seva programme. One of the organizing secretaries who had joined recently was given charge of the entire administration. Thus the stage was set. It was a wonderful and unique event talked about in town, and much appreciated. The *bhaktas* were in tears as this was their first experience during their long walking for weeks. On average 4000 bhaktas got the benefits daily from the camp of five days.

Even though I had not been keeping well because of heart ailment and burning legs, for five days and 24 hours and along with about a hundred *sevaks*, I stayed at the camp itself risking my deteriorating health day by day. On the fourth day of the camp I was faced with another problem. It was an incident of food poisoning. I had accepted and eaten in good faith some laddus offered to me by someone with malicious intentions. The resultant diarrhea and weakness unnerved me.

One of the trustees came to tell me that there was criticism around that I was impulsively spending too much money. Of course, I do have the bad habit of insisting some work I think needs to be done today, to be done today itself. I hate keeping work pending. For this bad habit it happens that we have to pay extra money.

This blame upon me for "impulsive spending" was an unexpected blow. On the sheer merit of 'begging' from my obedient and large-hearted devotees for donations I had arranged for the sufficient twigs needed to do this *yagna*. So I thought that I was eligible to pay off without bargaining for the works to be done at the right time. One of my disciples said openly, "Guruji, if I were in your position, I would have paid only 3/4th of the amount you paid now." I replied, "Yes, you may have done that, but the work too have been done only after a week or so. I wanted the work to be done now and here, so I paid a little extra."

The talks in the air were disturbing my composure, so I decided to withdraw myself from the *seva* activities, citing health reasons for needing rest and solitude. I never involved myself in the trust's seva activities thereafter.

Preparations for my birthday celebration would soon be starting. The Hindi version of my autobiography (Niyathi ki Chitha) was also getting ready for printing and was in the press at Hyderabad. Staying at the home of one of my disciples there, who was also general secretary of the trust, somehow in spite of the suffering from physical pain and burning, and as well as mental stress, I completed the final proofreading and put print orders, with the intention to release the book at the birthday event.

One of my disciples, owner of a farmhouse at a distance of about 40 km from Kurnool, who had donated the oranges during the *seva* program, invited me to host the program at the farm, assuring me that he and his family would take care of the details. After discussing with a few of my closest disciples, I agreed to this. Many dignitaries of repute were invited as well as the nearby villagers. A full-fledged medical camp was planned for the benefit of the people of the nearby village.

My disciples spent the lion's share of expenses for the program, and the expenses for the book-release function were met by

Abhaya Varada. With the backdrop of the beautiful countryside, we danced joyfully to the musical tune of the famous *bhajan* "*mallayya . . . mallayya..*", ode to Lord Mallikarjuna of Srisaila. Even though the program went well meeting the expectations of my disciples, the last phase of the event did not. The sponsor who had willingly shouldered the program now displayed unexpected and indifferent behavior, causing irritation. Contrary to the etiquette of a host, the near and dears of the host hurried to have their lunch even before the invited guests were served, or even before my *bhiksha*. They started boasting about having dined first. Adding fuel to the fire, they showed insensitivity in neglecting to arrange a vehicle for the timely return journey of the esteemed guests and doctors to Kurnool. I became concerned about facing the problem of the return journey from this far-off place of invitees, among them women, children and elders. By that time most of them, sensing the carelessness of the organizers, and not wanting to hurt me, decided to walk for a kilometer or so in scorching heat to catch a local bus to Kurnool from the main road. I reprimanded the hosts at the end of the program for this callous indifference and told them 'not to show their faces again' in the future and returned to my room exhausted and dejected.

The incident hurt me very deeply. In a pensive mood, I simply threw myself down in my room. My legs were aching a lot and my blood pressure shot up. I felt like I was in a tornado, feeling as if my head would burst. Astonishingly from the darkness I had a vision of my Guruji and felt some ease, till 'Amma' scolded me for permitting them to host such an event, which had only given me more stress and pain.

Yes, I had miscalculated. I should not have taken it for granted that they could organize such a program, which even went off well despite the difficulties to the disciples from softer lifestyles. But as always, the fault was mine alone. I told myself, "Forget it. It is your mistake but the *janma din* event and book release are now in the past, leaving a negative experience though. This may have happened because of my inflated 'ego' too, or trying to project myself as someone special."

Pouring Milk Onto A Neem Tree

Could anyone even think of irrigating a neem tree with milk? Is it not a futile exercise? We may disagree until our destiny turns some people to be hostile towards us. By nature the neem tree is bitter, through and through, from root to enticing fruit. Sometimes out of idiosyncrasy, one flaunts the strongest conventional wisdom advising against it. Though it is not a forbidden action, it seems almost as if we are driven by destiny to do so. When the sense of dispassion gets polluted, our intellect by default leads to irrigate that neem tree, and that too with life-sustaining milk. The faculty of thinking before rushing to act sometimes fails, and then we repent at leisure for our actions, and sometimes lifelong too.

The proverb of the cat stealthily drinking milk with eyes closed under the impression that nobody will see or know, comes to mind. Some people, keep their eyes intentionally closed, and venture to act like that cat—from the height of recklessness of ego-centered actions, powered by intoxication of material pleasure. And seeing themselves in a pool of miseries are then reminded of the past temptation and indulge in them. They are then given to lament: "Oh! I could have opened my eyes before doing such karmas." And even if a saint, however well-versed in his trade of knowledge, makes the mistake of blessing every person he stumbles upon, or takes for granted that the person is deserving, then he too is bound to pay a price for helping, gracing, blessing, or inspiring such a one at risk that may cost him his life. But this realization dawned upon me, when I had already burnt not just finger but my whole hand.

By sheer coincidence, true to heavens, I was introduced to one '*purohit*' or priest during my stay in Kovvur. I was extremely busy with work as the first set of my books were in press, with proof reading, editing etc. The priest was well-educated and probably a graduate. He was not a master though where rituals etc. were concerned. He used to visit me daily evening, doing *seva* to me by pressing my tired legs etc. Economically he was weak, and had some intentions to learn more about performing rituals so he could earn more. I started teaching him the rituals especially '*prayoga vidhi*' (practical part), and certain *mantras* for daily use. His repertoire of skills grew and he recorded most of my teachings on *Srichakra navavarana pooja*, and the *rahasya* (secret) *pooja* related to *Shakti saadhana*. He was initiated by me in Srividya too.

Time passed and he left the village to settle in Hyderabad, in search of better opportunities for his priest profession. I introduced my disciples in the city to him too. He had now a network among the city people and started earning well with his group of priests, and settled in the city. Those city disciples of mine also started *monthly satsang* on spiritual values, and I used to visit the city as a monthly routine. During that time the construction work of the room for my stay in Kurnool was almost ending. The disciple who had done the favour of constructing a separate building for my stay wanted to convene a housewarming ceremony on the same day. The *purohit* who I had helped to develop his *vrittis* was called to conduct the *vaasthu pooja*, *chandi homam*, etc. The *purohit* came with his 'gang' and performed the rituals that I had prescribed. At the end of the day, after all rituals and lunch were over, he came to me to settle the *dakshina* for the priests. I was shocked beyond belief when he demanded fifty thousand rupees, just for the *vaasthu pooja* and *chandi homam* alone. Yet I told my disciple who had constructed and convened the programme, "As you have spent a good amount for constructing these two buildings, pay him the amount he demands. Also, just think of this as an offering to a *Brahmin*." He paid the demanded amount. In that town, the maximum dakshina for such ceremonies would only have been around fifteen thousand. I had invited this purohit only because he was my disciple of mine, thinking that he would do the rituals with sincerity and devotion. Never did I dream that he would demand such a huge payment for a house-warming ceremony. I felt some guilt at this, as because of me the other disciple had to spend such a large amount. But money was not the issue, it was the way the *purohit* (who was my disciple) presented the bill to me. I said nothing, but a sense of disappointment in mind erupted because of this matter. A few of my disciples in Hyderabad told him that what he had done was not righteous.

By this time the same *purohit* was now facing some cardiac problems. He called me one day and requested my blessings for the open heart surgery that he was supposed to undergo. Just a couple of days before his surgery he tied and wore a *raksha kavacham* and transferred his clotting in aorta to me. The surgery was without complications and he was discharged from hospital. In the meantime he was getting ready to be married. Without even a second thought I travelled to Vijayawada with a few of my disciples to attend his marriage. A couple of my disciples, who are well versed in *panchangam* read his horoscope and told me that he did not have *putra yogam* (childless due to destiny). I challenged them and in due course, with a lot of prayers, he was blessed with a child. But his 'ego' was going up. Even though I had taught him the higher steps of rituals in Srividya and certain techniques in *Shakti saadhana* and the practical way of doing it, which is the asset of *Nambudiri* Brahmins of Kerala, he was never thankful or *krutagna* (ungrateful) to me, his guru. *Krutaghnata* (ingratitude) towards anybody will definitely pay back in a negative way. The same thing happened here as well. He paid a lot for his behavior towards his guru. Even though, I, the poor guru was backing him for his return to normal life, since he had lost a good number of his 'customers'.

Never give milk to a neem tree—while the milk will only become bitter like the neem, the neem will never gain the sweetness of the milk. One just cannot change the law of nature.

I had mistakenly poured the milk of my knowledge onto a neem tree. If he charged me the way he did, I wonder what he may be doing with others.

Put Small Fish, Catch Big One

It has now become quite natural to human beings, to feel no guilt in giving just a little, yet in taking as much as possible. People have become masters in being cunning. They have lost the precious element of innocence, which exists from the grace of God. Acting with duplicity, they manipulate and use others even for the pettiest selfish motives, but in very polished diplomatic ways. Once their selfish interests are met, they will never care to look back at their prey again, and move on to greener pastures in search of the next prey.

On my return to Kurnool from Gyanganj, I was trying to find someone to sponsor the publication and distribution of 'The science and essence of Srividya' which had received the blessings and approval of the higher powers in Gyanganj. As the book was rather voluminous, more than 500 typed pages long, it appeared that it was going to very difficult to find a sponsor with the estimated printing charges of around five lakh or more rupees. Neither I nor the disciple with whom I was sheltered could either arrange such a huge amount. During those days, I was confined to my room without meeting many devotees or disciples, concentrating only on my *saadhana*.

One day a seemingly-rich business magnate who was well-known locally, was introduced to me by one of my disciples. He was clad in white and wearing the external symbols of vibhooti and kumkum tilak which gave the appearance of a serious devotee. In our discussions I told him about the pending printing work of the book. He took the manuscript from me, saying that he wanted to borrow it just for reading. But to my wonder, only after one week the first proof of the book was in my hands. That devotee had decided to publish the book, and the printing work started to progress right away. On the day of Vijaya Dashami during my pooja, I received the first copy of my book. There was no limit to my happiness. The same person spent some more money and arranged a grand function to release the book. A convention on Sri Vidya was arranged too, and well-known dignitaries, scholars, and practitioners in the field of Sri Vidya were invited. Devotees and disciples assembled in large numbers, and the book-release program was accomplished well beyond my expectations. I felt as if I were on the top of Mt.Everest.

Months passed, and I had thoughts of bringing all the disciples together into an organized group, so that they could be channeled, encouraged, and inspired in doing constructive, and society-oriented activities. In modern terms a platform was needed to achieve this in the form of a trust. One day I sat with a small group of disciples to discuss and finalize the creation, and the modes and methods of registering a trust. The wealthy devotee who had published my book (by this time he had been initiated and become my full-fledged and very close disciple and meeting me almost daily with family) was also present at that meeting. All of a sudden he started saying, "*Guruji, aapki na beebi, na koi baccha, na bangla, na bank balance. Trust khadaa karke aap kahin chale jayenge, samasya poori hamaare sar par padegi.*" (Guruji, you have no wife, children, home or bank balance. You can easily set up the trust and leave, then we will be stuck with dealing with all the associated problems.) When I heard these discouraging words, I felt really sad and hurt, and ashamed at convening such a meeting. Another disciple, who happened to be very close to me, also supported him in this. So at the very outset the idea of forming a trust was aborted and kept in cold storage. But the sound of his words kept echoing in my ears.

I was in a nearby town to attend the funeral of the mother of one my disciples when I received a telephone call from the same wealthy person who had helped publish my book, requesting me to recommend the loan of a big amount from one of my disciples in that town who was a money-lender. Due to lack of judgment stemming from inexperience in worldly or *vyavaharic* matters, I innocently encouraged the granting of the loan. Not just that once, but several times did he take loans from him, using my name. I was unaware of this. After a year or two, the person who had lent the money came to me with the complaint that the other not yet returned a single *paisa* from his loan, even the interest. I was shocked to learn from another disciple that the person for whom I recommended the loan, who had talked to me roughly in the meeting in cruel and undesirable language, had now failed in his business and was in debt to the tune of crores of rupees. He had already become bankrupt.

I thought it my moral responsibility to make arrangements to return the amount of the loan to be repaid to my other disciple, who was also badly in need of money at that time. I requested a third disciple to make arrangements to pay off the amount to the person who had made the loan to the first disciple. Taking it as *guru aagya* or orders of the guru, that disciple sold off a few acres of his land and settled the account. Now the original borrower has to pay a good amount to the new person in the picture. But the condition of the borrower has gone to hell; he lost his bungalow, bank balance, etc. and it was difficult for him to meet both ends. The words he had used in insulting Guruji were now being repaid to him in the same coin. But the huge amount yet to be paid to my disciple has become a big burden in my mind. As the moral responsibility pinches me always, I think it is I who owes that amount to be returned. I as a guru, unaware of the pros and cons of dealings in money matters, am now in pain mentally, and feel disturbed always.

A few are like this: they show some coins to a prostitute to make use for their pleasure. Likewise they try to turn their guru into a prostitute as well.

The Return Journey

I HEARD THE SOUND of footsteps outside the room. It was dark. I lay on my bed as if I had been thrown there, unable to get up, my body throbbing in pain. I was immobile and in a state of total collapse due to a severe cardiac arrest. I witnessed the separateness of the body and myself for a moment, and then the consciousness joined again with the body. This was the moment of struggle between the body and the soul, the stage in between, when the feeble thread of breath links life and death. I had lost all sensation except that of sound. There was the same sound of those footsteps again, but slower. An unambiguous feeling of the presence of someone at the doorstep. But other than me, none else present there appeared to have any knowledge of that. "Who is over there?" I asked. But no reply came in return, and there was again the same sound in that strange silence. I felt strongly that somebody was trying to enter the room and that something or somebody was preventing him from reaching me. My eagerness to welcome and talk to him kept growing. Suddenly that code broke: it came to my mind that perhaps it was 'He'. Because such struggles could take only place when 'He' comes to 'Meet' us. Such struggle between body and soul take place in their fight to prevail. And the signs of preparation for my final departure were already starting to manifest in the form of cardiac arrest and excruciating pain in the body.

A few of the disciples present around my bed looked on helplessly, their hearts aching at being unable to do anything to reduce my suffering. But they did not know that when the orders are delivered from up high, no one under the sky has any say. It was dawning on a few that their Guruji was preparing to leave his body. It looked to me too that the end of a long journey was near. Amidst an invincible pain, they saw me talking busily with someone, and I saw tears in their eyes. I remember, it was around *Karthik Poornima*, one of the year's happiest occasions, similar to *Deepavali*. I presumed the time was near and was resolved to see that last moment of leaving this world, unexpected but the inevitable moment of departure.

The feeling of someone moving between rooms, here and there restlessly, continued. Now at the third time of the same sound of footsteps, I asked again, "Who goes there?" Now one of my disciples asked me, "Guruji, to whom are you speaking?" I murmured, "A friend of mine, waiting for me outside." They went out and looked around, but there was nobody. Someone said, "Guruji, nobody is there. May be an illusion?" But I was not hallucinating at all. The efficacy of my consciousness level was intact with all of its parameters. Since long, I had been counting on this friend's arrival to take me with him, even from day one of this life. He had been there with me always, walking along by my side, through the whole journey of this eventful life, but never displayed any interest in taking me with him to his abode, preferring to leave me here to suffer when he had many more legal chances to do so. He was the accountant witness of my every moment, other than my beloved Guruji and the Almighty Himself, in every pain and pleasure, in peace and tempest, and now I could feel his presence just at the door steps. There was total silence everywhere. I was on the bed, counting down the moments to the arrival of that friend, with whom I must now carry out the rest of the journey, the final leg. The unavoidable part, which everybody is destined to do. The journey to the other world, the last journey with my friend, Death.

For the last few months I had been confined to the bed, my movements restricted to minimum, and suffering the pains of repeated cardiac episodes. Breathing was difficult, and an oxygen mask was on my face. The other emotional masks efficiently decorated by my own people, had already been removed as I did not want to take them along. Four doctors, all dedicated disciples with life-saving medicines at their disposal, and scores of friends and disciples with moist eyes surrounded my bed. I was at Vishnu Township, Kurnool, in my hospitalized room. Those days the room had become like a full-fledged ICU, created by my disciples to save my life, or to extend my suffering. People from all walks of life came to me to see me at my last moments, the unavoidable sunset. From north and south, east and west, did my devotees and disciples come to visit. Even with all the pain, I was calm and composed, yet one could see a few drops of tears in my eyes. The Kurnool disciples arranged daily *suvasini pooja* and *kanya pooja*, by offering clothes, fruits etc. to the visiting devotees. I was not sleeping at all, and my cognition was intact when I saw a few saintly persons in *kaashaya* enter the room. Their appearance was unusual. They were well-built in body, and effulgent in spite of old age, with golden-coloured beards and matted hair. Clad in *kaashaya* or ocher robes, with *kamandal* or water-pot in hand, they looked like the *Maharshis* of yore, come here for us to hear about the Vedic scriptures. Their presence started working in me, filling me with an unknown devotion and exhilaration. To express my reverence, I tried to get up physically but it was not possible because already a lack of identity with the body had developed. I did not like to take the help of the body any more again. I could see that I had folded my astral hands again and again to them, as I was doing *pranaams* and submissions even though I was unable to recognize them. Their saintly look and presence compelled me to bow and prostrate, their being near my bed gave me a few pain-free moments. They smiled and one of them, very old, with white beard and matted hair touched my forehead. Just then, I felt a cooling-down in and around me and a deep serene silence pervaded within. Soon I was limping back to my dense worldly consciousness. The pain was started to recede.

One of my friends, a well-known doctor and professor at the

medical college came to visit and touching my body with his palms, started reciting the *mruthyunjaya mantra*. Just for a minute or so, I entered into a state of oblivion. I could see the presence of my Friend, of course everybody's friend, just near me. He touched my body, and I could see that I was out of my body. I heard the sounds of crying people over there, but here my journey had started. As I was not allowed to look back at my body, I just moved out of the room along with the friend. I started travelling through clouds colors, red, yellow, orange, and at last entered a vast area of deep violet color, where I could see only light predominantly in shades of blue or violet. He, the friend Death was not with me and I too was not there. No body, no mind, no intellect, no question of thought, only the 'I,' the existence was there. Ego lost and merged in colors, a sound of silence, then a pure light of golden yellow appeared. How long I was like this, I do not know. Then again I was not knowing. There was no time factor. Only a calm, cool, and colourful experience of 'Self'.

All of a sudden came a faint experience of loneliness. That was all—I had opened my eyes, or rather the eyes had opened themselves. I found to my dismay that I was on my bed, pain in my body. The disciples around were still grief-ridden and immersed in tears. I could see my Friend turning back and leaving the room. I felt like sitting up and with the help of some of the disciples, I sat leaning back on the pillows behind me. One among them asked, "What happened, Guruji? You have been unconscious for a long time. We were all worried." Even though my voice was very feeble, I was awake and murmured, "No, I was not unconscious, but aware of everything all the while about my being. I just travelled with my friend far, far from here to experience the 'SELF,' but I was here only." I had to say something to pacify them, because the situation from which I came back could not be explained at that time. I was so overcome from lack of energy and emotional freedom that any explanation was out of bounds for me. Nobody understood what happened, but the experience was full and final to me. I had gone there where everybody has to go one day, into the unexplored landscape of reality, the lap of 'the ultimate reality,' and was now back in the body. There might have been some dues, yet to be paid, and works to accomplish, or some more pains to be experienced, a balance of some kind in my account, that I was destined or allowed to return.

Three Stories To Remember

On one sunny evening, I was strolling through a village road which leads to a small and very old temple. I often preferred this road for an evening walk, as its loneliness is like the path towards the divine which also is trod by very few. Though I walked alone most days, that day an old man from the same village joined me. He was returning from town after purchasing some medicines for his ailing wife. It was nearing dusk. A calm prevailed, characteristic of any village at this time, for activities come to a standstill then. There were no villages within yonder visibility and at far I could see the inviting *gopuram* of a temple. It was dilapidated due to age and lack of maintenance, but had an elegant and wonderful look because of its age-old style of construction and architecture.

The old man who had joined me on the way after exchanging pleasantries, started asking me a lot of incongruous questions which I was not in the mood to answer for them, being just of trash value. But to him, his own opinion was intelligent and legitimate. I too was not interested in annoying him, a totally naïve person. So though I tried to divert him into other matters, but he seemed stuck like a worn-out gramophone record of olden days. When he noticed that I was uninterested in his questions, the old man started making up or telling me a story, in his feeble, shivering voice. I was forced to cut short my walk for the day, and we both sat under a tree.

Putting on an imposing air to as prelude, he started his sermon by saying, "There was an old man, on his death bed, with nobody either to look after or be looked after by, who was suffering a lot of the blessings of old age, called pain of all sorts. He saw a few old people gathering around him, with curiosity and expectation waiting to see the takeoff. The old man asked of them in his feeble voice, "Are you not that childhood friend, who has come here now to bid farewell to me?" One of them replied, "Yes, yes of course we were together with you in boyhood and youth. But you never cared to pay the least attention to us and abandoned us." Then the old man feebly said with curiosity, "Who are you?" They replied, "We . . . don't you gather? We are none other than your hopes and dreams that you never tried to fulfill, the talents and gifts which you never tried to use or tried to develop!" The old man said, feeling scared, "Then why are you here, to curse me or bless me in this last moment?" "Neither," they said, "We too are just bemoaning our destiny that we should die here with you not attending to our calls throughout life."

"Did you get the point, baba?" the storyteller in front of me asked. I nodded my head forcefully, conveying an option-less 'yes'.

I thought the story was over, and observed a politically-correct silence. We both remained in silence for some time. I was thinking these incidents were common in everyone's life, so why was this old man relating this pregnant and tragic story to me. I was wondering, bemused and trying to catch the intention behind it but failed. So I stood up to resume my walk. But with a gesture, the old man asked me to sit and started telling another story.

"Once in a forest a friendship developed between a dry clod of earth which looked like a human face, (which can happen by chance sometimes) and a dry leaf that had fallen from a tree. They became very close friends. Due to a drought, the face-like clod remained intact for many long years. Once they decided to go to Kashi for pilgrimage. They started walking together from the place of their origin toward Kashi. They walked many miles sharing their stories and experiences. One day along the way, there was a heavy downpour of rain, and the dry leaf draped itself over the clod like an umbrella and saved it from dissolving in the rainwater. The clod was moved at the act of friendship exhibited by the leaf. As they continued their journey, there was another test of destiny in the form a wild wind. The clod sat on the dry leaf to save it from being blown away by the wild wind. The journey continued for many days and one day as they walked together, the rain and wild wind came together. The wind blew away the dry leaf far away from his friend, and the clod dissolved in the rainwater."

The old man narrating this story then took a break. I opted to go into deep silence again. So there prevailed a silence between me and the villager for a few moments. I was a bit confused as to why this unknown old villager was narrating such stories to me. That odd main then said, "Babaji bear with me for another small story."

One small story! Now here again was a prelude with expectations. Now my mindset was different, as I too was curious to hear the peasant's next story. He embarked on his narration—"An old man in a village felt much pity at the plight of Mother Earth, as he was seeing her carrying a lot of weight in the form of stones and rocks, which he thought was a big burden on her. His unique sense of magnanimity and sense of duty prompted him to do something to reduce this burden to the extent possible. He had an idea when he saw a huge rock lying in front of his house, which had been there for long. Overpowered by his love for Mother Earth, and with much difficulty he hoisted it upon his head and stood in front of his house. He stood all day this way and everyone including his family members were amazed at the degree of his innocence, or idiocy so to say, but no one dared say anything. It was almost the end of the day when *sadhu* came walking through the small village road in front of his house and saw this unusual scene. The sadhu went near the old man, who was tired and sweating with the weight of the large stone on his head, and asked, "What is this? What are you doing with the stone on your head?" The old villager replied, "This is my humble service to Mother Earth in order to reduce her burden of weight." The *sadhu* smiled at his foolishness and said, "People like you are the real weight to Mother Earth."

The peasant had finished his stories, but I was clueless about the import thereof. Without saying anything more, and even without a word of farewell, the old villager just stood up and walked away, leaving me at the crossroads. It was almost dark. I was standing still for some time, a bit confused and racking my brains at the possible meaning and any conceivable link among the three ceremonious stories. It appeared he wanted to air some sarcasm.

Whatever it was, I was not able to take my mind off his words. I returned to my room thinking on the possible purport, his intention, wish or any moral of the story and lay down flat for hours in a thoughtless state of mind waiting for my mind or intellect to tell me the real meaning of those stories. Here I was left in the wilderness for showing a little affection to that old man out of compassion and respect for his right to equality.

So, a *sadhak* always should be careful in hearing stories which may be ambiguous in meaning, a dangerous situation. Doubt doubtlessly destroys. One who becomes a victim to doubt cannot hope to enjoy either this world or the next. Random discussions with any raw intellect harboring its own preconceived concepts, or ideas should be avoided at all costs. Thereby we can lose the *saadhana* of a whole lifetime. So says the lord—'*samsayatma vinashyati*' or the doubting soul is ruined. Do not do that with spirituality, for it is a great sin.

An Emotional Sunset

I WAS SITTING IN the shed across the street from my room at Vishnu Township in Kurnool. It had just stopped raining a few minutes before. The small bushes seem to be smiling and in a very happy mood, as if saying a thanksgiving prayer to the Almighty for the rejuvenating shower upon them. A stray dog passed on the road barking again and again for a reason unknown. Somewhere at a distance a crow cawed. It may have been returning to its nest, as the day was ending. A child's laughing sound came from the neighbor's house. In spite of that, a deep and serene silence prevailed. A refreshing cool wind carrying the soul-elevating aromatic smell of wet soil breezed upon me for a moment. And just as it had come, the wind left, leaving me engulfed in a strange loneliness. I felt as if there was someone around trying to talk to me, and convey to me some reality of life. As my being searched for that entity who was bearing that agony of life in its heart, my eyes fell on a flowering plant there. A few drops of water that had been on one of the leaves fell down. I could feel the loss of the leaf, from when the drop of water had been in its bosom. My eyes then sat upon a yellow flower lying on the ground which had been an object of adoration, enhancing the beauty and value of its mother plant. I too had much loved and enjoyed it till yesterday, but alas today, it had fallen down with nobody there to value it anymore. "No one loves a fallen flower," they say. It was waiting for the sweeper to dispose of it.

Who says you can't learn anything from a plant, thus came

the flash. It was that fallen flower, yesterday's hero of the plant community who was disturbing my whole being for a while. As has always been the case with me, I have loved even the fallen flower. But the fallen flower was asking am I the same as the flower attached to the plant? As the way of life goes, the sweeper came by, and that tiny beautiful yellow fellow bade me a happy goodbye. I, with wet eyes and heavy heart got up, but only to see the west where the sun was now setting, sinking like a hot red ball. And reminding, yes, that there is not much time for this sun to set too. The darkness is nearing us but not everywhere, because somewhere else it is morning, and the sun is going to rise there. Darkness is just a cover over the shining sun. The sunset of nature, the sunset of a guru is the same too. Does the guru's sunset attached to any time limit? No, he travels constantly to keep the world always in 'daylight'. Except that we are unable to travel at the speed of the guru-sun. So if we always would like to remain in 'daylight', we must make guru take us to his bosom. For a child cannot walk at its father's or mother's pace, that is what the Shukla Yajurveda says. But nobody is ready to take shelter in the guru's bosom or heart. It is only with that in mind that the scriptures say that the gurus are *avinashis*, the never-setting suns, and ever-travelling suns. They never die since they were never born. A guru's life is a never-ending journey between birth and birth, day and night, among places yet not in them. So for them there is no question of a beginning or ending. The guru manifests at the time of our 'days' (*saadhana*) or beginning of the universe. The guru never remains unmanifest. It may be that the eyes of sishyas or disciples are 'closed' (bound to a particular place in nature) so they see only darkness, and not the light of the ever-shining guru, the ever-travelling sun. Whenever they 'open' their eyes, they see their guru in and around them. I was with closed eyes for more than 25 years. When I opened my eyes at Mookambika, I saw that sun, the light, my Guruji near me, in me rather. Even now Amma is near, dear and in me. In and around me.

In the long journey of my life till now, I have faced and passed through a lot of experiences—bitter, sour and sweet. Though the flavours are never a reality, when I look back now I realize that they were all inevitable. It was only those experiences that turned me into a *sanyasi*, an *avadhoota,* and a *guru*, making me useful to others, and to the coming generations.

But the sun was about to set. The sun, tired from the long journey of dawn to dusk, needed to disappear from the sky for a bit only to return for another journey starting next dawn. My own journey has been much the same. Every day I died, and every day I am re-born. Every day I am travelling from dawn to dusk full of ever-new experiences. Yes, but now I feel the need for rest too. The eternal rest of the 'sun' happens only at the time of dissolution, or *pralaya*. And if at all there is a new beginning after *pralaya*, the 'sun' will come back with renewed vigour.

The room, which I stay at Vishnu Township has been designed according to Vedic *Vaasthushasthra*. In the middle of the room, a pit has been dug to place this body after my *samaadhi*. The entire piece of earth measuring 21'×21'×18' has been activated through *mantras*. A *parikrama marg* or circumambulation path has been made around it, and a small but beautiful garden in front of the room. As I am very fond of trees and bushes, the front side of the room is filled with small plants, some of them flowering, and some crotons etc. I can very well visualize the moments of my *samaadhi*: how they will remove the slab above the pit, how they will place the body, and how they will do the first *aarathi* to the *samaadhi*.

As has been true eternally, time heals every wound, but the scar remains. Sometimes when you see the scar, you remember the wound and the memories of pain are green again. All these are just repetitions of the last birth so to say. It seems as if it all happened only now. But the best part of life is that we have forgotten the previous *janma* or birth, and are conditioned to think only of this one, and never try to visualize the next birth. In the life of an *avadhoota*, he can, at his will, remember yesterday, today and tomorrow, if he wants to. Or he may completely ignore those happenings of yesterday, today and tomorrow. That is the reason he can be calm and composed, and that is why he is in bliss always. It is the stage of being *kaalaateetha* (beyond time and space).

So you all see there! It is becoming dark now. The night of yours is almost ready to arrive, and my journey to yonder is about to start, everything over! The dark blanket is spread on the body of mother earth. I look around and see the watchman appear to turn on the light. Of course he may turn on the external light. I asked him not to switch on the man-made light now. Let me be in darkness for some more time. It is an irony that the human with all his mighty science has so far been unable to create a man-made darkness, which is equally pristine like the light.

The light of the sun is not visible to others now. Only a few stars have appeared in the sky. A deep and transcending silence pervades around me with a mesmerizing song loaded in it. I should enjoy the song of that silence, sitting here, just alone in that divine darkness. The darkness is only seemingly external. Inside, the light of existence is burning with all its glory. It never blinks. It never bursts. It is, it was, and it will be, here forever.

Butterfly—A Messenger

It had been raining all night long and the courtyard filled with muddy water. I was sitting in my room, the dawn yet to come. The heavy rain slowed to a drizzle and then it stopped. The sun was up now and the rays of sunshine entering my room. A butterfly with some yellowish spots on a dark background was fluttering here and there in the courtyard. Because of the rain in the night, the flowers on the bushes were scattered around the courtyard. They would have been the source of food for that poor butterfly, which was now in search of an alternate source of food, or at least something to eat from the flowers. I opened the door and let the butterfly enter in the room. It was drenched and it seemed as if it was shivering from the cold. It moved around the room and slowly came near to sit on my shoulder. I felt it as some special moment, as if the butterfly was giving me some message.

On several occasions butterflies have come to me, and in different colors and designs. They come to my room and move around, and may sit on my shoulder, or head, or hands, or ears, and then move away after few minutes, and vanish. To my surprise I would see its dead body lying next day in my room, sometimes eaten by red ants.

I was in my Jammu ashram in those days, and working on drawings based on the *Lalitha Sahasranama stotra*, the hymn of the thousand names of the Goddess Lalitha. Every name in the Lalitha sahasranama has a *beeja mantra* hidden in it, and every *beeja* has its own *yantra*, (a geometrical diagram, in color). It took almost three years to complete the entire drawing work. Drawing each *yantra* on a wooden plank, I would do *japa* of the related *beeja mantra*, for a long time daily till I got the result.

I did not carry any money with me in those days, and I never had the habit of asking for money from anybody either. When Madan Lal saw me do the drawing with a pencil and keep it aside, he brought me a set of sketch-pens, a geometry-box, a few pencils and an eraser. Paramanandji had some drawing paper with him which he offered me. He had worked as a draftsman in the military, and enthusiastically helped me transfer the notebook sketches to the drawing paper, spending a lot of his time. The sketch-pen ink would dry up after some usage. I hesitated in asking for ink to refill them, or for a new set of pens. One day I had a wonderful idea to pour a few drops of water into the back side of the pens, and this worked to extend their life for a few days. With those faded colors and borrowed sheets, I somehow managed to do the drawings. In the nights I would do *japa* or meditate on the *beeja* on which I want to finalize a drawing next day. This work on the Lalitha sahasranama was a *tapas* of more than three years and took so long to complete, as I used to travel a lot in between to Samalkha or Indore or Omkareshwar or Srisailam.

I had also made plans to write interpretations of these *yantras* and *beejas* based on the *Lalitha Sahasranama*, but they were not materializing. After a few years though, during my stay in Kurnool in Andhra Pradesh, I was able to do the *vyakhya* or commentary on the *Lalitha Sahasranama*, based on Saubhagya Bhaskaram (Bhaskararaya's commentary), in the form of daily *satsangs*, and later as lectures that were released as a CD titled 'Srividya Vichar', sponsored by Dr. Srinivasa Reddy of Kurnool, and well-distributed among the Srividya sadhakas. But the language of lecture being a mixture of Hindi and a little English, it was not properly understood or used in South India.

I held on to those Lalitha Sahasranama drawings that I had done with sheer love, passion and struggle even lacking decent equipment such as color pen and pencils, or any such modern accessories or instruments. But the making of those had given me an immense satisfaction. Due to the absence of cooperative factors in turning them into a book format, I left them in dormancy in my room in the Jammu Ashram on top of my book rack, like a helpless mother might be forced to leave her newborn. I had to leave for a long stay in Indore at my friend Baba's *ashram* to continue my research work on the vibrations of *bindu*. The paintings had almost slipped from my memory when one winter, after my return from Indore, I did notice them while re-arranging books on the racks. The drawings had been stored on top of the rack and alas, had been eaten by termites. I verified each and every drawing sheet, but all of them had been damaged by the termites, and were full of holes. They now appeared like some modern art creation of an absurd mind. I wept for hours on end that day at the sight, and can even today remember the looks of sympathy on the faces of my disciples. They asked me to re-draw them, and were ready to bring fresh paper and colors, but my heart was broken. In the way of a father putting his only son on a funeral pyre for cremation, I burnt some of them with a heavy heart and tears in my eyes. Paramanand kept two or three drawing aside that had not been damaged much, and when I came to Kurnool I brought them along with me. Again thoughts of redoing the same drawings appeared in my mind, and Ramesh even brought a lot of drawing sheets and sketch pens. Though I tried several times, it could not happen, as one cannot bring back his or her dead child from a burning pyre. It was a heavy loss not only to me, but to the Srividya *sadhakas* and to the lovers of the *Lalitha Sahasranama*. In Kurnool, in my room in Brindavan Nagar, there is an almirah full of cassettes and C.Ds. They are audio and video recordings of my lectures on *Lalitha Sahasranama, Lalitha Trishathi, Saundarya Lahari, Guru Gita* etc (more than thousands of hours). There are also video recordings of the events of Guru Poornima, book releases, lectures etc. I used to tell my disciples in Kurnool that those old cassettes will meet the same fate as the drawings, by accumulating fungus which will ruin the tapes. I am much older now and not in a position to give lectures again on the same subjects, due to health conditions and faded memories.

Yesterday, a butterfly appeared again. It was in the hall in Baba Brindavan Nagar, where my stock of released books was stored, and where I sit to type the next part of the autobiography. It fluttered around the room, then sat on the books, moving on to the typewriter, then flew away to a corner and finally disappeared. But this time around it did not come to me, or sit on my body, or deliver any message.

When I entered my room this morning and sat down to resume my typing, I spotted the motionless body of the black butterfly, with yellow spots on its wings, lying on my writing table next to the typewriter. It seemed to be delivering a last message—in silence. Tears flowed from my eyes for a few minutes and I thought I should give it a proper cremation. I went into *mauna* or silence for a moment, sitting in my bedroom in voidness without a single thought, but with a prayer to the Almighty to give *shanthi* to that *atma*, who had been delivering messages for a long time, and who delivered its last message through its 'silence,' through its death. Yes, it will never come back to me again, never.

The Hamsa Gaanam

MYSTICAL EXPERIENCES TYPICALLY disturb the normal life of a spiritually enlightened person. I had heard and understood this as true of the great Ramana Maharishi too. His was so natural a life that no one fully knows or realizes what a volcano of knowledge he was. He never bothered to exhibit his powers, or aspired for any experience of mystical traits. The common man's idea and notion about and of a *sadhu* is one who has some kind of magical power to produce, show, or manifest things of unnatural kind to happen. There are vested interests who have planted many stories and uncorroborated experiences about *sadhus*, unverifiable and irreproducible, to the extent that it has become very difficult nowadays for a *sadhak* to carry out genuine *saadhana*.

As you progress in the path, you stumble upon so many such experiences which are very enticing, and if by chance you entertain them, it will become infectious.

When I finished writing the episode about my experience during one of my *purascharanas* in the Jammu ashram, that experience in which I had the *darshan* of my beloved Guru Devi, my mind had to virtually reach back to that date in order to write it. In doing so, that same ecstasy was reproduced afresh. Slipping backwards naturally meant that I would have her *darshan* once more. The impression of that incident was so intense and lingering, similar to the memory of the enjoyment of a good sweet, that it had engraved itself so deep upon my heart. It refused to leave. It is exactly in this way that human beings repeat incidents in their lives, engaging themselves to re-enact those events of enjoyment. So *the* emotional rapture of that experience got a second life just by me recalling it. I kept zooming into that stage for a few days, even without my cognition, but I was busy too with other activities as usual. In the meantime, for a few months I had developed some interest in Radha, Krishna, Bhagavatam etc., due to interactions with Abhayanand, who contrary to me was a Vishnu devotee. I am by default, a devotee of Maa Shakti. So that year we organized a few programs on Bhagavatam as well, all successful as far as my expectations were concerned. I had already been zooming in the bliss of my guru's *darshan*, and I was now over-writing that area of my memory with the new stories and newly acquired Krishna-related *sanskaras*, thoughts etc. It produced a wonderful incident which I would like to share with you all here in this episode.

I would not say it was at all a reproduction of the memory but a re-manifestation of the previous experience. I was not just merely recalling what I had, but re-enjoying and revisiting what I had previously experienced, under a specific state of mind and in specific circumstances. The reader should be clear about this in mind to be able to get the meaning hidden. In our scriptures it is termed *pratyabhingya* (recognition), itself the basis for self-realization. A *vedantin* considers *pratyabhingya* verily realization itself.

One day as I mentioned, some days after writing the episode 'Beginning itself is ending', I was alone in the room in Vishnu Township. It was around 1.30 in the early hours of the night, a deep silence pervading everywhere. I never forgot to turn off the tape-recorders etc. before going to bed, especially since I was recovering from a debilitating illness. I was not sleeping very well and wanted to make the conditions suitable and available should any occasion for sleep arise. Otherwise I would have to wait even for days together to see the face of this deity called sleep. There was no question of any music to play by itself at that odd time without my knowledge. So sometimes I would keep tossing on the bed all night due to non-advent of the deity called sleep, and it made me tired to the core in the morning. But that day it was not like that—I felt utterly relaxed, fresh, and agile in mind. I was not feeling the least necessity for sleep. I lay calmly on the bed, with no urge to turn and toss from vexation. It was neither a state of sleep, nor an awake state, nor a meditative state—I can claim to say that I was absorbed totally in some unique ultra-empirical but joyous and blissful state with full knowingness of things. Abruptly I heard the enticingly melodious sound of a flute, wafting gently from somewhere. It was one of my favorite tunes on Krishna. Initially the experience was one of hearing. Then the hearing experience was gone—transitioning into one of feeling. After a while the feeling transformed into a merging. I started accompanying the flute with my humming of the same tune. Suddenly I felt that I was losing cognition. I was forced into merging with something, and had lost the capacity to identify or to recognize whether I was the song or the flute. When I found myself dissolving into that unearthly state, I was struggling to make an identity of myself. And when that instinct for identity arose, I split myself into two halves: the one 'I' was intact and other half of me became many. When I saw the other part I saw Krishna in his full effulgence standing on a dais there. I exclaimed, "Krishna!" He exclaimed, "Radhe!" We were both overpowered by our respective *bhaavas*. This was a state of inexplicable bliss. The Radha *bhaava* in me started intensifying more and more. Now I started comprehending the music, situation etc. I was hearing and dancing with the divine song called *hamsa gaanam*.

Yes, the *hamsa gaanam*, the song of the swan, the ultimate form of existence, the song of the Self. The *naadam*, or never-subsiding reverberation of the cosmic voice of ecstasy, the rhapsodic effortless sound of everlasting cosmic flow. The self-clarificatory sound of knowledge, a heightened state of purity of heart, innocence par excellence of existence.

They say it is painful to hear 'it', the sound of the flute of Krishna, a sweet pain which only Radha along with her retinue of *gopikas* can experience. The *radha bhaava* in me was experiencing it at that moment in the *panchama raaga*, the ultimate one that has been vibrating within me from the very beginning. I was singing within me the Krishna *geetam*, '*Krishna nee beganey baaro*' (the famous devotional song, 'come hither soon, O Krishna'), the song of the *sakhis* or the *gopikas*. They were dancing in me to a rhythm, the rhythm of merging. It was the song of oneness, not of death but of the dissolution of the 'I' within me. The sound of the flute of Krishna merges in the rhythm of the steps of Radha. The song was divine and the rhythm divine. The steps danced to the *aadi taalam* and then to the *druta taalam,* then there was silence. And again there was the sound of the flute, as if from an unknown distance, from the very depth of the inner self.

It was not going to end, that song divine echoed as a pulsation: that divine pulsation empowered my existence. The *bindu* (third eye chakra) broke in me and I could easily see the Shiva and Shakti separating and merging together in me as *ardha nareeswara*, and that a new *raagam* of 'self' was emerging in me, the *raagam* of *viraagam*, the *viraha raagam* of experiencing the 'self' in search of the 'Universal Self'.

The swan, the *hamsa*, still singing. Every pulsation is a song in a new *raagam*, a never before experienced symphony—the symphony of the merging of Shiva in Shakti, and Shakti in Shiva, which is happening in me every moment which is the sweet yet painful experience that everyone awaits from birth, the final sound of self, the sound of another beginning, the ultimate song for the new dawn, the sound with a fragrance of my awareness in 'being,' my merging in 'me,' and coming out from the cosmic womb with a new fragrance of 'self-awareness of being in 'the self.'

Sounds like another mad day of an *avadhoota,* doesn't it? No, ending of the mad day of an ignorant fool from the clutches of the so called ordinary behavior, and awakening into the intelligence of an *avadhoota*, merging the intelligence in the self, in the cosmic self, the Shivatva, the ultimate reality of cosmic awareness.

A deep silence, serene, calm and composed moments, for long time, yes, the time factor vanished, no more space, a '*poornatha*' (fullness) filled '*soonyatha*' (emptiness). "Ekkada raa nee kettina medagulu, ekkada raa nee moha bandhamulu" . . . a sound of song disturbed from distance. It had the meaning of 'where gone your palatial buildings, where gone your attachments towards unreal things...,' is it telling me, is it telling you all, is it not the real enquiry of 'self,'- 'where in the winds gone the false identity, where in the water dissolved your desire for money and fame, where in the skies merged your false sounds of external steps, where on earth merged the fragrance you loved for long, where in the fire you burnt the desires of the birth to death, where in the self you merged yourself.

I started dancing to that tune of the song heard from far, sang by an unknown villager came out with his cows to take them for feeding in grounds. I looked around, 'where am I,' I found I am here where I was, where I am, and where "I" is!!!

Just the new dawn is on my door steps. Another day, another beginning, for another ending. Daily I look to the parijatha tree in front of my room, just at the gate, in my garden. It is full of white flowers, whole night spreading the marvelous, inviting fragrance. Mornings, one by one, like the rain drops the flowers falls down, as if it is doing an 'archana' to the Mother Nature. But after few hours the whiteness fades, fragrance vanishes in the air; the dry flowers fell down on the floor as useless. It reminds me about my life. Whole life I experienced the 'truth of being,' but when I share the experience none in the so called 'samsara' ready to experience it, as they are addicted to the 'unreal samsara.' Like the 'parijatha' flowers, I lay down in my room, calm, quiet, useless, good for nothing with a pain same as the 'parijatha' flowers have. I learnt a lesson from the 'parijatha' flowers, just give fragrance to others, never mind of your satisfaction, as the nature never minds the birth and death of that flower, as it is a natural process.

Break Not The Mirror If Thy Face Is Ugly

PEOPLE ARE BY default compulsive bug-passers, with the habit of blaming others for the mistakes committed by them. Of course all have their share of blunders and wrongs of all sorts during the short spans of their lives. It is true that to err is human, but the desire to rectify is divine—the desire to eradicate that tendency, stemming from the carelessness of the mind that refuses to pay a little more attention to the task assigned, at a particular moment. The first step in this direction of rectifying a mistake is to just accept that it was done by us. Yet how few are ready, or able to muster the courage at the appropriate moment to accept responsibility. We simply pass it on to another's shoulder. Or just make God himself, or destiny, the scapegoat. "It was because of this, or that perhaps, that it happened this way"- this is the common pretense and excuse we use to hide our lapses and we even invent innovative ways to escape!

It is all due to that dragon, the ego, which we have fondled and nursed since birth, that we never accept the mistakes. So after the unsuccessful smear campaign, the air of Ramnagar had become thicker by pounds. I noticed a change and a divide in mutual dealings of my devotees, and their interpersonal relations were getting a beating. The hidden operators behind the mission had become active again. So many people came to me, serving me up with relish the stories of their choice. I thought to myself that if even after so many gentlemanly explanations, they were not able to guard against cultural slander, then what else could be done to save them from the net of greed. This thought was eating me up day and night, so these days I was in an upset mood. I remained in that state of frustrated concern for the innocent *sadhaks* among them who were being disturbed.

I began wondering whether at all I was a fish fit to be in that pond. Such was the wide gap between my instruction, and their comprehension of it. Though not everybody can succeed in every situation, yet my abilities as a guru would be under-utilized, in the guiding and leading towards the ultimate reality of human birth. If they were approaching me with other inferior intentions, wishes, desires, goals that were not really my area of accomplishment, I would naturally end up as a flop. It is important to understand that worry and concern at choosing an unfit field of service, which happens to not be as per our abilities, doesn't imply that we are ineligible for anything else. So we have to search our hearts to understand our own language, feelings, and understandings and find work that suits our wavelength. So a doctor must not call an engineer an idiot, or vice versa. I do not have any attachment to the buildings etc. of the ashram, only love and concern for the few sincere *sadhaks* there. This being the first abode from where I had begun my evolution into *sadhu*-hood, it was the gratitude that was holding me to that place, towards who had helped me with pure love and affection for my *saadhana* during those initial days. But if I chose to continue in that atmosphere, I might be stunting my own way of going beyond, which would be a loss to them too.

So many options were coming to my mind, but mulling over the pros and cons made them all seem futile it that situation. One morning when I woke up, I felt a powerful call from inside that I should leave that place for the sake of peace. Since that feeling kept appearing repeatedly, my routines became harder to carry out, and so I decided to obey that inner guidance.

I was very much flummoxed at leaving my Jammu ashram. Of course I had no special affinity towards the buildings or temples constructed there, there was still an affectionate soft corner in my heart towards the few disciples whose *saadhana* was in progress. Once I left the ashram, their saadhana would definitely be adversely affected. But there was no other way than to accept the commands of cruel time. I was not aware of where I would be going and what the next step would be. I walked out of the ashram with just the clothes on my body, and with no intention or instruction of any certainty about my destination. At the *chowrastha* (four-way crossing) from where the road lead to the Pathankot, I spotted a three-wheeler waiting. I had nothing other than my *kappar, kamandal* and the clothes I was wearing, and not even a single *paisa* on me. Even though the disciples offered to help, some hidden 'ego' came up. I told the autorickshaw boy that I would like to be dropped off at the bus stand but that I had nothing to pay as fare. He said, "Baba, I am fortunate that you picked my auto to travel in. Because of this, I am sure that today my business will be better." I prayed that his belief would deliver his desire.

Even after reaching the bus stand, I was clueless about where and how and why to proceed. But even in that setting, there sprang to mind a habit I had developed just to boost my mood during my writing work. Yes, in those days I used to chew *betel leaves*! That habit was pushing me to beg now, when I noticed a petty *paan* shop owner opening up his shop for business that morning. I requested him to give me a packet of *paan paraag*, and he happily gave it to me. Standing at the bus stand, my mind was blank. Life is like a leaf in a stream, and I was not sure where it was taking me. A Delhi-bound bus, which was coming in from Katra (base camp of Vaishno Devi) entered in into the bus stand. An old woman traveling on that bus, got down and approached me in a friendly way as if she had known me since a long time. With a smile, she asked. "*Baba, kahan jane ke liye khade ho?*" (Baba, where are you headed for?) Even though I didn't know and had no place of choice in mind, the word just came from my mouth—"Delhi." Without any further ado, she promptly purchased a ticket from the conductor standing nearby and handed it to me. I sat for more than 10 hours on the bus till it reached Panipat, in the same blank state of mind.

When the bus began nearing the village of Samalkha, I felt an urge to get down there. I told the old woman about this intention to alight before reaching Delhi, but she didn't reply, so I got down at the Samalkha bus stand. And as if mechanically, I started moving towards Sharmaji's house. When he saw me at the doorstep without bag and baggage itself, he was very surprised at my sudden appearance. Smelling something wrong, he asked, *"Kya hua? Is baar keval bhiksha patra ke alaava hath me kuch nahi?"* (What happened? This time around you are here with nothing except *bhiksha patra* in hand?) Usually I came there in the company of someone from the village. I told Sharmaji, who was more of a friend than a disciple, *"Aap jaake jaroorat ke kuch kapade aadi leke aayiye."* (Please bring me some necessities like clothes etc.) By that time, Lata, Sharmaji's wife brought me a cup of tea. They could easily guess that something unpleasant had happened. I was in silence. Once he had brought me a few new clothes, toothpaste, brush etc., after a bath and some lunch I narrated to them what exactly had happened.

After a couple days' stay there, the news spread among the disciples and many came to see me. We all, Sharmaji, Lata, Varun (their son), and Brijalata (sister of Lata) sat together and after a brief discussion, Sharmaji offered me a few yards of land in front of his house itself to construct a room for my stay. I contacted a few of my disciples to arrange some money to construct that room in Samalkha, and the work was completed in a very short period, about one month or so. Sharmaji arranged a house-warming ceremony with *pooja*, *archana* etc and a few disciples joined the program. Though I started living there, my mind was still a little disturbed from the Jammu situation. A few days after, some of the Jammu villagers came to meet me with a request to return, but I was unwilling to accept their argument; it seemed like they wanted to play down the situation as if it were not a big issue at all. But I was firm with my refusal. Sharmaji as well gave them a dressing down for mishandling the issue.

But as is the case with most people, they put the blame on others. It is not unusual for the guilty to show an innocent face by placing the responsibility on someone else's shoulder. Being neutral after committing a blunder or mistake, and feigning innocence is definitely a crime.

Vyavahara

It was on my way back from Gyanganj. I was bubbling with the newfound bliss of having had the *darshan* of my Supreme Gurus at that protected seat of learning, Gyanganj. As planned already, one of my friends, a *mahatma* Swami Lalitananda requested me to do the installation ceremony of his Shiva Mandir which he had built in Samalkha. I was on my way there to fulfill my commitment. I reached Panipat (Samalkha) by the evening of the third day of journey and went to Surendra Sharma's residence who was there to welcome me. After two days' stay there, a few sincere disciples insisted I deliver them some enlightenment, and so I started a *satsang* session in spite of exhaustion from the long trip. This time they had arranged the programme at "The Punjabi Mandir" (known because the *mandir* was maintained by the Punjabi population there who had migrated to Samalkha). This time instead of taking a particular text for *satsang*, I lectured extempore on different subjects from the *Vedanta*, on *bhakti*, *yoga* etc. The program was fulfilling to everyone. After my lecture there would be *bhajan* and *keerthan* sung everyday by the people who had assembled. I sang only one *bhajan* on Krishna, "*adharam madhuram . . .*" which attracted a lot of people, even enjoyed by the youth present. Even though these people were not much interested in the lectures, by the time of my singing the *bhajan*, more and more people had assembled to hear me, though I was not a good singer at all!

By this time the final phase of the construction work of

Lalitananda's Mandir was also almost over, and he was preparing for the installation of the idol of Shiva. A *muhurta* was fixed for Shivaratri day. Well in advance, he had brought a very imposing 'Narmadeswar Shiva Lingam' from Dhavdi Kund in Madhya Pradesh, and kept it at one of his devotee's residence at Pitampura in Delhi. We all went there in a truck just a week before the installation day, performed a very good *pooja* at the house where the idol had been kept, and brought it to Samalkha with grand ceremony to keep at the newly constructed mandir, where a few local Brahmin priests did the needed rituals before starting the Shivaratri celebrations.

A well-decorated bullock cart was arranged to carry the big Shiva Lingam (since Nandi, a bull himself is Shiva's *vahana* or vehicle) for *nagara pradakshina*. I held the *Shivalinga* in my hands, and a band played *bhajans* as the procession moved. During the *pradakshina* I was not in body consciousness, and fully in *Shiva bhaava*. Accompanying us were young girls and women carrying 365 pots or *kalasams* on their heads that were well-decorated and filled with *gangajal*. It was really a wonderful scene, and worth seeing to see so many people participate with so much devotion in that program. The aspect of unity, love for others, discipline, and sense of sacrifice were well exhibited by the devotees in the name of Shiva. The next day being Shivaratri, along with the chanting of Veda *mantras* and 'Om Nama Shivaya', I myself installed the *Shivalinga,* and did *abhisheka* with the 365 pots of *gangajal*. The day was packed with various events and the program went on for the whole night with *bhajan/keerthan*. On the day after, the program concluded with a feast of common feeding or *bhandara* which was attended by thousands. My heart was deeply satisfied at this. In between I received a message from Jammu that they needed some guidance in the construction. So, after staying with Surender Sharma for a few more days, I went to Jammu (Kathua) Ashram along with him.

Upon reaching there I realized that it was not for work that I had been called, but to have my *darshan*; some devotees had sent some notes. They had heard of the big gathering and *satsang* at

Samalkha, and had thought I might settle there for long, due to receiving more love there. So at Jammu I now had routine normal life, with the construction work almost ending. Whenever I find a conducive atmosphere my heart automatically starts longing for a *saadhana* of deeper nature. So thinking along those lines, I felt that this place was also looking okay now, with no commitments and no obligations, I was free there. The burden of daily *bhiksha* was met too, as it was so arranged that daily one house in the village would take care of my food and other needs. I thought that now with the shelter and permanent arrangement for food etc., my *saadhana* should go well without a hitch.

But in a corner of my heart, there was a deep yearning to share with *sadhaks* of equal footing, all the experiences, enlightenments, enhancements, and clarity that I had received from the trip to Gyanganj. That was not possible here in Jammu though the arrangements for *saadhana* were perfect. That was creating the vacuum. I gave the heart a lot of toys to play with, but to no avail.

After a few days stay thus in that state of mind, and with the monotony and boredom, I took to thinking about the options for my destination. The Narmada began making her case forcefully with rights. So I asked one of my disciples to book a ticket to Indore, with the Narmada pulling me towards her once again.

The following week I started my sojourn to Omkareshwar via Indore. I do not know the reason for my attachment towards Narmada. Even though I had done long stints there, I was not still not fully satisfied! On the second day, I reached Omkareshwar and as usual went to Markandeya Sanyas Ashram for lodging. I felt the calmness in my heart, as if I was on the lap of my mother.

Be There Where You Are

THE SKY HAD been cloudy since the previous night. Even though the sun appeared, it was in hide-and-seek mode and the weather was sultry. There was a possibility of rain. But the dull sky affected my mood strangely; an inexplicable experience, like a cloud heavy with moisture but lacking other requisite factors, unable to pour down and just thundering occasionally. A cloudy sky is much like the writer's mind. The vaporized waters of emotions form the clouds of experiences. The rain is like the writing itself. When the mind finishes pouring out its thoughts through writing, the mind looks exactly like the sky after a heavy downpour. The clean, bright, and thought-free mind is like that spotless sky. It is only then that life becomes an effortless joyride. In our traditional literature they say that a deer starts to feel the pains of labor right from day one of her pregnancy, and the pain continues till the day of delivery. My mind's throbbing too was not much different from this.

The day I started thinking of writing the second part of my autobiography, that 'cloud' started to form and a sweet pain began somewhere in my heart. When a raincloud forms in the sky we, in our bodies, start sensing some pressure. Similarly when the mind forms that cloud, the heart feels the pinch. The cloud began to grow in size and empowered my instruments of expression (writing). The body, mind, soul, and intellect all came together to work to shape the concepts and themes into embryos of episodes, one-by-one, of my experiences along the long and tedious journey of my life. And my fingers started converting them into words that I transferred from my memory into my best friend's memory: a small laptop computer who has been a recent companion. Swami Abhayanandji, another friend, who though staying far away physically, is near my heart, and who of course through cell phone or e-mail has revived my memory with his wonderful vocabulary and his mature thoughts. I am grateful to these inventions which brings distant hearts closer, and thanks to these, we are both able to work simultaneously even with this geographical divide and exchange our views (sometimes we do disagree too).

A few years back, I was hospitalized in order to attend to a cardiac problem in a multi-specialty hospital. Investigations diagnosed a ventricular ectopic beat and also that I was suffering from lower chamber disorders causing chest pain. They planned for an ECG study and an angiogram. One Dr. Narasimha, a well-known cardiologist and a rare human being with much affection towards me was looking after my case. I was brought to Hyderabad in an unconscious condition. Apart from Dr. Satyanarayana, Mohi, Sujatha and Satyam were also with me. The other arrangements for my treatment at the hospital were done by D. Narasa Raju and Harikishore. After a routine check-up the doctors wanted to order an ECG study and even planned for a pacemaker. By then, Guru Poornima was around the corner. In fact I was not in a mood to undergo any type of treatment like surgery. But the angiogram and EPG study were inevitable.

Preparations were over and I was taken into the operation theatre which was well-equipped with all modern facilities. Usually any type of tranquilizer or even anesthesia has never worked on my body. As my body is 'yogic' with activated *shat chakras*, the chemical energy of pharmaceuticals are never able to impact me. A yogi whose *shat chakras* are activated with spiritual energy will never respond to any artificial energy. Or if it is required to work on such a yogi, he has to deactivate those *chakras*, which is dangerous. Doctors administered three or four units of injections to put me in an unconscious state, so they could do further procedures.

But I had forgotten to mention the crucial fact of the *chakras* to them, so in spite of all their attempts, they failed. Because of me they were all getting delayed on their schedules. So the irritated Dr. Narasimha asked me in frustration, "Are you a man or a devil or a god? For the first time ever, I am seeing such a person who has almost no response to even the heaviest of anesthetics." Then I remembered, and told him, "Dear doctor, you need not worry. I will get your job done. Okay, now you just mark the place of your choice with an ice cube (where you want to make the incision) for inserting the catheter. I will remove my mind from there, and you can proceed with your study." But he was not ready to accept my idea, and refused to take a risk, telling me that medical science does not permit such foolery. I argued, "When I myself have signed the necessary papers you can do it at my risk. You are a Hindu and believe in the existence of divinity, gods and in the words of our holy scriptures; then again you want them to comply with science which even now in spite of all its mighty achievements is just in its inception. Pray to your *ishta devata* if at all you have one, and please go ahead." Perhaps it challenged his knowledge base or perhaps I had touched on his belief, for he finally agreed. With some hesitation and caution, he agreed to mark the joint of my leg with an ice cube, and cut a little to insert the catheter. It took more than two hours to complete the surgery. The next day he paid me a special visit to understand how it could have been possible for a human being to keep in check his mind for so long a time. Instead of giving him the lengthy lecture he was expecting, I merely said, "It's possible. Only that one must have a Guru, and a staunch belief in the scriptures and an unwavering faith in the Guru." For, this is not an arbitrary science which changes its sayings and data according to whim. As a token of gratitude for the successful surgery and correction the ventricular ectopic beat, I placed my *rudraksha mala* which I had been wearing for a long time, around his neck. I could very well see various emotions on his face including that of astonishment, and his eyes filled up with tears. I learned that a few months later at a cardiology conference, he had presented a paper on this incident that he had come face to face with. After a few days, I was discharged from the hospital and came back to normalcy.

The dark and ominous pregnant cloud that had been hovering in the sky had now released and emptied itself. The rain had deeply saturated the earth, and the sun now shone afresh in his own glory. It is the perennial truth: if you have staunch belief in 'Amma', the Ultimate Guru, the impossible becomes possible.

To You, For The Motivating Assurances

It is not easy to bring a sentence to a 'full stop' with a period, after so many commas have been hooking together to form a meaningful statement. The journey from the first letter to comma was easy enough. Moving on from comma to semicolon was difficult, and from semicolon to period, very painful. But I have to put that period, that 'full stop'. The inevitable ending to my story. There is still a bit left of the journey, it seems. But I wonder whether it would be possible for me to pen down the rest of my story. Hence the full stop. It is a decision made by Time and I have to bow down and obey.

It has been raining again since morning. The sound of the thunder and lightning arouses a fear in me. Is this the end? I am at my writing table on my laptop, writing a few more words. A sound is heard—yes, it is that of my beloved Guruji, Avadhoota Taramayee, that echoes in the room. Maybe it comes from the inner consciousness, that home within where she dwells, in my very pulsations. They seem to say, "*Band karo, likhna padhna. Bas, bahut ho gaya. Kisko sunayega tumhari kathayen, kisko is ke prati sraddha hei. Bas re bas.*" (Stop all this reading and writing. It has been quite enough. Who are you telling all these stories to, is there anyone devoted enough to care at all? Put an end to it.) I look around. I have been in *maun vrata* since yesterday. I felt that need to be alone, not lonely. I need rest. So I keep to myself, locking myself in my room.

Here comes the end of the memories of an *avadhoota* with a vision, a *sadhaka* with a mission, a dreaming social activist with great love for the world, a guru with experiences to share, and a failed human being who only wanted to see his fellow beings live in eternal harmony and mutual love. I am sure my life was never successful in that last aspect, except for my *saadhana*. After I realized that there were a lot of devils dancing around me wearing masks of divinity, I tried to join them but mask-less, and failed. I was searching for my real face in that faceless crowd. I know that there will be no use to this book. They may read or they may not, and this will also end up as another 'pretty thing' in their bookcase. They will tell people, "Oh, my Guruji suffered a lot, and he wrote a wonderful account of it in his book." Another mask that they will wear on their occasions of dignity.

I have tried to share, and perhaps I have been wrong in doing so, in the intention of partaking my experiences along with the esteemed readers of this work. Some of those were bitter, some sour, and some sweet. I tried to be honest to the facts in writing this. I don't know if some of you felt hurt, felt happy, or felt angry with me for writing the truths. But it was inevitable. Even if a single person awakens from the deep sleep of ignorance, I will feel successful.

The time of my departure is near and I must embark upon my onward journey. So even if I want to, I will not be able to add any more words though there exists a full ocean to plunge into. I prefer to be free from the scorching sun of the loveless world, the selfish mob, the disorderly crowd, and feel free to be under the soothing shadow of my Guruji, always at her cozy bosom, at least during my last days. Let me be in *mauna*, the silence that speaks volumes. Let me be within myself, to make sure that the end will be calm, composed and serene. Let the end come in a state of full awareness, enabling me to be reborn with full awareness.

No more words—the words have merged into oblivion, merged in the air, in water, in sound, in earth, and in fire. And I too shall one day, merge into the cosmic soul.

And that 'roaring' will be in silence hereafter.

The Waiting

THE SUN MUST set. I had imagined an earlier sunset. Last fourteen years I endured the pain of lung cancer and many betrayals. Life was becoming heavier by day. I did not know when to put the full stop nor did I know how to put the full stop. Many a times, the seeming full stops ended as semi colons and I continued to breathe. Many times I thought, *'My only success in this life has been my saadhana. I failed miserably in the world otherwise. I failed in interactions with worldly humans while I was successful in my interactions with my Mother and the masters of Gyanganj. Two distinctly different worlds! The world of pretensions and the world of Truth!'*

Since a few decades, I have been walking this tedious path literally with blood in my mouth and 5th stage cancer which I had taken over from a woman who was dying from this painful illness. Even though I went for treatments, no cancer was visible on the X-rays and scans. The doctors were intrigued. I once explained this to Sujatha and some of my closest followers. When our seven chakras are fully activated and we operate in the superconscious realms, physical body is equal to *sukshma* (subtle). When cosmic energy is fully activated in our system, any kind of artificial energy, such as medicines or machines, will not work or will just get nullified. Medical science will not understand that.

The nagging ailment has been weighing me down for the last fourteen years. Many times, I requested Guru Mandala to allow me to step down. I told them "I am ill, I am tired." They would ask "Who is tired? This is our body. You are us."

I was aware of the fact that a Guru will have to come back if He leaves without handing over. If you read the Kailash chapter of the Autobiography of an Avadhoota, at one point Ma Tara Mayee tells me that I should find a worthy successor, hand over my siddhis (powers) and spiritual bank balance to him and, only then, I can be totally liberated. This successor would need to be someone who has the capacity and maturity to handle all that I have spiritually earned and to whom I can transfer it all completely.

Last fourteen years, I was in deep pain and agony to find such a successor to run the spiritual activities and seva activities started by me. Despite my nagging illness, I searched in the world for long, and had almost given up hope. I could not find anybody eligible to receive what I had earned through intense and long saadhana and with the grace of my Guru and the Masters of Guru Mandala. At the back of my mind, I was always feeling that the same tradition that made Nadananda will also find a suitable successor. How can I be the one to find the right one after all?

Meeting Mohanji

THE DAY BEFORE Datta Jayanti in 2015, at Dhar in Madhya Pradesh, Mohanji and family came to meet me. It was not planned in any way. I knew nothing about him except that he is from Kerala, my home state. My friend, Sri Nagarajan, from Varanasi played the catalyst here. He arranged our meeting. When Mohanji and group came into my room, he prostrated at my feet in deep reverence. At this first meeting itself, both of us were in a silent voidness for some time. There was a strange familiarity. There was an instant bonding. Something attracted me to him. He was humble and quiet.

I realized that Mohanji himself is a recognized Guru in the world spiritual arena and has his own following. His humility never displayed his stature. He never explained in detail what he does in the world and this was amusing to me. Usually, people are eager to display their achievements and credentials. Most of people in the world are in a hurry to prove themselves. Here is a different man, who has already attained a stature in the world, but never cared. He had no airs or protocols. He behaved as humble and a loyal disciple. This made things easier. There was no ego barrier between us.

I was not quite thinking about the divine design behind this seemingly strange encounter. I asked Mohanji rather bluntly to tell me the purpose of his visit and what he wants from me. His reply was instant: "I want nothing except your blessing. I felt a deep urge to see you, after I saw your picture in the book that Sri Nagarajan gifted to me. I have no other reason or purpose for this visit." I told him there are no coincidences. There is always a larger purpose. I also said not to worry, surely Mother will tell me. I arranged for their stay nearby and asked him to stay back for a day and leave the day after Datta Jayanti.

After they left my room, I was in isolation in my room. Suddenly, I had a vision of the great Mahatapa Baba of Gyanganj (also known as Mahavatar Babaji) and heard a murmuring voice: "Take care of Mohanji". I asked, "How?" But no reply was forthcoming. I got the meaning of it. The following day, the day of Datta Jayanti 2015, I announced my intention to honor Mohanji in keeping with the instruction of the Guru Mandala. I decorated him with a shawl and a Sree Yantra in front of all people present at the ashram in Dhar that day. Because I never told him then, Mohanji did not know anything about what Mahatapa said to me. Mohanji told me that none of this was necessary. He had no expectations or demands, nor did he ponder further on the purpose of our meeting. I also decided to let time reveal things.

Time went by. Mohanji and I were in touch regularly by telephone and through inner communion. My ailment was arresting my mobility most of the time. On Mohanji's birthday, as per the Indian almanac, in early March 2016, we met again and I initiated him to Sri Vidya. In June 2016, I was invited to join Mohanji in Shirdi for the inauguration of a vegan restaurant Ahimsa Vegan as well as Madhuban, both owned by some close disciples of Mohanji. I agreed to come not only because I support a non-violent lifestyle but also because I already had an insight that something very important was about to happen in Shirdi.

Trip to Shirdi

Before we embarked on the Shirdi trip, I phoned Mohanji and told him that two of us should walk the streets of Shirdi together. I knew his schedule would be busy due to the function for which many of his disciples would come to Shirdi. I asked him to ensure that he dedicates some time for our silent walk in Shirdi. He said: "Guruji, your wish is my command. Do consider it as done." Hence, soon after breakfast, two of us started walking towards the temple of Sai Baba, Dwarakamai and the Samadhi Mandir. I told Mohanji that we won't be going into the Samadhi Mandir and those who must meet us will meet us on the streets of Shirdi.

We walked seemingly aimlessly and only I knew the higher purpose for taking him alone through the sacred streets of Shirdi. While walking together, I pointed out to him how many thousands of people are eating their food in Sai Baba's name today. How many shops, restaurants, hospitals and schools get their sustenance in Sai Baba's name! While Sai Baba was in His body, he hardly had any food to eat. Hardly anybody offered him food or shelter, except perhaps a handful of people. Both Mohanji and I have experienced similar situations in life. Today, we may not have sufficient funds, but tomorrow, so many will thrive in our name. The likes of us receive discrimination and betrayal while living, and glorification after death.

As we continued to walk together in blissful silence, as one consciousness, I ensured Mohanji that I will never leave his hand. I revealed to him that our relationship was several lifetimes old and that I will always protect him and empower him to do more in the world, just like my Guru helped me. I could feel the pain of betrayals that he endured, just like I did, and told him that he will never have any problems in life. Guru Mandala will ensure that. Those who left or betrayed his trust lost him forever. It is their loss. Those who see only our terrestrial side will completely miss the consciousness and the tradition that we represent. Such people do not possess the eligibility to walk the Golden path of Lord Datta to the ultimate end. I thus encouraged him to just relax and do more for the world. I assured him that I shall be with him all through. This is a promise I was happy to make because I knew Mohanji well.

The walk continued until we finally stopped at the temples of Lords Shiva, Shani and Ganesha inside the Shirdi temple complex. And there he was, my beloved paramesti guru (Guru's guru's guru), Bhruguram Paramahamsa, with his matted hair and sparkling eyes, standing right in front of the Shani temple. As usual he was invisible to most people except perhaps me and Mohanji. Those who are subtle could possibly see a lean man with matted hair, a wandering saint or a Nath Sadhu, standing and looking at the entrance of the Lord Shani temple. But nobody except me knew who he really was and why he came.

I mentally prostrated to him and told Mohanji that he is the one who was waiting for us. I took out the 100 rupee note, which was prepared for this way back, wrapped up in the cloth around my waist and placed it into Mohanji's hand. I then instructed him to give it to this sadhu. Mohanji took the money and walked towards the great Bhruguram Paramahamsa who then turned and looked deep into Mohanji's eyes. He received the money from Mohanji and graciously bowed down to him. We walked on. I was filled with deep joy and awe. I said nothing to Mohanji at that point in time nor did he ask me the significance of what happened just now. One thing about Mohanji is that he hardly sought explanations for anything and almost always never asked WHY about anything. I was just deeply contented for I knew what this meant. Bhruguram Paramahamsa, as you know from my Autobiography, is the guru of Bhagawan Nithyananda and my direct connection to Gyanganj. When Mohanji gave a dakshina to Bhruguram Paramahamsa, which he accepted, he made a direct connection with Gyanganj. Thus my job was over.

Soon we left the temple. While walking back, I revealed to Mohanji that Shirdi Sai Baba was the 37th pontiff of Gyanganj. I am the 48th. Now I am not well. It is time for me to remove this mantle. I am waiting for orders. The power of this incarnation will remain and multiply for 300 years after leaving the physical form. Same with Sai Baba. Same with me.

I wanted to make sure Mohanji understands that his existence has a different flavor than mine but that we are one in consciousness. I made it clear to him that I do not touch money. When people give me money, I use it for serving the needy. I do not have a bank account. But he is different. He is a grihasti. He has a family and responsibility to take care of them. I told him that he must lead a different lifestyle than me and live like a regular householder.

I always treat Mohanji as my brother, not as my disciple. When an older brother is transferring everything he has to his younger brother, he has faith in him. I told Mohanji why I sign off my mails to him with "brotherly, Nadananda." I do not want to have any barrier between us, not even that of guru and disciple. I am like his elder brother. I come to him. He need not come to me. He need not take any effort anymore. He has already come to me, come back to me. Now it is my turn. I come towards him running, just like my guru came running to me and took over my life and destiny. I thus told Mohanji to just be available. Just be there.

I later revealed to Mohanji what had happened in front of the Shani temple at Shirdi. I could make out that Mohanji recognized from the eyes of the sadhu that he was no ordinary wandering saint but his gateway to the ultimate reality. He understood that this man belonged to Guru Mandala, but did not know his full identity. I then told him that this was Bhruguram Paramahamsa himself, the one who took me to Gyanganj. He is the one who guided me. He is eternal.

The Revelation in Mookambika

The final confirmation about Mohanji being my successor happened during my trip to Mookambika on Guru Poornima in July 2016. It was my great wish to undertake this final trip during which I would visit all the places sacred to me, the places that I formerly visited with my beloved Guru Tara Mayee. It was a wonderful experience. I relived the times I spent with her years ago. On the eve of Guru Poornima, while at Mookambika, Bhruguram Paramahamsa suddenly appeared in my room. With his unique firmness and clarity, he told me: "You can step down now. You have found a successor."

I knew what this meant. I had the first confirmation from Mahatapa, second in Shirdi and now in Mookambika the final confirmation happened. Everything became crystal clear to me. He has come to receive from me. He was sent. This meant completion for me. Fourteen years of my waiting for a successor was thus arriving at a fulfilling completion. Instant joy and relief filled my inner space.

It was clear to me that Mohanji has been chosen by the Guru Mandala to be my successor. Usually, every Guru gets raw marble to carve a suitable idol. Here, I got a ready-made one. Mohanji hardly needed any chiseling. I waited for fourteen years and Mohanji came as a ready vessel, ready to receive. I was asked to confer the title of Brahmarishi to Mohanji.

The handing over ceremony of my spiritual powers to Mohanji was originally fixed for Datta Jayanti in December 2016. Due to my health challenges and as per the instruction of the Guru Mandala, I moved the ceremony earlier to Vijayadashami, which fell on October 10th, 2016.

I explained to Mohanji how important this function would be. I told him that it will be life changing for him and for me and that his family members should join us. I then made it a point to personally invite his parents from Kerala and wife and daughter from Europe over the phone, one by one. All of them were happy to come and in the end more than 80 devotees of Mohanji from different parts of the world decided to join.

I explained to Mohanji and his family that this is not an ordinary day, ordinary title or ordinary function. All has been arranged by the Guru Mandala. After this function, Mohanji will never be the same again. I will step down. He will climb up.

The handover ceremony on Vijayadashami

I knew very well that such a ceremony has never happened in public in the past. Mohanji is already known in the world and I found it my responsibility to declare to the world about his new status. It was my responsibility to position him properly so that he could easily do his work in the world. I knew there would be many distractors who would try to belittle this function or belittle Mohanji and me. For Mohanji's sake, it had to be public and official.

As per the instructions of the Masters of the Guru Mandala, which I represent, it was my privilege to ordain Mohanji with the title of Brahmarishi. This was the last function that I intended to perform in this lifetime. The auspicious day of Vijayadashami, which marks the end of the 10-day celebrations honoring the Divine Mother as well as the Mahasamadhi day of Beloved Shirdi Sai Baba, was chosen for the function.

I and the ashramites of Siddhaganj in Kurnool worked hard for many days to prepare for the function. When close to hundred international guests arrived from different parts of the globe, the ashram was buzzing with activity as all experienced the warmth of heartfelt hospitality at the ashram. It was beautiful to see all basking in the love of the Mother as one family.

A day before the actual ceremony, on the morning of Saturday the 9th October, I gave my last public satsang to the people who assembled at Kurnool for the ceremony. In the evening, I led the Guru Mandala pooja, a powerful invocation and worship of Guru Mandala. Mohanji was at my side. In an extremely heightened state during the Pooja, I witnessed my beloved Guru Tara Mayee and the Masters of the Guru Mandala appearing in the room. All felt them and many could see them. It started raining right after the Pooja. No more signs were needed. Guru Mandala was happy with our offerings and our work. Rains could destroy our plans. I went out and called Lord Indra to withdraw the clouds. The rain stopped instantly.

Mohanji and I met alone in my room at 4am for the actual handover of powers. I performed a special Homa for this purpose. One of my closest disciples Sujata was present as well to assist me. As I performed the Homa, the sacred flame went towards Mohanji and I transferred all my energy to him. The full process would take 21—51 days though. It all came from Guru Mandala, from Datta Bhagavan to him. Why he is selected is none of my business, and it is none of his business. It has been decided by the higher authorities of Gyanganj, by the sacred Guru Mandala which I represent. I was thus relieved from all my responsibilities and noticed that my blood pressure immediately went back to normal.

I was relieved. I felt totally relaxed, a big burden lifted off my shoulders.

The energy accumulated during years of intense saadhana in the Himalayas would not go to waste after all. I would not have to come back to Earth to complete my tasks. I also paid my debts to my Guru when I handed over to an able successor. The beloved Guru Mandala ensured that. It is my sankalpa that Mohanji too reaches Gyanganj. I have no doubt that it will happen. On this auspicious day Mohanji was included into the sacred Guru Parampara (the lineage of the Guru), the image of which was introduced to the public for the first time.

Before the public function started, I arranged for another special ceremony which was, in a way, blending the energies of East and West. I wanted to express my deepest gratitude to Acchan and Amma, Mohanji's parents, for bringing Mohanji to Earth and into my life. I told his father that Mohanji has come with the power to lift seven generations before him and after him. The beauty of this process was transcendent and touched the hearts of all present. Amma was visibly engulfed by the most blissful energy and indeed looked like a Devi. I did my job.

The public ceremony started in the afternoon when more than 300 people gathered in a marquee which was specially erected and decorated for the function. After the launch of the first volume of the international version of my book "Autobiography of an Avadhoota" and several other books in local languages, I adorned Mohanji with a shawl and conferred upon him the title of Brahmarishi. Mohanji then delivered a speech that brought tears in the eyes of all who were present.

The speech ended with the silence. Deep cleansing happened in the people present at the function. As I was leaving, I could see some of the people who met me for the first time literally sobbing. Something deep within them was stirred. Divine willed it that way. But that was not the way Mother would want the function to end. She wants to see her children in bliss, celebrating life and radiating Her Love.

Gokulanji, one of my loving devotees who is a gifted musician, and a group of talented fellow musicians poured out their love in musical art form on the stage. The beauty of bhakti expanded all the hearts. I thus decided to go back to the marquee. Sadness was replaced by a big explosion of joy, which was celebrated through endless dance.

The function ended in the mandir with a ghungroo (when Avadhoota Nadananda dances with ecstasy wearing anklets and a garland of bells around his hips). I went into the exalted state of the Divine Mother and we celebrated Her grace, beauty and elegance in the vastly expanded state of Consciousness. My feet moved in Her graceful dance to the powerful beat of the drum by my beloved disciple Swami Ajayananda, as the purifying essence of frankincense engulfed all of us. This was the beautiful ending to an unforgettable day.

The next day in the morning I initiated Devi Mohan, Mohanji's wife and disciple, into Sri Vidya. This was the last initiation that I performed in this lifetime.

The Farewell

For the last fourteen years I was focused on selfless service as my main saadhana. I was seen in the slums, among the street dwellers, railway stations, in hospitals where people were suffering. For fourteen years, I was not doing any pooja—service to the poor was my pooja. In Sanskrit, our Gurus taught us, "Atmano mokshartham jagat hitaya cha" It means: "Whatever you are doing, it should be for the betterment of others, it should definitely be for self-realization." But, I forgot the self-realization part for the last fourteen years. I don't care if I am realized or not; but what I have realized is that our life can be an inspiration to others. If the helpless people see people like me come out and wipe their tears—that's enough.

Now I am 76. This body is tired. I need to withdraw from public life, go back to myself and merge with the supreme consciousness. I shall be in isolation. I am going to withdraw and simply be in me. It's not an end—it's a beginning, except that it's a beginning for me.

Two years before, I had declared Mohinish Divekar from Chowl, Maharashtra as my spiritual successor. He is taking care of that part since then. Mohanji is holding the beacon light to carry forward the seva activities. Last Sivaratri, a brahmachari was sent to me by Maa Narmada to fill the vaccum in Siddhaganj. He was initiated into the Tirtha tradition of Sanyasa and given the monastic name, Swami Ajayananda Tirth. He will be my successor at Siddhaganj. That's all. Thank you all.

I close with Mohanji's speech in the title conferment ceremony:

"He was here . . . He is here . . . He will be here . . . He was, is, and will be with us always . . .

Last 40 years he was seen among the street dwellers, slum dwellers, footpaths, railway stations, bus stands in different cities as one amongst them - to feed them, to clothe them, to treat them for their ailments, to give solace to their sufferings, to teach their children about the preliminary 'samskars' of Bharath. Yes, He is always with all of us. That is our Guruji—Avadhoota Nadananda.

Now, after decades of moving here and there, travelling a lot, working almost 18 hours a day for betterment of suffering people, now . . . He is tired physically. Even though His body was being eaten away by cancer, suffering its unbearable pain, vomiting blood and pus for the last 4 years, He was continuously travelling to meet people, conducting gatherings, creating teams, arranging funds etc., to work for the suffering people around. May it be in Kurnool or Vishakhapatnam, in Dhar or Bangalore, his tireless work yielded results as the street or slum dwellers, rag pickers, beggars and other needy get food, medicine and clothes, education etc., regularly.

He is tired . . . physically . . . He needs rest and medication in this evening time of His physical existence. Now He has reluctantly agreed to His beloved devotees and doctors that He is retiring from all social activities. In Bangalore, when I met Him last month He told me: "The inevitable sun set is near..."

Entrusting all responsibilities on the shoulders of all of us, He is retiring from all activities, and will be confined to his room at Siddhaganj, Kurnool in meditation and medication. He will be available every Thursday morning for an hour or so to meet all of us. He assured us of that. Let Him take rest. All of us will shoulder the responsibilities entrusted on us. May it be saadhana or service... let us pledge in front of Him that we will definitely deliver our duties of saadhana or service with utmost care... and will yield a positive result.

As a father, a mother, a guide, a Master, He will be with us as the Pure Consciousness. I am sure.

Let Him be with us as the Awareness of Existence"

As a parting word, let it be known that Avadhoota Nadananda loved each one of you and will love you through time into eternity.

Parting Thoughts

Deep within the recesses of my memory, there still lie impressions of incidents that I have not called forth. At the repeated urging of my disciples and others, eager to hear more such stories, I have travelled back into memory lane. Here in the epilogue are scattered reminiscences that will hopefully satisfy their hankering to know more details of my itinerant life. If they prove to be food for more reflection, I shall have trupthi or satisfaction.

Sparks Of Oblivion

BEFORE ENTERING

It was only a fortnight before that 'Roaring Silence', the second part of my autobiography was released in Kurnool on *Makara Sankranti* day. That same night I left for Hyderabad to travel to Delhi and then onwards to Samalkha near Panipat, in the company of Abhayanandji and Sharmaji. A group of devotees and disciples gathered at Siddhaganj and waited till late in the night to see me off. The moments of farewell were full of emotion. I too was in an unusual mood.

I had already bid farewell to my thoughts. That is why the last line in 'Roaring Silence' reads "... the roaring will be silent hereafter". But for the past few days I received numerous calls from some well-wishers, disciples and devotees, and the common sentiment was: "Guruji, we feel that the book is incomplete. You are still hiding something from us. Do tell us about the remaining episodes of your life". Then the same words, in another tune, came from Abhayanand's mouth as well—"I am sure you will write more. Do it. I will do the repair work."

And so this morning, in the early hours before the gods awaken, here I am brooding again with my thoughts in my room at Srikul (Samalkha). I have that itch inside my head. Perhaps there is still something remaining to be shared, some more thoughts left to tell. I tell myself. "Yes, I am starting my writing work today, on *Poornima* day, opening the doors to a new dawn, I will begin now."

So here is the beginning of SPARKS OF OBLIVION. Unforgettable experiences of my journey of yesteryears. The never ending journey of an avadhoota, with experiences in all flavors— bitter, sour, sweet, hot. In reality, there is nothing to be conveyed to you all. This is just an *'aatmagaatham'* – a talking to self. And if at all you have overheard, I have no problem with that. The sound is yours, the words are yours, the emotions are yours and yours only. I was merely a witness, and am now merely trying to collect the sparks. The sparks may take the form of a fire. It may burn you or it may warm you.

So let us enter . . .

Spark 1

. . . AND AGAIN

And again, the story doesn't seem to end; every day ends with new experiences that are stored. When I recollect those stored experiences, I think they must be in black and white, to be in words, in order to be shared.

One may regard useless the telling of such stories of an *avadhoota*, or even the reading of them. But let that reading be a 'reading between the lines' for therein lie a few morsels which may prove useful to the reader, and of course to the coming generation. So, here I go again!

I was on the banks of Narmada in those days, roaming here and there simply, not as a *parikramavasi*, but as a *sailani* (wanderer). In fact my inclination was to move around in 'Soolpaneeswar Jhaadi'[23] for some time. Carrying nothing in hand except my *khappar* and *kamandal*, I left Omkareshwar with no aim in mind. In a few days I had reached Khalghat where I camped under a tree on the north bank of the Narmada. For food, I used to go to the nearby village once a day. A few villagers had cautioned that my stay by the river was not at all advisable, as there might be disturbance from snakes or drunkards. It was true as both are dangerous beings with

---

23 Soolpaneshwar wildlife sanctuary located in Narmada district, Gujarat.

poison. In spite of the warning, I made up my mind to stay by the river banks.

It was near the end of the day that I saw a sadhu, possibly a *parikramavasi (*one who circumambulates the Narmada river*)*, approaching me. The appearance was of an old man with well-built body, white beard and hair, and he wore just a small piece of cloth. He somehow seemed very familiar.

Saying "*Narmade Har*", he offered *pranaams* and I too reciprocated. He sat near me and opening his small shoulder bag, offered me a packet of biscuits. I was surprised and when I looked to his face for a minute, I recognised him—he was Achyuthanand Giri! We had previously met in Kashi during my *saadhana* at Manikarnika Ghat. Achyuthanand was born in a remote village of Bengal and had been doing his *Tara saadhana* on the same *ghat* where I too had stayed for *saadhana*.

"Are you on Narmada *parikrama*?" he asked.

When I told him that I was just roaming around he was happy to share that he too had come there for the same reason. We talked for some time about our *saadhanas* and shared biscuits too, as dusk approached.

With sunset, the Narmada was covered in a blanket of darkness. I just lay down on the sands and Achyuthananda sat near, humming a Bengali tune. Then he was silent and seemed lost in his thoughts. A deep silence prevailed with only the 'har . . . har . . .' sound of the Narmada punctuating it. He broke the *mauna* with the words "Why you are not going to Kamakhya for your saadhana?" A few days ago I had indeed been thinking of visiting Kamakhya, but lacking the money to purchase a rail ticket to Gauhati, I had scrapped that proposal of my mind. Now this swamiji was suggesting too that I visit Kamakhya.

"Why Kamakhya in particular?" I asked.

In a beautiful voice, as if it was coming from the depth of his heart he replied, "That *yogini Brahmani* was enquiring about you".

Yes, I remembered her quite well. She had helped me a lot during my previous visits to Kamakhya, and helped mold my *shakti saadhana*. She was the one who had introduced and initiated me into certain *veera saadhanas* at Kamakhya on the banks of the Brahmaputra. If she was remembering me, there was definitely some important reason behind it, I thought. Keeping myself in silence for a few minutes, I replied—"Yes, sure, I shall visit Kamakhya shortly".

I felt deeply drowsy and my eyes, feeling heavy, closed under their own weight. A gentle breeze from the Narmada seemed to embrace me and I fell into a deep sleep.

Feeling a peculiar kind of waxy coolness on my body and the sensation of something crawling on me, I opened my eyes. It was almost dawn and I could see a long black snake on my body making its way towards my head. I screamed in fear, "Help, Help!" Achyuthananda was sitting near me, eyes closed as if in deep meditation. I was shivering in fear, and in a moment he lifted the snake and tossed it into Narmada. I sat there, gasping in deep breaths.

"Afraid?" Swamiji asked.

I nodded as I wasn't able to speak, my throat having gone dry. "Yes, very much", I murmured with difficulty.

The villagers had rightly cautioned me against staying there as the place was frequented by snakes. My mind was now a bit upset and ready to move from there.

Achyuthanand asked me to go with him to Khandwa or to Indore, and was even willing to get me a rail ticket to Kamakhya, but at that moment I was still not in the mood to leave Narmada. I replied, "I would like to be at the Jhadi (the forest) for some more time. I will plan my trip to Kamakhya later".

Doing nothing and being empty and alone, I wanted to be at Soolpanneswar Jhadi for some time. I too stood up and after bathing, started making my way towards the Jhadi which although not very far, was not very near either.

Spark 2

NEITHER HERE, NOR THERE

He had been in a pathetic mental state when he had last met me. I had initiated him a few years ago into *shakti saadhana* and I thought he was making good progress. In spite of a long life in study and *saadhana* and stay with famous *sadhus* and *sanyasis* of the time, he was still very much addicted to his wife and children. A Brahmin by birth, he had done several *purascharans* of the Gayatri, but was impoverished as far as domestic finances were concerned.

"I would like to be initiated into *sanyasa*, please do something Guruji", he said.

I was in one of the ashrams in the city, totally engrossed in my research work in those days. He sat in front of me as if awaiting my reply. I stayed in silence for some time.

He repeated "Will you please help me to be initiated into *sanyasa*?"

All of a sudden I replied, "No, not in the least, I will not."

Startled, he asked, "Why, why not? Tell me what is wrong with me."

I had been busy doing some drawings on a few *yantras* related to my research work. Putting aside the pencil and eraser, I looked at him and said, "You need an answer? Yes, here it is. You are very much attached to your family, or addicted rather."

He had never expected such a response.

"Of course you are a good *sadhaka*. Do it and keep going. But why do you want to commit to something that is not possible for you at this moment?" I said without any hesitation.

He left me without saying anything. I too left the city after the completion of my work which took a few months. For a long time I heard nothing about him. When I visited the city about a year later, he came to meet me. He was now in orange robes.

He said "You refused me *sanyasa*, yet I have obtained it. I was initiated by . . .". I congratulated him for his success in his mission of wearing saffron robes.

"Nowadays where you are staying?" I asked with curiosity.

The reply was very discouraging.

"I constructed a room in the courtyard of my old house."

"And bhiksha?" I enquired again.

"At the same house where I stayed before *sanyasa*. The children bring it to me."

Actually a sanyasi is not even supposed to go to the village where he was born or where he grew up. He is not to receive *bhiksha* from any relatives. But in this man's case, the *shastras* had now become mute. I tried to convince him that what he was doing was a sin, and asked him to go to North India where thousands of *sanyasis* stay in ashrams. But his attachment was so deep-rooted, that he was not in a position to even imagine leaving the premises of his old house or family.

It seems he was unhappy with my comment on his state of *sanyasa*. He left me in a bad mood. After a week or so I too left the city. By this time my wanderings had come to an end. My thesis was complete, I had a doctorate in Srividya, and was settled in an ashram made by my disciples in Jammu. On one Guru Poornima, the same *swamiji* came to my ashram for a long stay. I was happy that now at least he had left his caged life of attachments to do peaceful *saadhana* in my ashram.

One day he came to me and said, "Guruji, I would like to leave this place. My saadhana is getting disturbed by the crowd around you, as well by the sounds of the microphone."

My ashram being new, naturally there were daily *satsang* and *bhajan* sessions and a crowd was around me always. But none of the other ashram inmates had ever complained about it. He got ready to leave, and one of my disciples informed me that he was heading back to his home.

In North India such type of *sadhus* are known as '*fasali*' (*fasal* means crop or harvest), as they roam around ashrams and collect a lot of things and money, and then return to their homes during harvest season. For them every day is harvest time really, whether ashram or village. This *swamiji*'s case was also not much different, I thought.

Years passed. I was at another one of my ashrams in South India, where my disciples had started a few social service activities such as rehabilitation of poor children, or medical camps. I was busy writing my autobiography. During one of the functions, the old *swamiji* came to meet me. He had become very old and weak. The bloom on his face was gone.

"You look very weak", I wondered aloud.

Now he narrated the pathetic story of his wife and children's untimely deaths, and about his stay now with his youngest son and family. He was very unhappy with his present life.

"I could not adjust to any of the ashrams", he said speaking of his weakness.

That was true. He had lived free as a householder (in saffron robes) but not as a sanyasi. The life of a *sanyasi* is structured differently. That was the reason he had not been able to adjust to any *ashram*, even though the *Guruji* who had initiated him into *sanyasa* was from a well-established *ashram*. He requested me for some financial assistance, and with the help of a disciple I made sure that he received some amount.

Later, when I left all my established ashrams in North and South, freeing myself with the intention of returning to the Himalayas, I was staying with one of my disciples temporarily. This swamiji was back again. The son with whom he had been staying until recently, had died in an accident. The daughter-in-law and her two children were suffering a lot.

"There is nobody to look after them. So, I have to stay with them."

I nodded my head after hearing the story. Once again he requested, "Guruji, I am badly in need of some money for the education of my grandchildren."

From where on earth could I, a sanyasi, bring money to help him! Of course I had saved a small amount for my Himalayan journey. I told the disciple with whom I was staying to give that amount to him. The swamiji was happy. Before leaving he said, "Be always merciful to me like this."

That means he was expecting more financial help from me in the future.

That night I wept in grief thinking of that old swami again and again. What was in store for him next, and for how many more years would he have to suffer like this, for his wrong doing—he was getting the payback for his attachment and addiction, which a sanyasi should never ever keep.

Spark 3

MERGED IN NATURE

Those were happy days in Jhadi. I used to stay on the Narmada sands and go around the villages for my daily *bhiksha*. The villagers were primitive tribals, dependent upon the forest and the Narmada for their existence. Small *parnasalas* or thatched huts were used for shelter and the single room functioned as kitchen, bedroom, and living room with no partitions. The villagers seemed content with what they had, appeared pure in mind, and wore only a single piece of cloth on their bodies, their children moving around naked. Without any modern facility, they lived their life in nature with all its pluses and minuses, and without any grievances. There were no schools in the forest and so they were illiterate, but they were god-loving.

I stayed in that forest for one month, subsisting upon whatever they offered me. My saadhana during the nights went well, adding more value and depth. Collecting a few dried logs from here and there, I would light a campfire (*dhuni*) at dusk daily and sit by it till midnight, or until sleep overcame me.

As I possessed nothing valuable other than my kappar and kamandal, I had no concern about thieves. There was though, the danger of wild animals visiting the river at night to quench their thirst. The fire was helpful in this regard, as it kept away the wild animals since they fear fire.

But one night it did happen. I had been wandering in the forest the whole day and was tired, and fell into a deep sleep shortly after making the campfire, lost to the surroundings. It may have been after midnight that I heard a roaring in the silence of the night. I woke up, but it was dark since the campfire had gone off and nothing was visible around. In the dim light of the stars in the sky, I could see that some animal was reaching for me. For a second I thought it was a leopard or a jackal. With a ferocious roar, it jumped upon me. My mind and body were almost paralyzed, but I shouted 'Narmade Har' and tried to jump into the Narmada. But the wild animal had caught hold of my left leg. In spite of that, I managed to loosen the grip and jump into neck-deep water. My body was shivering with fear and from the coldness of the water. The animal reached into the water, looked here and there, maybe for me, drank some water and left. I continued to stay in the river shivering in the cold waters, in fear of encountering the animal again on the shore.

It was almost dawn when I dragged my legs to the shore. My left leg was hurting, from a large wound that was the *prasad* of that animal. I was surprised to notice that there was no bleeding from the wound, perhaps due to being in the water for a long time. But the pain was unbearable.

I walked to the nearby village and a bunch of villagers gathered around me. I narrated to them the happenings of the previous night. One old man came near and looked at the wound keenly and left. He returned in a little while with some leaves in his hands, with which he made a paste and applied to the wound. In just a few minutes I started to feel relief. A village woman too brought me some hot black tea made from forest herbs and salt. The experience had upset me and I now wanted to leave the forest. The villagers told me that such incidents were not uncommon and they took it quite lightly. I, however was not convinced with their logic.

So the next day I pulled out from the Jhadi and walked towards Omkareswar with an intention to go to Kamakhya.

Spark 4

EXPERIENCING ADHANAREESWARA

Kamakhya was crowded as it was a holiday. I walked from its railway station to the temple situated on the top of the hills. Due to the crowds, I avoided visiting the temple and climbed down the other side of the hill to reach the bank of the Brahmaputra. It is one of the few rivers which has a male name (the names translates to Son of Brahma). In the monsoon season it rushes down, flowing wildly in full flood but that day it was silent. I wandered here and there in search of that Aghora yogini but she was not to be seen. I knew her from a time long ago when I had stayed in Tinsukia. I used to reach there on weekends and stay during nights for saadhana. I had never tried to learn any other details about her, and regarded her as a maternal figure, a guide and companion in my spiritual life. I sat there for a long time hoping to meet her. I was hungry and sleepy from the long journey and slipped into deep sleep.

"Oh! You are back!"

I woke up to the sound of these words. It was almost evening and I saw the yogini mata sitting near me.

"Son, you have come back to me. In fact, I wanted to meet you before leaving this body."

"Maa, Swami Achutananda told me that you were remembering me so I have rushed to you," I murmured.

Age had taken a toll on her body, and it had become weak.

Her eyes were no more shining, and she was shivering. She had brought me some roti and dal from her *kutia*.

"Son, eat this. There is a lot that I want to talk to you."

I sat in *mauna*, eating slowly, and she continued, "I want to teach you a different but important saadhana, you stay here with me and practice it and find the result here itself."

By the time I finished eating, she had already started explaining in detail about '*aghor yogini saadhana*' which she wanted me to do. She concluded saying, "This saadhana has to be accomplished within twenty-seven days of starting it, and after that you may leave. I shall initiate you with the mantra on the next *asthami* day." I agreed to this. She added, "You need not worry about your bhiksha. I will take care of it, you just concentrate upon the saadhana."

On *ashtami* day she initiated me as promised, but it was not as easy as I thought. I use to do japa from sunset to sunrise and sleep during the daytime. The yogini mata would sit by me till midnight every day, observing my saadhana.

I was slowly making progress, but after about twenty days beginning to feel a little tired and weak. One day during my japa I saw a reddish light appear in front of me and in no time it took the form of a woman. But when I looked into that manifested form it was neither woman nor man. It was the form of inseparable Shiva and Shakti (*ardhanareeswara*). I got up immediately and did pranaam to the form in front of me.

I heard a voice say, "What are doing this japa for?"

I replied, "For you. To have the experience of oneness with you."

All of a sudden I felt my form take the form of a flame, like that of a pyre. The 'I' was gone—my body, mind, intellect, consciousness were all lost. I had become like a flame in a *deepam*, a small one and moving towards the bigger one. I was not there but wondering who then was experiencing this thing. It was just the 'I' now, the trine transformed into single. I experienced the 'I' in a moment, when everything had disappeared.

I heard the voice of the yogini mata say, "Oh! You have got it. You got the experience of 'being'. Keep it up."

On the day of the completion of the twenty-seven day saadhana, she invited a few saadhaks to have prasadam. The yogini mata had herself prepared rice, dal, curry, and sweet rice for all. She looked happy that I had completed my saadhana successfully.

I told her, "Maa, I am tired. I would like to be with you for a week or so for rest."

She agreed and took me to the Kamakhya temple for darshan. I could easily see that her health was rapidly deteriorating. Most of the time she was confined to her bed, yet the japa on her lips was going effortlessly. I cooked for both of us every day and fed and served her. It seemed like she was happy in my company.

It was an *amavasya* day when I realized that her departing time was near. Her body was shivering with weakness. I called a few sadhaks staying nearby. She called me near and putting her hands on my head, took a few deep breaths and tried to speak to me but the sound was feeble. I could hear only the sound of '*hreem*'. She caught my hands for a few moments, and I felt as if some current was passing through. It was indeed, for my body had become hot in a moment. Was it a *shaktipat*—was she transferring her deposit of energy into me? I heard again the '*hreem*' sound from her mouth. I saw her hands dropping from my hands and everything was over within minutes. There was a deep silence all around. I wept for a long time, and the other sadhaks started consoling me. Together we carried her body to the Brahmaputra, and gave her a *jala samadhi*.

I returned and sat in silence as if I had lost everything and was left in a void. After leaving my Guruji Avadhoota Taramayee at Mookambika, this *aghora yogini* had taken care of my saadhana. She was as good as my Guruji, or rather was my Guruji herself in this form. One of the sadhaks asked me to stay back in the *kutia*, but I was unwilling, feeling an emptiness there without the mata.

I decided to leave Kamakhya. And the next day I took the train to go to Haridwar.

Spark 5

AT KANKHAL SMASHAAN

I am back in Haridwar after a long time. As I had no plan in mind about what I was going to do there, I wandered here and there and reached Kankhal. I tried to find accommodation at some ashram but did not succeed because I did not know anybody there. I decided therefore to stay at the Ganga ghats and found a place under a tree near the Kankhal *smashaan*. In Haridwar, food is never a problem for a sadhu, but accommodation is. I was happy though, with my stay under the tree.

For some time I sat near the Ganga, staring at her and then had a bath. I collected my bhiksha from Anandamayee Ashram and slept under the tree for a while.

"Are you not Nadananda?" The sadhu sitting near me spoke. I looked at him blankly.

"Do you not remember me? I was with you when you were in Devprayag," he said.

Now my memory did a rewind. Yes, I could recall that he was the sadhu I had initiated at Vyas Ghat and who had served me during my stay in Devprayag.

"Sorry, since we are meeting after a long time, I failed to recollect," I replied.

He was now staying at a *kutia* near the smashaan ghat (cremation ground) at Kankhal. I felt neither happy nor unhappy at meeting him. I kept myself neutral remembering his behavior which I had never liked. He requested me to go with him and stay in his kutia.

"No, I am fine here and you need not worry about me," I said. He left me in a bad mood.

All day and night I sat under the tree doing nothing, leaving the tree only to collect the bhiksha. But slowly sadhus and devotees started reaching me. It was happening only because of that swami spreading the rumor that a *siddha* from Narmada was staying near the *smashaan* ghat. Now because of the visitors my solitude was getting disturbed and I wanted to leave, but something was stopping me from doing so.

One day a sadhu living in the *smashaan* came in contact with me. Since long, he had been at the *smashaan* doing *tantra saadhana*. He was from Assam, a calm, quiet, and advanced sadhak known as Taranand Brahmachari. I talked with him about my saadhana in Kashi, and he wanted me to instruct him further in saadhana. I initiated him into *shodasi mahavidya*.

Taranand had a good idea to restore my solitude.

"Just come and stay in the smashaan, no one will come and disturb you, so please come along with me," he said.

So I shifted to stay under another big tree at the smashaan. Though in those days I never knocked on the door of any ashram that imposed its rules as conditions for stay, I still had to depend upon the ashrams for food.

I observed that Taranand never slept during the nights and was fully involved in saadhana. One day he said, "Let us go to Tara peeth."

I declined saying I was feeling quite blissful in that solitude. With no visitors to disturb me, I was enjoying the seclusion. One day Taranand left for his *gurusthan* as well. Now other than the occasionally arriving corpses, I was all alone in that cremation ground.

Instead of simply wasting time, I wanted to continue my saadhana, though not a *purascharan*. I opted to meditate for some more time. This was the place where I perfected my meditation and of course remained in ecstasy or in trance for long periods. In fact I felt reluctant even to collect bhiksha because of the bliss state from the trance.

One day a sadhu, a longtime acquaintance, came to meet me. He was born in Kerala, but staying in Saadhana Sadan to pursue his Vedanta studies. He was known as Anand Saraswati and was full of ego of his studies. He would quote Adi Sankaracharya for everything we talked about, and fed me Vedanta, but I used to keep quiet as I wore no label of being a Vedantin. He sarcastically dismissed my stay at the smashaan grounds. With his sadistic nature he contaminated my equipoise. I lost my temper and shouted at him,

"Mind your business, your way and mine are poles apart. I belong to the *Siddha Parampara*. I am not a person like you, who eats from great acharyas saying's and vomits out the words he was never able to digest. You people are merely 'masters of mental masturbation'. So get lost."

This incident had unfortunately kindled some negativity in me. I was disturbed and made plans to move to Rishikesh in search of a more secluded place.

I was happy to see Taranand return at night. I told him about my plans, and that I had been disturbed by the so-called Vedantin.

He reassured me, "I will take care of it now. Nobody shall come and disturb you anymore. Continue here." So I stayed back. Now Tarananda had taken the responsibility to collect my bhiksha too. My saadhana was going result-oriented.

It was the rainy season, and the Ganga was in full spate of flood. One morning I heard a shouting and screaming at the ghat. I rushed there to discover Taranand caught right in the middle of the fierce flow. The situation was beyond anybody's reach, and Taranand drowned. All were standing there helplessly, witnessing the tragedy.

The next day we discovered his body in the nearby bushes and resubmitted it to the Ganga as *jala samadhi*.

I stepped on to the road to Rishikesh, walking alone in an aimless and mechanical sort of way, my mind in a state of distress.

needed a cup of tea and he happily offered to get me one. While sipping tea at the roadside make-shift tea stall, he talked about his stay at 84 Kutias.

This 84 Kutias Ashram was built by the well-known Maharshi Mahesh Yogi for his disciples' saadhana. For the last few years however, the ashram was functioning below normal and facing closure. There were many *kutias* (huts) that had been constructed to accommodate one sadhak in one hut. Each had an attached bath, was well-ventilated and situated ideally in the middle of the forest. The huts were in the shape of *shivalingas*. Food for the inmates was provided by the Ashram itself. This brahmachari had been staying there for saadhana since long. He insisted me to go along with him so he could arrange my accommodation there too.

We met the person in charge of the Ashram known as Satyananda Swami. He spoke to me at length on Maharshi's life and how the ashram activities were going on. Swami said,

"I am pleased to offer you a spot here. We follow TM (Transcendental Meditation) and happy to initiate you tomorrow."

This is the system everywhere in India. They initiate or introduce their guru's teachings or system of saadhana to the inmates. I had heard about TM earlier. Swami gave me a book on TM and took me to a nice-looking hut and opened it up.

"Now, this is your place for saadhana. Please keep the room and surroundings clean and concentrate on your TM. I will initiate you tomorrow."

He seemed in a hurry to impart to me the TM techniques and left with smile on his face.

It was almost evening. I was tired and a bit hungry too. The *brahmachari* brought a broom and helped me clean the hut. I placed my belongings on the wooden cot.

"After 7 pm, there will be a bell from the kitchen for dinner. I will come and escort you there."

Then pointing to a building nearby, he continued,

"That is the kitchen and dining hall." He left me.

I sat on the cot looking at Ganga.

"Oh Ganga Mayya, all this is due to your *kripa*," I murmured.

Spark 6

84 KUTIAS

After a long walk, exhausted and with aching legs, I reached Rishikesh. I was not at all in the mood to go to Shivananda Ashram where I had stayed during my earlier visits to Rishikesh. I crossed the Ganga by boat. At the other bank too, I made no effort to search for accommodation in any ashram. I simply sat on the ghat for some time.

'Let Ganga Mayya decide my fate at Rishikesh'—I thought.

After bathing I went to Swargashram and collected my bhiksha. I sat there on the ghats the whole day without any purpose, and without any particular thoughts.

I felt like having some tea, but I had no money in hand, possessing nothing except for my khappar and kamandal and a pair of clothes. I was climbing up the steps of the ghat leading to a small congested road, when I heard a voice call out -

"Nadanandji, just wait!" I looked around to see who it was, and oh, it was a *brahmachari* from Karnataka who I had known from long before.

"Where were you all these days? You have been missing since long."

I said nothing. He continued, "When did you reach here? Where is your *asan*?"

I briefed him about my stay at the Kankhal *smashaan*. He seemed happy to meet me after a long time. I told him that I

There were no buildings near the kutia where I was put up. At a few yards' distance, there was another kutia.

The dinner was fine. I had rice, dal and curry. There were only a few there, about five or six other inmates. I knew one among that group in the dining hall, a Swami Viswanathanand. We had known each other since long. He had been staying there for the last few years and was an advanced TM practitioner. After dinner, this swami introduced me to the others.

I returned to my *kutia*. I had no bedspread or blanket to sleep. Covering myself with one of my clothes I slept on the cot. I might have slept for a while when I heard a knocking on the door. It was that *brahmachari* with a pair of blankets in hand.

"I did not see any *asan* in your hand. This is for you. These blankets are unused. I received them in a *bhandara* last week. Now they are yours."

This is the way of sadhus in North India. Their *seva bhaav* [serving nature] to their brother sadhus is wonderful. I experienced this love and affection from them (even from strangers) several times during my stay in North India. The brahmachari spread the blanket on my cot and arranged my *asan* for sleep. I wonder sometimes at the love poured on me by some sadhus. It has been an unanswered question. Why—why do they love me? Why do they do *seva* to me? Even though I have never loved them? I know I have nothing with me to repay their love and affection. It was due to their inherent natures that they were like this—it was perhaps my ignorance that was not allowing me to experience it.

I was initiated into TM in the evening. Satyanand Swami briefed me again like the previous day, but at length.

"Do not leave your *kutia* till you reach a goal in your saadhana." I nodded my head as if in agreement. In reality I had wanted to be somewhere safe and secure. Now by the grace of my Guruji, I was getting a place to stay where my food and other things were taken care of.

My days went well at 84 Kutias. Brahmachari and Viswanandanatha use to sit with me for some time daily during the evenings on the bank of Ganga. We would discuss upon spiritual matters, journeys to *teerthas* etc. One of the sadhaks staying there was planning to go to his *gurusthan* after vacating his room. He came to me with his stove, tea leaves etc., and passed them on to me.

"I am leaving for my Gurusthan. Keep these things with you and make use of them. You may give them to any sadhak if you feel like leaving from here."

I decided to keep them. So far I had possessed nothing but slowly *samsara* was now creeping in: first it was the blankets, now the stove etc., what was next? I was perplexed. One day the food stock ended. I went to purchase sugar etc., and was returning with a plastic bag in hand when all of a sudden, a group of monkeys attacked me. One of the monkeys pulled out my bag with sugar, and another one attacked me on the shoulder. A person walking behind me came to my rescue and drove away the monkeys. He took me back to the market, and got my wounds dressed. This incident opened my eyes making me rethink on why I had now begun living like a householder. Purchasing essentials, storing them and finding ways to use them. I felt this type of life was against the nature of a sanyasi. Those monkeys had reminded me about the essence and glory of *aparigraha*.

"You give this stove to somebody. I don't need it anymore. The way I was heading towards is against a sanyasis life", saying this I handed over the things immediately to the *brahmachari*.

Once again I felt the bliss of leaving unwanted possessions.

TM saadhana was in good progress with encouraging results. Satyananda Swami was off and on instructing me into the further steps of saadhana. But the problem was the real core Srividya saadhana was getting lost in the process. And a guilt consciousness had slowly started developing in me. It was not possible to do both saadhanas together for they were poles apart. Being thus in a dilemma for a few days, I finally discontinued TM and decided to leave 84 Kutias. Viswanathananda gave me five hundred rupees. Satyananda swami did not want to let me go, but by an impulse from within, I left 84 Kutis towards Omkareshwar to continue my saadhana.

Spark 7

LOST IN NATURE

Instead of going to Omkareshwar, I changed my mind at reaching Indore, and decided to go to Amarkantak.

Amarkantak is a small town near the Mekhala hills in Madhya Pradesh, in dense forest and surrounded by small hills from where Ma Narmada originates. This place is known as '*Mayee ki bagiya*' and is a pilgrim center as well as a picnic spot. There are a few ashrams, temples, and shops and not much population making it a beautiful place to stay, relax, and do saadhana. I tried in vain to find accommodation in an ashram by the road. While walking around in the manner of a stranger, I remembered being told that there was a small ashram named Tureeyashram belonging to Swami Ramanandji Maharaj of Omkareshwar. On enquiry, one of the shopkeepers gave me directions to that ashram situated in '*Mayee ki bagiya*'.

Swami Prakashanand was the *kothari* or person in charge of Tureeya ashram. We had met at Omkareshwar previously. He happily granted me permission to stay there. This small, but convenient, ashram was built by Swami Anand Puri, a well-known scholar in Vedanta, a few years back and was handed over to Ramanandji Maharaj recently.

Prakashanand was staying there all alone. He started cooking *khichri* for the both of us. It is a food preparation popular among sadhus that is easy to make, consisting of rice and dal mixed with salt and chilies, and occasionally potatoes as well.

"Are you in *parikrama*?" he asked.

"No. I came to stay for some time here, if you permit so," I replied.

My reply brought a smile to his face. He took me to the small room where I was to stay, and we talked for some time about my various journeys and also of his lonely stay there in that forest. He was of course, much older than me. In his *poorvashram*, Prakashanand had been a school teacher living with his family at Mortaka, near Omkareshwar. After his initiation into sanyasa, he had been staying here at his Guruji's orders for the past few years, to take care of this ashram.

"Very rarely does someone come to stay here. The *parikrama vasis* do of course visit, but only for a couple of days or so," he said. He seemed a bit unhappy at being there alone.

"It is a good thing. Nobody will disturb your saadhana," I said.

He replied with silence.

"How many days would you like to be here?" he said breaking the silence.

"Till you tell me to go away!" I said.

He laughingly replied, "Why should I ask you to leave? Be here always, and for as many days as you choose."

We talked for some more time. Now he was ready to go to bed and I was tired too. The nights in Amarkantak are chilly. I just pulled my blanket over my body and slept.

One day an old swamiji came to the ashram. He was a *naishtik brahmachari*. He had brought a letter from my friend, the Baba at Anandmayee Ashram in Indore. It was with a request to me to initiate the bearer of the letter in Srividya. This new swami was a jolly type of person, full of witty talk and jokes. He was also retired from service, and was doing Gayatri saadhana since long. After initiation, I observed the he was fully and sincerely engaged in saadhana, and was also doing seva to me every day. The number of inmates were now three. We cooked together, ate together and lived together happily.

By birth I have always loved nature. In my childhood and youth I was in a village full of greenery. Then after meeting my

Guruji, I stayed with 'Amma' in the forests of Mookambika on the banks of Sauparnika. Later during my saadhana in the Himalayas most of my time was on the scenic banks of Ganga, or later by the Narmada. So it was only natural that I enjoyed the Mekhala hills and the forest. Amarkantak, in the deep woods is full of greenery, with big trees and plenty of wildlife, very reminiscent of my stay with my Guruji in the Mookambika forest. Every evening, I used to walk around in the forests for some time. Not far from the ashram we stayed, there was an *adivasi* or tribal village that I visited once or twice. Even though the tribals were poor in terms of material possessions, they were happy in that unpolluted life in the lap of nature. One of the tribal families sold milk to our ashram, and a few of them prepared 'Gulbakkavali oil' which is used for treatment in ailments of eyes. In all of India, this 'Gulbakkavali' plant is available only in this forest. They sold it in that small market to earn a few rupees to meet the day-to-day needs of their families.

That new *naishtik brahmachari* was showing good progress in his Srividya saadhana. He stayed with us for a few more days and then left for Indore.

"I will be back in a few days," he told me before his departure.

Prakashanand and I were again the only two living in the ashram. Almost two or three happy months went by this way.

"Guruji ... Guruji ..." I heard the sound of somebody calling me. It was late at night and the weather was chilly. I opened the door and lifted up the lantern to see who it was at this late hour. Oh! It was Mohi, one of my disciples from Maharashtra. Somehow he had learned that I was staying there, and came to meet me with his parents. Swamiji made some tea and served it with biscuits, and made arrangements for their stay.

"Please come with me. I came to take you to my village. Let us do saadhana there," said Mohi.

A few years ago he too had been initiated by me into shakti saadhana. When morning came, I took them around Amarkantak to a few temples, to 'Mayee ki bagiya' or the origin of Maa Narmada, and to a few ashrams. He pressed me again and again to go with him. They had come there by car with plans to return to his village next day, along with me. After lunch we were ready to move.

"When will you be back?" asked Prakashanand.

He had had my company for the last few months and had been most happy. He never liked solitude, so felt depressed at my leaving.

"Let us hope very soon," I replied.

With a smile he added, "Let it be in a week or so."

Now it was Mohi's turn to reply, "Not in the very near future. I am taking Guruji along to live with me so I will be benefitted in my saadhana."

The smile on Prakashanand's face vanished.

"Okay, Narmada mayee ki icha. Narmade Har!" he said.

I said my namaskars to Maa Narmada and the car started heading for the main road in the direction of Chowl village near Alibagh, Maharashtra.

Spark 8

IN THE NAME OF GENERATION GAP

I met him last during the book release function a few months ago. The second part of my autobiography, 'Roaring Silence' was released on that day. He looked very weak, and was walking with the help of a stick. Old age and malnutrition were his main problems. Adding insult to injury he had suffered a heart attack too a few years back.

I had known him for a long time. Even as early as youth, he had fought against social injustice, and worked for the welfare of the downtrodden. Though born and brought up in a well-known *Vaishnav* and *zamindar* family, he was known for his work in the society. I used to visit him whenever I happened to visit that area where he was settled. A few years ago he had returned to his home in the village where he was living with his son, daughter-in-law and grandchildren. We were very close friends and shared similar views on social issues. In fact he was one among the elders who had helped me realize that service to those who are suffering, is the real form of *pooja*. I adopted this as the motto of my life, instead of sitting for hours in meditation or *japa*, but a few of my disciples, friends, and well-wishers looked at me with doubt. Some of them even left me, calling me a communist. I never bothered about caste or creed, and accepted bhiksha from anybody who served me with love and affection. This old man's impulses were very worthwhile and had made a positive impact in my life.

I had seen his sufferings too. I was there with him at the time of his wife's funeral. He was very much upset, and that was only natural. He withdrew from all his activities, confined himself to his room, and stayed alone, reading a few spiritual books or doing *japa, dhyaan* etc.

Once I was sitting with him and we were discussing details of some of my work for the society. His daughter-in-law was rough in behavior. Even though his son and daughter-in-law were 'well-educated' (the so-called modern convent education that teaches how to discard moral values), and well-placed in society, her behavior with this old man was not at all positive. That pseudo-modern lady, with her latest modern outfits and fashion, who lead a life of hypocrisy (which modern society applauds), never bothered to take care of the needs of this old man. There in his house, I witnessed a pathetic scene. The old man was standing in front of the kitchen with his plate and glass for collecting his lunch and the maid servant served rice, curry and *sambar* onto his plate. He took the food to his room and started eating it with tears in his eyes. Never had his son or daughter-in-law sat down with him to eat a meal together. They were serving him food with aversion, but she served 'pedigree' food to their pet dog with full 'devotion' as if she were offering *naivedyam* to God. In this modern time of so called external development, and the pseudo-culture or imposed westernization of convent education, dogs have more status than parents or in-laws. Several times did I witness the abusive treatment by his son and daughter in-law towards this old man. They forgot that he had lived like a king once and that he had given up his properties in the service of his suffering fellow humans.

He was taking his lunch with tears in his eyes. I was in silence. His grandson aged three or four years of age came in the room with a packet of banana chips. While eating the chips, the boy offered one of it to his grandfather. The old man also offered a little rice mixed with curry into the tiny mouth of the child. Watching this, the daughter-in-law appeared in the room shouting,

"What the hell are you doing? With that dirty unhygienic hand, you are feeding my son!"

She kept on shouting for some time, which was unbearable. It looked like she might slap the poor old man. He looked at me in tears, at the humiliation in front of a friend. I too began shouting at that lady, rather abusing her with rough words. Hearing this, his son arrived at the scene too. I spoke to him,

"Of what use is your nasty education? Be ashamed. What you are giving now to your father, you will get back in the same coin!" He looked at me with anger.

"This is our private family matter. Perhaps you are a friend of this old man. Don't interfere in our family matters. Get out!" He said.

At his yelling, I grew so angry that I felt I must kill this idiot who was treating his father in such a despicable way. But, controlling my anger and without saying a word, I just left the room without answering him.

My friend, the old man used to visit me now and then. Or I used to invite him to the programs organized by our ashram. He would stay for a few days whenever he came to me. But never did I visit that house again, where he was being treated so cruelly.

"You be with me. I will take care of your needs. Like your son, never will you be insulted by me or my disciples," I told him once.

"Maybe he is a rough guy, but still my son. Even if he does not love me, I love him," he replied. I kept quiet.

"This may be because I had never bothered to serve my parents in my youth. I was so involved in social activities and politics that I had no time to look after them. As my house was well-settled and there were servants, I thought they would take care of them. Yes, it is only due to my mistake that I am suffering now," the old man concluded.

I told myself –'*karmana ghano gati*' (the ways of karmas are very deep). What you give, only that you get!

I met him last on the occasion of the release of my autobiography. Even though he was walking with difficulty, he looked fine in appearance.

The life of this old man made me think about myself. Once during a moment of leisure, I shared this incident with my spiritual brother Swami Abhayanand. His perspective on this incident was different.

"Never mix *dharma* and *karma*. Both have their own ways. You have studied the Upanishadic saying—'*Dharmo rakshati rakshita*' meaning, 'if you can protect *dharma*, it will protect you.' Never involve yourself too much in such things."

Yes, I was looking at the incident through educational values. I thought that I need not contemplate anymore on such happenings. Let 'time' or *niyathi* take its own decision.

Thank you Universe for my life.

Thank you for my mother, father, teacher & good

Thank you for my health, wealth, relations

& happiness

Thank you for all my experiences both good & bad

which made me mature & loving

Thank you for filling my heart with love

compassion & kindness towards all being

of earth.

Thank you for removing anger, jealousy, revenge

& selfishness from my heart forever

Thank you for the cool water, sunlight, food & for

everything that has made my life easy & good

Thank you for the world. Thank you, thank you.

Om Om Om Om

In the early morning I meditate upon my essential Self clearly experienceable in my heart cave.

- That which is existence in knowledge & bliss in nature that is the Supreme gold the Paramahamsa's state.

- That which is the 4th plane of consciousness: Turiya which constantly illumines all experiences in the dream, waking & deep sleep states.

- I am that indivisible Brahman not this configuration of elements that is my body

6) My shaktri will always be with me to guide, correct & protect me as she is the Universal Supreme Power, same as me.

7) If we are not giving such value to ourselves and Divine mother, the beliefs and practices we do, don't seem anything and the practice will not provide much / any results.

8) The readings are not to stick on one's lower nature. If it is to give clarity of value to the shaktri, that we adore, trust & elevate

1) I belong to Divine Shakthi. I cannot fail.
2) Divine Shakthi chooses me towards Success.
3) I have to be Truthful to my Soul and the Divine Mother in me and the victory is for sure as She is the Embodiment of All Victory. I need not serve some small ideals of the ego.
4) If I fail I will rise again by the Will of my Mother.
5) I have to satisfy my Soul's needs. I will have Titiksha (endurance) to go through any affliction or discomfort to the very end of Divine Journey.

Spark 9

SPIRITUALITY OF SWARNA BHASMA

I had known him from the time of joining the group of wandering sanyasis. In Northern India, groups of sadhus and sanyasis travel by foot and stay a few days in selected villages at the invitation of devotees.

A senior sanyasi was the head of this group and his devotees made arrangements for the stay, food, and satsangs. He was a young man, known for his total detachment from external things like money or material possessions. I joined that group along with one of my friends, another swami. This young sanyasi was in charge of the daily *pooja* and *arathi* ceremonies in a makeshift temple of Shiva that the group carried along with them in a truck or tractor.

In a short time, the young sanyasi and I became very close friends. He had become famous among the sadhus in the group, as well as among devotees for his *virakti* or *aparigraham*, a type of non-attachment practiced by sanyasis. We ate together, and talked for hours on matters of saadhana. Like me, he too was fond of rice, curd and green chilies in bhiksha. We followed the strict discipline of the group and walked along with other sadhus all over North India, especially in different villages in Punjab.

After several months, I left this group to travel alone to selected pilgrim centers. Upon my return after a few years, I met a few of the sadhus at Haridwar who I had known from that group. They were returning to the group, and I too planned to return with them. By this time the senior swamiji who had been the head of the group passed away tragically due to snakebite. Now the young sanyasi, who was my friend had taken charge of the group. With more devotees and more facilities, the group was enjoying and passing time without any proper saadhana. They were stationed at Dehradun when I returned to them. Of course my old friend welcomed me, but I could easily discern the drastic change that had occurred in him. He had travelled the length and breadth of India with his group, even staying in metropolitan cities for long periods, from where he had generated a good amount of funds too. The notable change in him was that he had developed 'ego' and lost the simplicity of his old lifestyle. It seemed as if he had forgotten the friendship we shared and did not bother to sit down with me for some time to talk on saadhana, like in the old days. The dealings with the members of the group was also quite mechanical and hypocritical.

I felt terrible at seeing this type of change in him, but continued to stay with the group in hope that an opportunity would present itself when I would be able to talk to him, and bring him back to his original nature. But it was looking unlikely as he was spending most of his time with his own devotees, especially ladies. His behavior with them was not at all appropriate for a sanyasi. But he needed the sanyasi group with him as a 'mask' or cover for his earning money. This bunch of sycophants that he kept close, would 'butter' him and close their eyes to all his wrongdoings.

I was sure that my relationship with him was deteriorating. Those days his food was specially cooked for him, and he also started staying a little away from the group, if possible in a separate room. Though I tried to reach out to him twice or thrice, my words of *upadesha* were ignored.

He travelled a lot, and of course by foot, but a few vehicles followed with essentials. The group also walked along with him. I too was in the group. He started avoiding me but perhaps because of being old acquaintances, he never told me to leave. I myself now wanted to quit the group in my own interest, witnessing his attachment to *kamini* and *kanchan* (women and wealth). The original concept of sanyasi life was broken and he was living as a pseudo sanyasi, with external show only.

I left his group in a disturbed frame of mind, having failed to bring him back to his previous life.

He had transformed into a different person now, with thousands of devotees, and collected a lot of money. The present generation is going after such hypocrites who suck blood in the name of spirituality. Such so-called gurus not only give nothing to society but take a lot, in fact loot a lot, and not merely for their survival. They are earning a lot of wealth and making bank deposits in their relatives' names. He wanted to falsely represent himself as a 'non-attached' or *virakta,* but I had uncovered the truth. His food was being prepared separately in the name of *upavas* or special fasting food. Since he was getting old, he had started taking *swarna bhasma* (an anti-aging ayurvedic medicine) which was very expensive. The number of sadhus in the group was reducing, and he had also started behaving roughly with the devotees from whom he earned a lot.

He finally returned to his native village, and opened up a posh ashram with all modern facilities, forgetting the roads he had travelled so far. He was awarded a high position in the society of sanyasis, and even known as a 'great aacharya' but in reality he was one who didn't even know about *aacharana,* or proper conduct.

It is not due to any envy for his so-called external development as a millionaire, that I am writing this episode, but just to tell devotees in the path of spiritualism to be aware and beware of such foul elements in society, so spirituality can be kept pure, or rather be saved from pollution.

In the present generation, we can see such people actually being worshipped as '*bhagavaan*', but those of us in the path of spirituality who have the misfortune to witness such incidents consider ourselves as '*daurbhaagyavaan*'.

Spark 10

LIVING IN VOIDNESS

I was suffering from depression in those days. The symptoms had developed slowly to the point that sometimes I felt I should either run away from where I had been staying for a long time, or commit suicide. After consulting with a doctor, he cautioned some of my disciples not to leave me alone even for a moment. That doctor started me on a few high-dose medicines which made my body swell up. I used to keep to myself most of the time, shedding tears for unknown reasons. Sometimes I even got violent and was afraid if anybody entered my room.

A few months earlier, one of my disciples had suffered badly and with the same symptoms. I had done a few *poojas* for his recovery and that disciple was now back normal, but his symptoms were now appearing in me. A few months passed thus with deep suffering from hallucinatory dreams, violent thoughts, suicidal feelings etc. Once I felt that I was returning to normalcy, I thought of going to Kashi for a change. I informed my friend Ramakrishnanand, who was then in charge of Shankar Mutt at Kedarghat, about my present condition and my need for his assistance for accommodation and food at the Kedarghat Mutt.

The stay at Shankar Mutt was fine, and my friend took care of my needs. Every day he would take me for a walk on the Ganga banks and we would sit for hours together at Harishchandra ghat. I expected that there would be a speedy recovery due to the change in climate and scene. But it was not as I thought. The symptoms started aggravating. My days and nights were so bad with so much mental and physical suffering that I felt I was not in a position to bear anymore for even a minute. Some unknown fear developed in me and I wanted to run away from Kashi to somewhere else. I was not eating or sleeping properly and my health was deteriorating day by day. The body began swelling again. Sharmaji and Lata from Samalkha came down to Kashi after hearing of my bad condition. They stayed with me for a couple of days at the Mutt where I was staying. I was paranoid about allowing them to go for a bath in Ganga as I was afraid that they might drown. When they did go, I sat at the ghat in deep fear, such were my hallucinations. Sharmaji was worried about what to do next. He took me to Samalkha after two days' stay at Kashi.

Sharmaji arranged for my treatments at Samalkha. He consulted a homeopathic doctor and started medication. Slowly I began returning to normalcy. The homeopathic medicines had worked very well and in a few days I started eating and sleeping properly, yet the swelling of body had not reduced. A few more weeks of medication produced results. Now I thought I had almost recovered and wanted to leave for Kurnool.

I was back in Kurnool, after two or three months stay outside. All were happy that I was better now.

Spark 11

RETURN OF VOIDNESS

The happiness and relief at my recovery from the present illness of depression was not long standing. Following the advice of the doctors, I had discontinued the medications, but in a week or so the same symptoms returned. This time though the symptoms were not violent, I was still in the melancholic state. I wept a lot whenever I happened to be alone in my room. My disciples used to try to make sure that I was not left alone, and someone used to be with me always. The fear complex had developed in me once again and I wanted to leave Kurnool. I preferred Kashi as I felt I could be in the good company of my friend Ramakrishnanand at Kedarghat Mutt.

With all love and affection, he scolded me gently for leaving Kashi before I had fully recovered. It was summer, and without moving out, I continued staying with him at the Mutt. The depression symptoms continued to linger. I used to do '*namah shivaya*' japa most of the time, sitting alone in the room. We both would take evening walks everyday on the ghats of Ganga and sit at Harishchandra ghat for a long time, just like in my previous visits.

The problem of depression was only increasing day by day. Sleepless days made me more restless, and food consumption had become very low. My body started swelling once again and grew weaker. Once again I felt I must run away from the Mutt. One fine morning without telling anybody, not even my friend

Ramakrishnand, I left the Mutt. I left all my belongings like clothes, pooja books, *Sri Yantra*, *bhiksha patra* there, and taking just my purse and cell phone I left the Mutt and reached the bus stand. I heard the voice of the conductor of a bus call out, "Lucknow, Lucknow" and got in the bus mechanically. The journey was long and by sunset I reached Lucknow bus stand. With the help of the conductor I purchased a ticket to Haridwar on the night bus. I spent another sleepless night in the bus worrying at what was happening to me. In the middle of the journey from Lucknow, I called Ramakrishnanand at Kashi from my cell phone and told him that I was leaving for the unknown.

"I have never seen a fool like you! At least you should have told me before leaving," Ramakrishnand shouted. I was not in a mood to apologize to him. By early morning I had reached the Haridwar bus stand and made a phone call to my spiritual brother Abhayanand, saying that I wanted to meet him. He was in Rishikesh those days, and asked me join him there. All of a sudden the sound of another bus conductor was heard. He was calling "Sonepat ... Sonepat ...." I went near him and asked whether that bus' route was via Samalkha.

"Yes Maharaj, be seated. The bus is about to leave," the bus conductor told me.

Once again I called Abhayanand and told that I was heading towards Samalkha. He sensed that there was something wrong with me. Then I told him of my present condition. Another call was made to Sharmaji at Samalkha that I was coming to him and to meet me at the bus stand.

"My health is not all good. Be at the Samalkha bus stand. I do not know where I will go! I am very much upset mentally," I told Sharmaji over my cell phone.

By afternoon, I had reached Samalkha. Sharmaji was waiting at the bus stand. He took me to my room adjoining the courtyard of his residence. Everybody at Sharmaji's home was worried about my pathetic health condition.

In a couple of days Abhayanand came to Samalkha. At his suggestion I started on some Ayurvedic medicines. He asked me to go with him to Himachal which he thought might change my mood. We went to Himachal Pradesh to meet the ashrams of some sadhus we knew. For one or two weeks we were together in Himachal and Punjab. By this time, there were notable improvements in my health. Abhayanand brought me back to Samalkha. He stayed with me for a couple of days and then left for Rishikesh.

I stayed back in Samalkha for some more time. I was almost better and wanted to go to Kurnool. Sharmaji came with me up to Kurnool. By this time the insomnia problem had reduced and I had started eating and sleeping properly. But the medicines were to be continued for a long time for full recovery so as to not to have a relapse of the symptoms again.

Spark 12

TO AND FRO

I was returning to Ramnagar ashram after ten years. Sharmaji and family were with me. We reached a day before *Shivaratri*. It was our desire to visit the ashram as I came up to Samalkha. We engaged a car for three days and reached there. The reception was encouraging. A lot of devotees and disciples had assembled there to receive me. Omkaranand was already there. All were awaiting my arrival with garlands, flowers, *arathi* and sweets in their hands. After I had darshan in the temples of Maa, Shiv, Hanuman, Radha, Krishna etc., inside the ashram known as Srividya Gyana Peetham established by me with the financial help of my devotees from all over India a few years ago, I simply sat down with my devotees for some time in the open courtyard, talking about their wellbeing. Everybody complained that my absence had been painful for them. One of the devotees asked me,

"You took more than nine years to return to the ashram. It is unworthy of you to keep us waiting for such a long time. As a guru, how can you forget our love and affection towards you?"

I told them, "A lot of water has flowed down the Ravi in the last ten years. It never returns. A guru is also like that. You have to make use of the water in the Ravi when it is there. So with the Guru too. Make use of his presence for the progress of your saadhana."

I too was aware that my absence in Ramnagar ashram had indeed been for too long. In fact my mindset was different. I had never liked the inner politics of the devotees. The ego-driven politics had harmed the ashram and its atmosphere earlier too. That was the reason for my leaving the ashram twelve years earlier, and handing over the charges of the ashram to my sanyasi disciple Swami Omkarananda, declaring him as my successor to that ashram known as 'Srividya Gyana Peedham'. For the past twelve years he had been looking after the activities of the ashram with the help of the devotees in the village. On and off my spiritual brother Abhayananda would visit the ashram to conduct a few satsang sessions.

I was certain that there would not have been much change in the attitudes of the devotees, or in the governing body of the ashram either which I had set up before leaving Ramnagar. The so-called 'ego' of certain people was the main hurdle for the development of the ashram. I had always disliked this, since the activities of these negative elements were damaging the purity, serenity and calm atmosphere of the ashram.

Secondly, I had been busy completing my work on Srividya (my thesis on Srividya for doctorate) and writing my autobiography for the past eight years. A few phone calls would brief me with updates on the ashram's functioning. Though I was informed that a few more temples had been added, and the grounds cemented, I felt that all the progress was only at an external level. What about the progress in saadhana, which I initiated to the disciples there? It was almost at a big zero, I knew.

Finally due to the insistence of a few devotees, I had reached there now. My spiritual brother Abhayananda had also been putting pressure on me to visit that ashram at least once.

"It will boost the mood of the devotees who are totally dedicated to you, as well as to the ashram. Just visit there once, and I too will join you," he had told me. That was the only reason for my presence there that *Shivaratri*.

The *Shivaratri* program was well-organized with four poojas at night. During the satsang that night, I spoke to them:

"When the Ravi is in flood every year, the whole village goes to the banks to witness it. But if the flood was a scene visible all year long, nobody will care to go and view it. That is exactly what is going on here too. I have come after ten years, and you are all present here. But if I choose to stay back here for a long time, it will be as it was. So, better that I visit you all only after the gap of a long time."

In fact, this was really my response to the pressure for staying back at the ashram. To be frank, my love was not for the bricks and cement, even though I had collected them to construct the ashram. I was always affectionate with my devotees and taking care of their needs in the spiritual as well as materialistic worlds. During the Shivaratri function too, I could smell the mean politics among the devotees. Some of them felt the Guru was their own, and not for others. A feeling of possessiveness had developed in some, and they thought the Guru must obey their decisions. They were pressuring me to be with them, or were surrounding me most of the time, during my three days' stay there.

The next day, after Shivaratri, there was a *bhandara* (common feeding) arranged by the ashram devotees. I wanted to leave the ashram as early as possible, as the behavior of some of the devotees was suffocating me. In the morning there was Shiva Pooja and a *havan*, and then there was lunch.

"You seem to be very busy. Now that your lunch is over, you may leave if you so desire."

This remark by one of the senior disciples, who was in charge of looking after the ashram, stabbed somewhere in the core of my heart. Did he mean for me to 'get lost'? I am not sure, but I sensed he was implying that. Sharmaji gave him a befitting answer, using some choice proverbs.

We prepared to return immediately. A few of them were deeply unhappy during the moments of farewell. I called Abhayanandji and told him,

"It is due only to your pressuring that I have visited the Ramnagar ashram. Now I am returning with some bitterness in mind. It is clearly evident that they have still not been able to understand their Guruji well. I am seeing more than five in-groups functioning here, none of them happy in the presence of the other.

So once again I bid goodbye to this ashram. Please do not ever ask me to return here."

Yes, it was true—each group was unable to tolerate the presence of the other. These factions had not existed a few years ago when I was living there. Even though they were just starting to function at that time, it was not possible for them to come out as openly as they were doing now. But was that my doing? Or someone else's?

Spark 13

IN SEARCH OF MY ROOTS

This was my third stay in Gangotri. A swami I knew had arranged accommodation at his ashram, newly built for the service of pilgrims visiting Gangotri. Being tired from the long walk from Rishikesh to Gangotri by foot, I preferred to rest in my room for a couple of days. Every time I traveled by foot in those Himalayan hills, I reveled in the natural beauty of those serene, calm and quiet hills. Looking out through the tiny window of the room, I was again enjoying the beauty of those snow-clad hills.

In my childhood I had heard stories of Himalayan hills from the elders. The origin of the *Namboothiri* clan in Kerala is said to be a village named 'Kalap'. There is a legend among the *Namboothiris* that on their arrival from the Himalayan hills to '*Bhargava kshetra*' (known as Kerala later), Rishi Parashurama had to cut off the head of his own mother Renuka at the order of his father Jamadagni. As a result, Parashurama was afflicted with the sin or *paapa* of *brahma hatya*. Rishi Narada told him,

"To atone for the sin, locate an unused piece of land on earth and give it as *daanam* or donation to *brahmanas*."

Parashurama wandered here and there on earth to locate such a piece of land. But it was not possible, as the entire land area was being used by someone for one purpose or the other. Now Parashuram requested the God of the Ocean to retreat a little and give him some land for the purpose of donation. But the God of the Ocean declined. In rage, Parashurama dried up a part of the ocean with his *tapa shakti* and threw his *parasu* or axe in. The region from where the land emerged from ocean came to be known as *Bhargava kshetra*. Bhargava is another name for Parashurama. Now with the land is in his hands, he wandered here and there in search of *brahmanas*. They were everywhere, but the concept of a true '*brahmana*' is one who is a *brahmagyaani* (*brahmagyanethi brahmana*—one who has personal experience of the ultimate reality). Narada rishi appeared again with advice,

"Go to the Himalayas. There is a village there known as Kalap which is not too far from Gangotri. All the villagers there are true *brahmanas* or *brahmagyaanis*."

"But how can I confirm that they are indeed *brahmagyaanis*?" Parashuram asked.

Narada replied, "That is easy. Even a small boy of five or six years age can converse with you about '*brahma tatva*'. That can only happen in the village Kalap for which you are searching."

Parashurama had to do a lot of searching but was finally successful in his mission and located the village Kalap, and at his request the 108 *brahmana* families living there came down and accepted the land as *daanam*. Parashuram divided up the land among them before donating. After accepting *Bhargava kshetra* as their own, they asked him,

"You have brought us down from our state of '*brahmagyaana*'. Now tell us through which *upasana* or spiritual practice we can regain that state of *brahmagyaana*."

Parashurama constructed 108 Shakthi temples in that divided land and told them,

"Do *Shakthi upasana*. Try to realize *Parabrahma* through *Shakthi*."

Parashurama then returned to the Mahendra hills for doing *tapas*. The Kerala *Namboothiris* are basically '*Shaakthas*' with initiations into the *Shaakteya Maarga*. But most of those temples went into oblivion and some of the *Namboothiris* adopted different systems of *upasana*. Even today, a few of those temples can be seen in Kerala, and some branches of the *Namboothiri* clan continue to do *Shakthi upasana* as Parashurama prescribed. Srividya in Kerala belongs to that tradition.

I was musing on this legend, as I lay on the bed in the ashram room in Gangotri. Slowly an idea grew in my mind. Why am I not going in search of my roots in the village of Kalap, if at all it exists now?

The next day I made enquiries about Kalap with some old villagers settled in Gangotri, but in vain. I continued my search and one day, maybe after three or four days of enquiry, an old man who was a priest in Gangotri temple, said,

"Yes maharaj, there is indeed a village known as Kalap. I have heard my grandfather talk about it. I think it is somewhere up ahead from the village of Nilang. I do not know the exact location as I never visited that village."

I decided to go to Nilang village which was a bit further up from Gangotri. The road was fine and I walked a few days to reach there. The scenery en-route was lovely with the picturesque beauty of unpolluted nature. As I failed to locate any village nearby, it was very difficult to get some food on the way. It will be a wonder if you happen to see any teashops at this high altitude area. I had with me a few rotis and *sabji* but those I had finished the previous day itself. Now I had only had water from the small waterfalls in the hills which were plentiful. Even though I was tired from the continuous walking without food, and uncomfortable sleep on the path, my mind was made up. I had to reach the village I was in search of.

Finally it looked like I had reached a village. At a short distance I could see a small village on top of the hills. Such was my eagerness to trace the roots of my lineage that I felt like running to my destination.

But in the Himalayas, distances are deceptive, and one may think a village very near but only when one starts walking towards it, realizes how far it really is. Before sunset I finally reached the village.

"Is this Kalap village?" I asked a woman standing just in front of the first house in the village. She nodded and went inside the house ignoring my presence. I walked a few yards more to sit under a small tree, probably a *bhojapatra* tree, and looked around at another small house near. A young man came out of this house and approached me uneasily, probably a response to the rare presence of a stranger. This is always the case with the villagers in the Himalayan hills. They are suspicious of any stranger at first sight, but once they give their trust, it is forever.

"I have come from Kerala on a pilgrimage to Gangotri. I thought of visiting this Kalap village as my ancestors are from here," I told him.

He appeared surprised at my words. He invited me to his home which was the third or fourth one from the entrance of the village. In fact it was a small village of only some ten or fifteen houses. I sat in front of his house. Tea was served, and I felt as if I was drinking nectar. By this time a few men and women and some children had appeared and they sat in front of me.

"I am hungry, and have not eaten for the last two days. Will you please---?"

My sentence was interrupted as one of the ladies said,

"Maharaj, in just a moment I will bring you *roti*."

She went to her house to bring it. A few minutes later I was being served with two rotis made of *cholai* (corn) and curry made of potato. Of course the curry was full of chilies, but the villagers eat this type of spicy food to keep warm in the snowclad hills. The temperatures at those high altitudes run subzero. I was enjoying the food served, and observed while eating that the number of people around me had grown to around twenty or thirty now. I narrated the purpose of my coming to their village.

"We all are Brahmans," one of the old men said. Now they started feeling that I was one among them. I was not familiar with their language but recognized a few Garhwali words that I had picked up during my stay at Dehradun. I tried to use the words in my conversation in Hindi with them. They liked that, and it is quite natural that locals enjoy it when strangers attempt to speak their language, even with mistakes.

It was almost dark and the village *syana* (head of village) arranged for my stay at his house. Even though it was a small one, the house was neat and clean. That old man, his wife, daughter-in-law and two grandchildren were living there. The son was working somewhere in Dehradun.

"He comes here only once a year," the old man told me. He was unhappy that his only son had to leave the village to stay in the town.

"Town life pollutes the people moving down from the villages located in the high altitudes. The people here are very innocent and generous," the old man said with a different expression on his face. He told me there were no basic facilities like a medical dispensary or school and one had to walk up to Nilang for needs.

"So our children and grandchildren are illiterate and have received no education at all other than what we have taught them, which we in turn learned from our parents."

Even after so many years have passed since India's independence from the British, basic needs of citizens are yet to reach the remote villages of the Himalayas, or in the forests of the Narmada. This is one face of India. And the other face is of the so-called English education imposed by Christian missionaries which has polluted the culture of *Bharat*.

"Are these the last villages of Hindustan? Are we near the Tibet border?" I asked that old man.

"Yes, of course, we are near the border. But there are two or three more villages a little further up from here, closer to Tibet," he replied. Usually these people confine themselves to their own villages, straying only as far as the nearby forest. They connect with other villages only when they have to go there to attend a marriage or something.

"Oh! What are they, the names of those villages?" I queried again.

"Naga, Jadung, Angar . . . all are small villages like ours," the old man continued. But I was drowsy and stopped talking, and fell asleep.

I woke up a bit late next morning. The sun was up and shining. It had been extremely cold at night. Covering my body with the blanket offered by the old man at night, I sat under the sun in front of the house. The old man's wife offered me some black tea. By that time the villagers whom I met the previous evening assembled again. Some of them asked me to repeat the story of my ancestors of that village. I told them the story of Parashurama and how he brought the Brahmins of Kalap to Kerala. Now they started feeling a kinship with me, and I too had the feeling of a homecoming.

"Stay with us for few days," one of them said. But I wanted to return to Gangotri. The mission had been successful. I stayed back at the village for a couple of days, telling them stories of my journeys, and other matters. One of the villagers told me,

"I too was planning to go down to Dehradun. We both can go together."

I agreed as a companion on a long journey is always a good idea.

We started the return, moving on foot only. There was no bus service to that area.

"Only rarely do buses come up to Nilang," he said. He was carrying roti and *sabji* for our journey. So though I wasn't starving like the last time, the villager walked at a very fast pace. The inhabitants of that area are used to walking at speed up the hills. Sometimes he opted for a few shortcuts, climbing up and down those snowclad hills, which was not at all easy for me. During the nights we stayed either by the road side or in a village known to him. On the evening of the second day, we reached a village from where buses were available to Uttarkashi. I bid farewell to the villager who had been in my company the last two days and resumed my journey on foot. In a carefree mood I walked towards Gangotri and reached after a couple of days.

As I had vacated the room in the ashram, it had already been given to some other pilgrims. It was difficult to find another room as the ashrams were fully packed due to pilgrimage season.

I decided to return to Uttarkashi.

Spark 14

CHALLENGE TO TAPA SHAKTI

I had just returned from the balloon angioplasty surgery for my heart problems at Sai Baba's hospital in Puttaparthi. Then for one month I went to stay in Hyderabad at a disciple's residence, in order to recuperate. Even though I had not fully recovered, I decided again to travel to Samalkha to stay and rest at Sharmaji's place. I stayed there for more than two months before going to the Ramnagar ashram. Sharmaji and family took care of my needs as much as they could.

One of the swamijis of my acquaintance hailing from Kerala, hearing of my ailments, visited me during those days. He pretended to be a *siddha* even though he possessed nothing on account of saadhana. I was unable to lay down due to respiratory problems which I suffered from in addition to the cardiac issues, and had to rest on an easy chair for months together, with the support of a few pillows. Sharmaji and other disciples had a tough time taking care of me. One day this swamiji said,

"I can stop this electric fan that is running in this room in just one moment with a look."

A few of my disciples were sitting around me. This swamiji stared at the fan for a few moments and of course, it stopped moving. I merely laughed at this, and I too looked at the fan for a few moments, and resumed its running as before. My disciples were struck at all this. Then I told them a story, in front of that swamiji, with the intention of puncturing his ego.

"Once a *siddha* arrived at Sri Ramakrishna Paramahamsa and boasted about his *siddhis*. He was claiming that he could walk on the Ganga and reach the other shore. He demonstrated this as well. Ramakrishna simply took a country boat to do the same act of crossing. Then he asked the so-called *siddha swami*,

"How much time did it take you to master this?"

"Twelve years," the *siddha swami* replied.

"I crossed Ganga by paying just one *ana* to the boatman. To do what you could have achieved easily with one *ana*, you have wasted the siddhi that took twelve years to accumulate," said Sri Ramakrishna.

My disciples laughed at hearing this story. *Siddhis* are not for exhibiting or making money. They are to be used for the welfare of deserving suffering people and the Almighty will shower blessings in turn. But in the present time, a few of the so-called sadhus attain certain *siddhis*, and use them to earn a lot from ignorant devotees and live a posh life, which in turn will turn such *siddhas* into beggars in subsequent births.

The days passed in intense suffering. I was pessimistic about my chances of survival. But the service rendered by Sharmaji and family helped me come out of the deep waters.

On one day the disciples had planned a *keerthan Sandhya* (evening recital) and satsang at Sharmaji's residence. It was evening time and they had arranged a *vedi* or altar for satsang with pictures, *deepam*, and decorated with flowers. Many devotees had assembled to attend the satsang and keertan when all of a sudden dark clouds appeared in the sky and there were peals of thunder. Looking at this, everyone's moods too went dark. I was in my room and Sharmaji came to say,

"Let us cancel this program. It is going to rain heavily. See the sky."

I just looked out to see all the people sitting there to attend the satsang. The *keertan* had already started.

"Let it continue. Nothing will happen. No rain will disturb us till the program concludes," I told Sharmaji.

I knew that he believed and trusted in me. I sat alone for a while in the room and prayed to my Guruji to keep up my reputation (*izzat*). It worked. My Guruji has always done favors to me, supporting me in all my altruistic acts.

The satsang continued and concluded with my lecture at around ten that night. Nothing happened. But as soon as the *prasad* distribution was over it began to rain heavily. It was difficult for my devotees to return to their homes. The rain showers continued all night long.

The so-called *siddha swami* was also present there.

"How did you manage to stop the rain?" he asked.

"I have done nothing. I have no *siddhis* like you. But my Guruji can do wonders. I just prayed to her to save my *izzat* and she did it. It was all *guru kripa*."

My reply was very casual.

"No, no! I will never believe this explanation. You have some siddhis to control Nature. You might have mastered the control of the *panchabhootas*.

I kept silent. But he was eying me with envy. He wanted to dig out details of what exactly had happened. I never bothered to offer any further explanation to him.

A few days after this incident, I left for the Ramnagar ashram.

Spark 15

IN SEARCH OF MY OWN FACE

I was returning to that village after a long gap. A few years ago, I had stayed there for some time. Most of the villagers would attend my lectures on spiritual values, and shared their pleasures and pains with me. Now I was back again.

I stood at the gate facing the village road which lead to the main road which would take you to the city. It was winter and the mornings were chilly. For hours together I stood at the gate. Not a single familiar face was seen. Time passes at its own pace. Children become youth and youth grow old. I was wondering where they had gone. Not a single known face was passing in front of me through that road.

An old man passed on his bicycle. Yes, I know him, I thought. The face was familiar. At the gate he stopped for a while, glanced at my face and moved off as if I were a stranger. I too wondered for a second if I should call him or not. But by that time he had moved off on the bicycle.

It was a day in January, the peak of winter. I felt that simply standing there and staring at the moving people had no meaning. Why should I stand here? The answer was there.

"You are in search of a familiar face," I told myself.

"For what," I asked me.

There was no answer. I just stood there for a long time. Slowly the fog withdrew and the sun that came out looked at me as if he was also a stranger.

"Yes, we are strangers to our self. What do we know about ourselves really? About the family lineage? About the anatomy of the body? About the earnings? About the so-called friends?" A lot of questions erupted in the mind.

I just spotted him, an old man hobbling on the road with the help of a broken walking stick. I knew him very well. Once we had lunch together at his residence. He had been very close to me previously. He had visited me and we had had lots of talks on spiritual matters. Now time had changed his appearance. He looked old, lethargic, tired, and helpless. I wanted to talk to him.

"Hi, just wait!" I called out to him.

He looked around for the source of the sound. He stopped and stared at me.

"Are you not remembering me?" I asked. He looked at my face once again and shook his head.

"But I remember you. Time has changed you and me! That is why you are not recognizing me," I said trying to explain.

Once again he showed no recognition. But he tried to submit a smile. It was a dry kind of smile, lifeless, empty, and tired, as if he were trying to smile for a smile. I too smiled as if I was his best friend.

He moved away slowly with shivering legs and pale face.

"Where I have lost this face?" I asked myself. The answer was a deep silence. I could see he had walked a few yards beyond me.

A cart came at speed. It was pulled by a single, dark, dirty looking buffalo. The cart man was also in a black *dhoti* and shawl. The buffalo cart stopped just near the old man. The cart man helped him into the cart.

Looking back at me the old man asked,

"Are you coming with me?"

"Where to?" I asked.

"For the long journey. The inevitable one. Join me, let us go together," the old man said.

Before I could take a decision to go with him or not, the cart moved away. I could easily hear the voice of the cart man say,

"His time is yet to come. Let him wait."

I was wondering what was happening. The cart disappeared at the curve of the road. I was still standing at the gate suddenly sweating and shivering with a fear of the unknown.

A schoolboy, perhaps studying in class one or two, on his way to school, appeared in front of me, looked at me, and tried to walk away at speed.

"Hi, just wait! You know that old man just disappeared on that cart?" I asked the boy.

"Are you dreaming? Nobody was here, no cart, no old man," the boy answered. He also walked passed.

Now I was all alone again, standing at the gate looking to the void of the road. Nobody was there now, it was like an ash ribbon. But my mind was in a different mood. I felt as if something was lost in oblivion. I had to search out what I had lost.

"Is it my face?" I asked myself.

"May be. The identity of self," I replied to me.

Since dawn I had been standing at the gate all for nothing. Looking to the road, it had been just a waste of time, waiting for something unknown.

"That is life! To wait for the unknown, even knowing it will not get here. Absurd thoughts, yes?"

Somebody was talking with me from within.

"Yes, of course! But I want to stop this waiting. Either IT should be mine, or I should be IT'S. How much time will it take?"

Here I recall a story. Narada was doing *tapas* to be in oneness with Lord Hari. Years and years passed, yet nothing happened. One day Narada saw Garuda, the vehicle of the Lord. Narada requested him,

"Please ask the Lord when I will get salvation."

Garuda on return from the abode of the Lord met Narada again. Narada was doing tapas under a tamarind tree.

"Have you asked the Lord about my salvation? What did he say in reply?" Narada asked.

"Yes, the Lord replied that you will get salvation after some years," Garuda replied.

"But how many years?" Narada asked again.

"Look to the tamarind tree. As many as the number of leaves on this tree. You have to wait that many number of years!" Garuda said.

Narada started dancing happily chanting the *Harinaama*. (name of Hari)

"Why you are dancing? You have to wait for so many years," Garuda asked.

"I am sure finally one day I will get salvation. I am ready to wait for it. It is confirmed that I will be liberated!"

Narada continued chanting the Lord's *naama japa* and dancing.

I laughed at myself. I too was not at all sure about when I would get IT. But I am sure I WILL.

I stopped searching for that lost face of mine and returned to my room, leaving the gate, in a very cheerful mood.

Spark 16

THEIR ACTIONS, BUT WE SUFFER

Such a thing happens when the parents act without proper thinking. It happened in my life too. Ours was a joint family. Namboothiris in Kerala used to follow *marumakkathayam*[24]. In those days the family used to be ruled by the maternal uncles. The father did not have much voice in any day-to-day administration of the family.

My uncle was a politician and was running a tutorial college in the nearby town. His daughter was my childhood friend. We played together, and lived together. Sometimes during informal sittings of the family members, the parents and especially the women told us,

"This girl is yours. You will marry her."

That was the old system among Namboothiris. Marrying the daughter of an uncle was prevalent among them. But what did we children know about their talks and commitments on marriage? But something did 'click' in our minds. It was a seed of thought planted by the parents in the bare fields of our minds about our family life.

When I think back now, that seed must have started slowly

---

24 Marumakkathayam—matriarchal form of society—form of social organization in which the mother or oldest female is the head of the family and descent are reckoned through female line.

sprouting then. I am not sure whether I will call it love or not, but we were good friends. We shared every moment whenever we met. During my college days one evening, sitting on the verandah of my ancestral home, I told her,

"I have decided to leave all behind to be initiated into *sanyas.*"

"What! *Sanyas*!!" she exclaimed.

"Yes, I mean that. It's my destiny. I must go. I don't want to live in this *samsara* of hate and envy."

"You mean you are really going to be a *sanyasi*?" she asked, full of doubt.

I was quiet for a few minutes. It seemed like my words had shaken her mind, created a sort of tempest. It appeared she was not ready for this. Though our parents had been preparing us to think that we were 'made for each other', such feelings had never taken root in my mind at least, from the beginning. But I was unsure about her mindset. She may have thought she had a future with me.

I left home to become a sanyasi, travelling all over India as a *parivrajaka* in search of the Self. Time passed thus.

Once I was on my way to Anantapur to attend a disciple's marriage ceremony, when I received a call on my cell phone.

"My commitments are now all over with—the education of my sisters and their marriages. I have built a house for myself too. Now you can come back to me."

It was she, my uncle's daughter, the one with whom I had played in my childhood, and with whom I had lived. She had been waiting all these years for me to return to her. She was yet unmarried. I began wondering what was happening to me.

"Nothing doing. How can I return from my *sanyasi* life? Ha, you can join me and be initiated into *sanyasa* instead, and stay with me as a disciple. Or if you become a *sanyaasin*, I can also arrange for your stay at an ashram for women in Haridwar," I replied.

But she felt otherwise.

"I do not believe in your gods who have given me such suffering my whole life. After my father's death, I underwent a lot to bring up my sisters and get them married. None of your gods extended their help to me. Never talk to me about your absurd *Vedanta*," she said.

Of course, I was able to understand her mindset. But I too could not go back to her to lead a householder's life. I had travelled too far to reach where I was now.

"Let go then. If you cannot come and stay with me as a *sanyaasin*, better forget it. But don't ever call me back," I told her.

She never did call me again. I had learned about her sacrifices in life, on how she had worked as a teacher to bring up her three sisters, and settled them in life. She had forgotten to live for herself. She had lived only for others.

All this had come to pass because of the way parents try to influence the children's future. Never do the parents give a thought to what will happen to the children's tender and impressionable minds, when they sow such seeds with their own expectations and plans for the future.

I am able to forgive my parents who unwittingly created this chaos in the life of two youngsters. But I am unable to forget the impact on her life. Sometimes it wrenches my heart when I recall her pain. They acted, and we are suffering.

Glossary

Aachamana—A purifying ritual done to the throat by the ceremonial sipping of water and touching the various parts of the body.

Aacharana—religious conduct

Aadi thaalam—One of the most popular rhythms in Carnatic music.

Aahuti—Sacrifice offered to the ritual fire or homa.

Aanandashru—Tears of joy

Aasha rahita—desirelessness

Aashirvadam—Blessings

Aatmagaatham—Talking to oneself

Adi Shankaracharya or Adi Shankara—Hindu philosopher of mid to late 8th century CE, widely accepted as incarnation of Lord Shiva. Author of over several hundred texts that are the foundation of Advaita Vedanta school of Hinduism. He cleansed the Vedic religious practices of ritualistic excesses, and ushered in the core teaching of Vedanta, which is Advaita or non-dualism. Also known as Bhagavadpada Shankaracharya.

Adivasi—Ethnic and tribal groups

Akasha Vritti—a life without asking anything from anybody for day-to-day needs, and only accepting the minimum

Aksharabyasam—A ritual making a baby start writing, done at a temple using rice to write with the baby's fingers. Usually done at the first birthday.

Alphy—A long shirt like dress made of country cotton fabric

Amalaki—The fruit gooseberry

Amavasya—New moon

Amma—mother

Ananda—extreme happiness, one of the highest states of being

Anna(s)—Obsolete currency where 16 annas equals one rupee

Annadanam—an offering of food

Annakshetras—almonries

Antyaja—of inferior class/tribe

Aparigraha—concept of non-possessiveness

Apavitrata—Impurity

Apmaan—Insult

Arathi/Aarathi—worship ritual in which light, usually an oil lamp is offered to the deity, to the accompaniment of chants

Archana—Personal puja or prayers offered by a temple priest to the deity, on behalf of a devotee, to invoke blessings and guidance

Ardha nareeshwara—Lord Shiva and his consort Shakti in unity in the form of half man and half woman.

Ardhanareeshwara—A composite androgynous form of Shiva and his consort Shakti

Artha—refer to Purushartha

Arunachal/Arunachala/Arunachal Hill—A holy hill at Thiruvannamalai in Tamil Nadu, revered as the Kailash of South India

Asan/Asana—seat (used as a seat or bed in a cave)

Ashadha masam—fourth month according to Hindu calendar, between June-July, when the south-west monsoon hits India

Ashrama—stage of life

Ashtami—eighth day following the nine nights of Navaratri

Ashtavakra Geeta/Gita—Song of Ashtavakra is a classical Vedanta scripture and is written as a dialogue between sage Ashtavakra and King Janaka, which is a treatise about Self. Astavakra is a sage mentioned in the Hindu scriptures is described as born with eight deformities of the body. Astavakra literally means"one having eight bends"

Atma—soul or the higher self.

Atma Gyana—Knowledge of the Self

Avadhoota—A mystic saint and a liberated ascetic who has gone beyond egoic-consciousness, duality and common worldly concerns and acts, and is often without standard social etiquette.

Avatar—a manifestation of a deity or released soul in bodily form on earth; an incarnate divine teacher

Avinashi—indestructible, immortal

Ayurveda, Ayurvedic—system of medicine with historical roots to India.

Baala—child

Baba—An ascetic/saint is addressed as Baba/Father

Badha—obstacle

Bala mantra—Chant or mantra of Balatripurasundari a form of Srividya

Balavat—Behavior as innocent as a child

Beedi/Bidi—Indian hand-rolled cigarette

Beejam—Seed, or foundation

Bhagavat Gita—Literally, "song of the Spirit", it is the most famous of Hindu scriptures in Sanskrit, and is in the form of counseling by Lord Krishna to Arjuna. It is a section of the epic Mahabharata.

Bhagawatam—Religious text

Bhagvan Nityananda—A highly revered Siddha Guru who has an ashram in Ganeshpuri, Maharashtra.

Bhagvaan/Bhagawan—Literally God, Sometimes one's Guru is referred to as Bhagvan

Bhajan—songs with religious theme

Bhakti kavi—A poet who writes poetry of devotion

Bhakti yoga—The yogic path of devotion to deity that leads to union with the Divine

Bhalu—White Himalayan bear

Bhandara—Food prepared on large scale, as a religious offering to the gods and eaten in a community setting

Bharat—Ancient name of India

Bhava—feelings

Bhikharin—Beggar woman

Bhiksha—Alms

Bhikshu—Monk, usually Buddhist

Bhrashta—immoral conduct, fallen into depravity

Bindu—Sanskrit word for point or dot.

Brahma hatya—the act of killing a Brahmin

Brahma Shakti—The force of creation

Brahma sutra—Foundational texts in Sanskrit, of the Vedanta school of Hindu philosophy

Brahma tatva—Supreme Truth

Brahmachari—celibate on spiritual path. A brahmachari is a student of the Vedas, committed to celibacy and leading a virtuous and simple life of meditation and training for spiritual living.

Brahmagyaani—Knower of the supreme truth

Brahmana—Refer to Varna

Brahmanatwa—State of orthodox Brahminhood

Brahmin—Commonly understood as a person belonging to the Hindu priestly class, but can also be viewed as one who has realized the Brahman or Self

Chaadar—Blanket

Chaar dham—Literally four abodes/seats, the names of four pilgrimage sites in the Himalayas—Badrinath, Kedarnath, Yamunotri & Gangotri—that are widely revered by Hindus

Chaitanya—consciousness

Chakras—The Sanskrit word Chakra literally translates to wheel or disk. In yoga and Ayurveda, this refers to the wheels of energy that exists throughout the body. The wheels of energy in a body corresponds to the nerve centers.

Chandan—Sandalwood paste

Chandi Paath—Religious text describing the victory of the Goddess Durga over the demon Mahishasura. It comprises 700 verses spread over 13 chapters. A ritualistic reading is often done during Navaratri celebrations and during Chandi Homam. Considered a powerful reservoir of mantras.

Chaturmas deeksha—Deeksha given during Chaturmasya

Chaturmasya—holy period of four months (July to October)

Chaturvarna—Varna' is a Sanskrit word which means type, order, color or class. 'Chatur' means four. The society was classified in principle into four varnas: Brahmins as priests, scholars and teachers; Kshatriyas as rulers, warriors and administrators; Vaishyas as cattle herders, agriculturists, artisans and merchants; Shudras as laborers and service providers.

Chettiar—merchant caste

Chiti yantra—Yantra is a mystical diagram and Chiti yantra refers to Nadanandaji's research and treatise on Sri Vidya

Crorepati—millionaire

Dabba—container

Dakshina—Donation or payment for the services of a priest, spiritual guide or teacher, and ideally an offering of gratitude without expectation of personal gain

Dal—Lentil (a warm gravy food made out of cooked lentils)

Dal Baati churma—A speciality food item from Rajasthan which contains semi-sweet churma, lentils and fried poori.

Dal vada—fried lentil fritters

Dand—Long staff carried by some but not all sanyasis, depending on sampradaya

Darshan—Sighting of the idol of the deity

Dasaamsa japa—Japa or chanting in divisions of ten

Dasamsh havan—Recitation of mantras, after completion of the main japa, for a number of times equal to one-tenth of total number of japa mantra recitations

Dashami—tenth day following the nine nights of Navaratri

Datta Bhagwan—referring to Lord Dattatreya, considered to be an avatar (incarnation) of the three Hindu gods Brahma, Vishnu, and Shiva, and as the exemplary type of the avadhoota. He can also be considered to be combining three figures in a paradigmatic way: the ascetic, the guru, and the avatara. He is often depicted with three heads and accompanied by a cow representing mother earth and four dogs representing the four Vedas.

Deepam—lamp

Deepavali—Major religious festival, falling in October-November, and the day of closing of the Badrinath temples for winter

Devi Bhagavatham—Durga Saptasati or Chandi Paath/Devi Mahatmyam—religious text describing the Goddess as the supreme power and creator of the universe. It is also known as 'Chandi Paath'.

Devi Pranav Deeksha—Spiritual initiation with the mantra of the Goddess

Devi pranava—The seed mantra/chant to invoke Devi
Devi stotra—Recitation to the supreme Mother
Dhaba—Roadside eatery
Dharma—Duty
Dharma—refer to Purushartha
Dharmashala—Rest house for pilgrims
Dharna—a peaceful demonstration
Dhavani—Upper garment, as worn in South India
Dhooni/Dhuni—Sacred fire, often kept lit perpetually. Symbolizes the purifying inner fire of Divine Love
Dhyan/a—Meditation
Diksha or Deeksha—Spiritual initiation
Dourbhagyavaan—misfortune
Druta taalam—two count beat in a rhythm of music/musical instrument
Durga—Principal form of the Mother Goddess, in her warrior manifestation
Dvaita bhava—seeing others as different from oneself, duality in beliefs
Ekadasi—Eleventh day of waxing or waning moon phase
Ekakshari—Chant/mantra of one syllable
Fasali—Harvest
Gaali—scolding
Gaddi—Cushion
Gajagamini—gait of an elephant
Ganeshpuri—City in Maharashtra, India—Ashram of Bhagwan Nityananda
Ganga jal—Water of River Ganga

Ganga, Ganges, Ganga Mata—The second largest riven in the Indian sub-continent, the river is revered and considered the heart of Hindu religion, tradition and living.

Ganja—Cannabis

Gayatri—Sanskrit word for a song or hymn having a vedic meter of three lines. Also a highly revered mantra from the Rig Veda.

Gayatri Saadhana—Spiritual practice of chanting Gayatri mantra

Geetam—melodious song

Ghat—river bank or piece of land for a particular purpose; ground

Giri Pradakshina—Circumambulation of the Arunachala Hill

Giri Pradakshina Veedhi—The path for the pradakshina or circumbulation

Gita or **Bhagavat Gita**—Hindu scripture in Sanskrit world renowned for its philosophical significance

Godavari—the second longest river in India, starts in Maharashtra and flows eastwards emptying into the Bay of Bengal. It is called the Ganges of the South.

Gompa—Tibetan monastery—a set of small Tibetan temple buildings and other places of worship or religious learning

Gopika—cow herdess, also friend or lover of Lord Krishna

Gopuram—A pyramidical tower, usually ornate, at the entrance of any temple, especially in southern India.

Goshala—Cowshed

Gotti or Goli—marbles used for play (like checker game) mostly on the roadside

Gulbakkavali—an ayurvedic plant; ginger lily

Guna—Merit, also means quality or attribute

Gunny sack—Burlap

Guru Gita—Song of the Guru

Guru mandal/mandala—The fraternity of sages, rishis and gurus who had themselves acquired a very high position in the hierarchy of spiritual evolution. All these sages were an 'Awakened' lot and formed a spiritual league to help humanity enjoy the divine bliss which they had themselves experienced.

Guru Mantra Deeksha—Initiation by the Guru who imparts a secret sacred chant of the Gurus.

Guru Parampara—The spiritual tradition or lineage of Gurus or Spiritual Masters

Guru Poornima—Guru Poornima is an Indian festival dedicated to spiritual masters and is celebrated on a full moon day in the month of Ashada according to the Vedic calendar, sometime during July-August

Guru shishya sambandha—The relationship between the master and disciple

Gurubehan/behen—Fellow female student of the same spiritual master/lineage, considered as a sister

Gurubhai—Fellow male students of the same Guru, and so considered as brothers

Guruji—Spiritual Master—'ji' is added as a mark of respect

Gurusthan—literally, place of the Guru

Gurutatva—The principle that the guru is the element that causes spiritual awakening within oneself, through a transmission process beyond the reach of the human intellect. The Guru is to be acknowledged as not a physical being but God Himself manifesting in a personal form to guide the aspirant

Guruvayur—A famous and religious temple of Lord Krishna in Kerala, South India

Gyana marga—the path to spiritual knowledge

Gyana Shakti—the creative power of spiritual knowledge; the power to know

Gyanagni dagdha karmanam—burnt by the fire of knowledge/wisdom (chapter 4.19 of Bhagavad Gita)

Gyanganj—Legendary city-kingdom of mysterious immortal beings, from ancient Indian and Tibetan mythology. It is said to be inhabited by yogis and saints of high order, and is also a place of spiritual training. Situated in a valley somewhere deep in the Himalayas, and though hidden from the world, still influencing it in various subtle ways when necessary. It is said that Gyanganj is cunningly camouflaged or may even be existing in a completely different plane of reality.

Halwa—a sweet dish

Hamsa—literally swan, but also a mythical bird with knowledge and represents the individual soul or spirit.

Hamsa gaanam/Hamsa ganam—celestial song by the swan

Havan/Homam—Religious ceremony performed in temples and in homes that involves worship through the use of a sacred fire, and with recitations of mantras

Havan/Homa kunda—Fire altar into which the homa offerings are made

Hindi—India being a large country where several languages are spoken, Hindi is the national language and is spoken widely in the Northern part of India. However, Nadanandaji grew up in Kerala which is a state in South India where Hindi is not widely spoken.

Hindu—Religion followed by many in India

Hindustan—India

Homa agni—The fire blazing in the homa pit

Homa kunda—Fire altar into which the homa offerings are made

Hreem—the seed mantra for Sri Vidya

Iccha—Desire

Iccha Shakti—the force or spiritual energy of desire

Ishta Devi/Devata—Literally 'cherished divinity' taken from the words iṣhṭa which means desired, liked, cherished or preferred and devi or devatā while godhead, divinity, tutelary deity is a term denoting a worshipper's favorite deity within Hinduism

Iswara—God in the male form

Jagat—whole world

Jal pathra—Kamandal—Water vessel carried by sadhu

Jal Samadhi—Internment in water—Dead bodies of saints are interned in flowing water

Janma—birth

Japa—Chanting of sacred mantras

Japa chakra—Prayer wheel

Japa mala—A string of prayer beads

Japa Purascharan—A vow to repeat a mantra a fixed number of times, usually a very large number, with complete concentration and rigid discipline, with the aim of spiritual progress

Japa Samarpan—Offering of chants

Japa sankalp—Vow to recite mantra a prescribed number of times

Jaunsarbavar—A hilly region near Mussoorie in Dehradun, India

Jeeva—Living being (literally, that which has life)

Jhadi—Forest

Kaali—Black one, or Goddess of Time, the destroyer of evil forces

Kaccha—Unpaved, not properly constructed

Kafni—A knee-length, loose robe-like garment

Kailash—Mountain peak in Tibet, legendary home of Lord Shiva and Parvati

Kala Kambaliwala/ Baba Kali Kamli Dharamshala—A resthouse for wandering monks/saints in Rishikesh, North India

Kaliyuga—Age of the Kali or demon or age of vice, is the last of the four stages the world as described in ancient Sanskrit texts

Kama—desire

Kama—refer to Purushartha

Kamandal—Oblong water pot used by ascetics or yogis to store and carry water

Kambal—Blanket

Kanya Pooja—worship of young girls representing Mother Goddess

Kappa—Tapioca

Kappar/Khappar—Vessel for receiving alms carried by a sadhu

Karma bhoomi—Land where the prevailing culture aids and supports a spiritual seeker in neutralizing his karmas through ritual and penance

Karma phala—Fruits of karma/destiny

Karma Yoga—Yoga of selfless action or service, whereby detaching oneself from the fruits of actions and offering them up to God, one learns to sublimate the ego

Karthik poornima—Hindu festival celebrated on the full moon day in the month of Karthika per Vedic calendar (November-December)

Karuna—Compassion

Karyalaya—Office

Kasba—Walled Township

Kashaya—Saffron, orange coloured robe

Kashaya dhvaja—Saffron flag

Kashayam/Kashaya vastra—Saffron-colored clothing typically worn by sanyasis

Kashi—Another name for the holy city of Varanasi

Keerthan/Keerthanai—Bhajan singing by an individual

Khajoor—dry fruit Dates

Kheer—Pudding made with milk, sugar and broken grain

Kichadi/khichadi—Rice and lentil gruel

Kothari—Owners/caretakers of large granaries/storehouses

Koupina—loin cloth

Krama deeksha—Step by step initiation process, moving into higher sadhanas

Krishna—Eighth incarnation/avatar of Lord Vishnu

Kriya—spiritual practice

Kriya of Shat Chakra bhedan—The activation of the six chakras

Krupa/Kripa—Grace

Kshama—Forgiveness

Kshamta—Capability or competence

Kshatriya—Refer to Varna

Kumkum—Vermillion, red powder worn as marking on forehead, made by combining turmeric with lime. It is offered to the goddess in puja/worship

Kutia—A hut, dwelling place

Lalitha Sahasranamam—Sacred and powerful hymn of thousand names of the Mother Goddess Lalitha

Lalitha Tripurasundari—Highest manifestation of Goddess Adi Shakti and the primary goddess associated with the Shiva–Shakti tradition.

Lalitha Trishathi—Most secret and sacred of the chanting of Mother Goddess Lalitha. This stotra recounts the 300 names of the goddess.

Lamas—An honorific title applied to a spiritual leader in Tibetan Buddhism

Laxmi Narayan—Lakshmi and Vishnu

Laxmi/Lakshmi—Goddess of wealth, consort of Vishnu

Leela—Divine play, or all reality, including the cosmos, as the outcome of creative play by the divine absolute

Lord Rama—Incarnation/avatar of Lord Vishnu and hero-king of the famous epic Ramayana

Maa—Mother

Maalik—Master

Maayee/Mayee—Mother

Maha Tapa—The Head of Gyanganj, Mahavatar Babaji

MahaKali—Goddess of time and death

MahaLakshmi—Goddess of abundance and prosperity

Maharaj—Sadhus in North India are respectfully addressed by this title

Maharaja—King

Maharashtra—State in the western part of India

Maharshi—A geat saint

MahaSaraswathi—Goddess of the arts, knowledge, and wisdom

Mahatma—Literally great soul, or person of advanced spiritual stature

Mahavatar Babaji or Babaji—Indian saint and yogi, believed to have revived the ancient science of Kriya Yoga, Head of Gyanganj

Makara Sankranti—A Hindu harvest festival that marks the transition of the sun into the zodiacal sign of Makara (Capricorn) on its celestial path. The day is also believed to mark the arrival of spring in India.

Mala—necklace

Malayalam—Language spoken in south India, predominantly in the state of Kerala

Mama—Mother's brother; uncle

Manasarovar—Freshwater lake in Tibet near Mt.Kailash, bathing in and drinking its water is believed by Hindus to cleanse all sins.

Manasik pranams—Paying obeisance mentally

Manava—Human being

Mandali—Group of sanyasis

Mandir—Temple

Mantra—A sacred utterance, sound, syllable, word or phonemes, or group of words in Sanskrit believed to have psychological and spiritual powers. The sounds may, or may not have literal meaning.

Mantra deeksha—Initiation with a mantra or syllable

Mantra Shakti—the divine energy or force of mantra

Masala—A powdered blend of spices

Mathadipathi—Head of a Mutt or Ashram

Mattadhipati—Head of the mutt or ashram

Mauna/ Maun Vrata/ Mouna—Vow of silence

Maya—Name, fame, wealth—created by the obscuring power that conceals the true character of spiritual reality. The manifested world of creation is constantly changing and thus considered unreal.

Mohi—A devotee of Avadhoota Nadananda

Moksha—refer to Purushartha

Moksha—Salvation or freedom from rebirth

Mookambika—The Kollur Mookambika Temple located at Kollur, Udupi district in the state of Karnataka, India, is a Hindu temple dedicated to Mookambika Devi.

Mookambika, Chottanikara Bhagavati, Kodungalur Bhagavati, Vaishno Devi, or Nayana Devi—Different names of Goddess Parvati or Shakti

Moorthy—Idol of God

Moorti sthapana— Installation of the idol with rites and rituals

Mritunjaya mantra—The Maha mrityunjaya mantra is a powerful hymn in the ancient Veda which has the power to conquer death.

Mudra—Symbolic hand gestures used in Hindu and Buddhist ceremonies, movement or pose in yoga

Muhurtam—auspicious time

Mukhiya—Village chief

Murukku—a snack

Muthessi—Grandmother

Mutt—Ashram

Naadam/ Nada—energy of music

Naga sadhu—Shaivite saints, who live in the Himalayas and occasionally come down to the plains

Naishtik brahmachari—a staunch celibate, not caught in the sway of desire

Naivedyam—Food offered to a Hindu deity/guru as part of a worship ritual, before eating it

Namaskar—A traditional Indian greeting or gesture of respect, made by bringing the palms together before the face or chest and bowing

Nambudiri/Namboothiri—The Malayalam speaking Brahmins of Kerala

Narmada—A River that flows through Central/Western India

Navami—Ninth day of the fortnight in the Hindu Lunar Calendar

Navaratna—Nine gems

Navaratri—Literally 'nine nights' in Sanskrit, *nava* meaning nine and *ratri* meaning nights. The Goddess Shakti is worshipped in her different manifestations for nine nights and ten days. This is a major Indian festival occurring in autumn (September-October) and spring (March-April)

Navavaran Pooja—The highest Pooja ritual of the Goddess, aimed at removing the nine concealments or obstructions to self-realization that are within one's mind and ego

Nirakara—Formless

Nishkaam karma—Selfless action without expectation or agenda, non-attached action without obligation

Nishkalankata—Quality of purity and innocence, and being selfless

Nitya karma—Daily ablutions

Niyati—Rule of destiny

Niyogam—Plan or destined arrangement

Omkar/Omkara—the primodial sound "Om"

Omkareshwar—Hindu temple dedicated to Lord Shiva, situated on an island called Mandhata or Shivapuri in the Narmada River

Oottupura—Temple dining hall

Paan—A preparation combining betel leaf with areca nut and sometimes also tobacco. It is chewed for stimulant and psychoactive effects.

Paarayana—Chanting in groups

Pachadi—food item, like a dip made of vegetable, yogurt etc.

Pada—As in padyatra, pilgrimage on foot

Paisa—One hundred paisa equals one rupee

Pallipatty—a snack

Panchabootha—five elements of nature

Pancha maha yagna—a daily ritual to be followed by Hindus. Offering food to five deities—God close to heart, God of the family, the animal, reptile family, ancestors and Guru.

Panchadasi—Devi mantra of fifteen letters

Panchajanyam—Periodical, popular in Kerala, South India

Panchakarma—Ayurvedic medical treatment using oils and herbs

Panchama raga—one of the tunes in the Indian classical music

Panchami—Fifth day of the moon

Panchang—A Hindu calendar and almanac which follows traditional units of Hindu timekeeping, and presents important dates and their calculations in a tabulated form.

Panchayat—Village governing body, assembly of village elders

Panditji—Priest

Papa—sin

Papad—Fried lentil wafers

Para Loka—World beyond death

Para Vidya—Higher or spiritual knowledge of the inner world, as opposed to knowledge of the material world

Param guru/ Paramaguru/Parmeshti Guru—Guruji's Guruji (Master's Master—Grand Master)

Parama virakt—Person with absolute indifference to worldly pleasures. Renouncer of all material things.

Paramahamsa—literally means supreme swan; symbolizes spiritual discrimination and refers to one who has attained realization of the true Self

Paramanu—Atom

Paramatma—The Supreme Divine Soul

Parampara—A succession of teachers and disciples in traditional Vedic culture; guru–sishya tradition.

Parasu—Axe

Paratpara Guru—Guruji's Guruji's Guruji (Great Grand Master)

Parigraha/m—intention to accumulate material possessions for future use

Parikrama—Circumambulation

Parivrajaka—Wandering monk

Parnasala—Hut made of leaves

Parvat—Mountain

Pathankot—City in the Indian State of Punjab

Pathra—Vessel, utensil

Pathrata—Eligibility

Payasam—Pudding sweetened with sugar or jaggery, and made with dairy or coconut milk and broken grain

Peepal—Ficus religiosa or sacred fig tree

Peetham—University or academic institution

Pishachavat—Sudden fits of anger etc. Literally means like a ghost. A realized one who is a loner and exhibits strange behavior and hence feared by people because they do not understand such a one

Pitthu—Large backpacks

Pongal—Dish of rice, moong lentils cooked together with spices and clarified butter

Pooja pathra—Utensils used for worship in the Temple

Pooja samagri—Materials used for worship

Poojari—Priest

Poojya—Respected, honorable

Poori—Deep fried wheat bread

Poornabhisekam—ritual conducted by pouring liquid (water, milk etc.) on the idol of the God or the body of the person to whom it is performed.

Poornima—Full moon

Poorva janma karma phalam—The result of the deeds of one's previous birth

Poorvashram—Previous stage of life, before Sanyasa/renunciation

Pottli—Small cloth bag

Pradakshina—A ritual of circumambulation around the inner sanctum in a temple

Prakruthi—Nature

Pralaya—dissolution

Pralobhan—Temptation

Prana Shakti—Prana (vital energy), Shakti (Awareness), in this context, the awareness of the vital energy

Pranaam—Greeting with respect; Namaskaar

Pranava—'Om' mantra considered the symbol or representation of the individual soul which sanyasis must always chant

Pranayama—Science and practice of control of breath as part of yoga

Pranta Karyavah—Official of civil organization

Prasadam—Food that is a religious offering, consumed after worship or religious ceremony

Pratibhijna—recognition

Prayaschita puja—a worship for atonement of sin committed

Prayoga vidhi—Method of usage

Presh mantra—Standing in water, this mantra is chanted as a vow of renunciation of the world, worldly relations and material wealth.

Preta yoni/atma—Ghost state after death

Pujari/Purohit—Priest who performs puja

Punya karma—Meritorious deeds

Purascharan—A vow to repeat a mantra a fixed number of times, usually a very large number, with complete concentration and rigid discipline, with the aim of spiritual progress

Purushartha—It is a key concept in Hinduism, and refers to four goals of a human life—Dharma (righteousnous), Artha (prosperity), Kama (pleasure), Moksha (liberation).

Puttu—food item, steam rice and coconut made in a tubular special vessel

Radha bhava—In the mood, emotion or devotional state of mind of Radha the beloved of Krishna

Ragam—The six basic musical modes which express different moods in certain characteristic progressions, with more emphasis placed on some notes than others, *of Indian classical music. A scientific, precise, and aesthetic melodic form with its own distinct ascending and descending movement, consisting of combinations of notes of the octave. One raga is demarcated from another in the way the notes are combined. The music created by a raga is known to color the mind in a particular way, creating distinct moods or feelings.*

Rahasya—Sacred Secret

Ramana Maharishi—A renowned and revered Indian sage who lived in the Arunachala hills of Thiruvannamalai, Tamil Nadu

Rishi—A seer who realizes eternal knowledge beyond the mundane world and gives expression to those truths in the form of hymns, many such hymns are found in the scriptures, the Vedas.

Rishi runa—Runa means debt. When highly evolved souls have a debt to the Creator, they come down to earth and lead a life of a human being to satisfy the debt owed.

Rishikesh—Ancient pilgrim city, Dehradun, Uttarakhand, North India.

Roti—Unleavened wheat flatbread

Rudri—Rudram or Rudri is an important text in praise of Lord Shiva.

Runa—Debt

Saadhaka/Sadhak—An accomplished spiritual practitioner

Saadhana—Daily spiritual practice

Saakshatkaram—self realization

Saatvic—Pious, virtuous.

Sabji—Cooked vegetable dish

Sadguru—An honorific title given to an enlightened Master

Sadhu—Hindu monk; an ascetic, holy man

Sadhvi—Female ascetic

Sahaja—spontaneous

Sahasrara—Crown chakra is generally considered the seventh primary chakra, according to most tantric yoga traditions and is the one which integrates all the chakras with their respective qualities. It is the last milestone of the evolution of human awareness.

Sailani—Wanderer

Sakamata—The desire to gain something materialistic

Sakshatkara—Realization

Sakshi—witness

Saligram—spiraled ammonite stone, worshipped as iconic symbol of Vishnu

Samadhi—Stage of union with the Divine, the highest bliss

Samadhi mandir—When an enlightened being leaves his mortal body, a temple is built over when the mortal remains are buried.

Samaj seva—Community service

Samatva bhavana—Viewing all beings impartially, without attachment or bindings

Sambar—a lentil-based vegetable stew made with tamarind and spices

Samhar—Annihilation and reabsorption

Sampraday bheda—Differential treatment pertaining to spiritual tradition

Sampradaya name—Traditional religious title

Samsara—Terrestrial

Samsaric—worldly; endless cycle of life and birth

Samskara—purificatory ceremony; imprints or past life impressions

Samyak nyasa—To renounce worldly and material aspects of living and lead a life of intellectual contemplation

Sandhya Aarati—(Refer to Aarati) Aarati performed during evening time

Sankalpa Siddhi—The power to fulfill desires or wishes effortlessly

Sankalpam—Solemn vow or determination

Sansaris—Worldly people

Sanskara—rite

Sanskrit—Primary sacred language of Hinduism

Sanyasa—State of renunciation, asceticism

Sanyasi—Renunciate

Saptaha—Seven days, usually period chosen to perform a chanting/reading of spiritual text.

Sari/Saree—A female garment traditionally worn in India

Sarva Sanga Parityaga Sanyasi—One in complete freedom from all attachments, unruffled and immune to all temptations, because of seeing the Self in all

Sashtanga namaskara—A form of salutation where the eight limbs of the body, namely, two hands, two legs, two arms, chest and forehead, touch the ground. It symbolizes the nullification of one's ego before Guru or God.

Sat-chit-ananda—Truth, consciousness, bliss

Satram—A resting place for pilgrims where rooms and food are provided by a charitable institution for nominal rates or for free

Satsang—A gathering of people for spiritual discourse

Sauparnika—River flowing near the Mookambika Temple, Kollur

Seva—Service

Shaakteya—A sub-sect of Hinduism in which the followers worship Mother Goddess in Her various avatars and incarnations.

Shakha—Branch

Shakta—Worshipper of Shakti

Shakthi upaasana—Worship of Shakti

Shakti—The female principle of divine energy, especially when personified as the supreme deity.

Shakti saadhana—The spiritual practice of worship of Shakti, Mother Goddess

Shaktipat—Spiritual/Divine Energy transfer from Guru to disciple

Shanthi—peace

Shastras—Scripture

Shavasana—Supine corpse pose in Hatha Yoga

Shiva Mahimna stotra—A Sanskrit composition in devotion of Lord Shiva

Shivalingam / lingam—Abstract or an iconic representation of Lord Shiva

Shodasi mantra/vidya—Knowledge of the sixteen-lettered mantra of the Goddess, recitation of which leads to liberation. This is considered secretive in nature, and only to be imparted by a Guru on initiation.

Shuddhi—Purity; righteousness

Shudra—Refer to Varna

Siddha—masters who have acquired siddhis and achieved some degree of spiritual perfection or enlightenment.

Siddha bhoomi/sthaana—Land or place of the adepts; spiritual energy vortex

Siddha Parampara—Traditional lineage of adepts, and ascetics who have achieved enlightenment

Sishya—disciple

Smashaan Ghat—Cremation ground

Soham Dhyan—Meditation on the Soham mantra, a central mantra practice of Yoga Meditation.

Soundarya Lahiri—Hymns of the Mother Goddess written by Adi Shankaracharya

Sparsan—Touch

Sramadan—Donation of time and effort, excluding money, for a good cause

Sravana Samadhi—Listening bliss (going into a blissful state while listening to a spiritual discourse)

Sri Chakra—a sacred geometrical construction of nine levels representing the Cosmos within which the Mother Goddess is considered to manifest herself along with Her parivara (family) yoginis. The Shiva and Shakti aspects of Consciousness and Awareness reside on the peak at the Navama (ninth) Avarana (level) called Bindu. Visualization and internal contemplation of the manifestation of this Sri Chakra within the physical body in a subtle form is the secret of Sri Vidya.

Sri Raja Rajeswari—Presiding deity of Sri Chakra, the Divine Mother

Sri Vidya Sadhana—Sri Vidya is an ancient and influential school of Goddess-centered Shakta Tantrism. The goddess is worshipped in three manifestations, as the beneficent deity Lalita Tripurasundari/ Raja Rajeswari, through her mantra and through her yantra known as Sri Chakra.

Srishti—Creation, emanation, projection

Srividya—Tantric or Shakta theology where the Goddess is worshipped as the Supreme, transcending the cosmos that is her manifestation.

Stithi—Continuation and maintenance

Stotras—Sacred hymns

Suvasini Pooja—Worship the Mother Goddess in the form of a married woman

Swabhava—Nature or habit

Swami—An ascetic/saint is addressed as Swami

Swami Vivekananda—Hindu monk and direct disciple of Ramakrishna Paramahamsa and a major force in the modern revival of Hinduism. Founder of the Ramakrishna Mission

Swamy Ayyappa—A Hindu deity worshipped as Manikandan or Sasta. The famous temple of Swamy Ayyappa is located in Sabarimala in Kerala

Swapna—Dream

Swarna bhasma—an ayurvedic compound prepared by using pure gold

Tamasic—negative

Tamil—Language of Indian state of Tamil Nadu

Tandava—cosmic dance of Shiva

Tantra/Tantric/Tantrik—An ancient Indian tradition of beliefs and ritual practices that seeks to channel the divine energy of macrocosm of God into the human microcosm.

Tapa Shakti—The spiritual power obtained by the practice of meditation

Tapas/Tapasya—Connotes certain spiritual practices in India related to asceticism, including meditation, austerities, body mortification and penance. **Tapasvi** n.

Tapovan—Forest of austerities or spiritual practice. In this context, the area above Gangotri

Tara Mayee—The Guru of Avadhoota Nadananda

Tara Peeth—A famous tantric temple in West Bengal for worship of Maa Tara

Tarpan/a—Offering/ritualistic worship made to departed entities (ancestors)

Teertha—religious pilgrimage

Teertham—Holy water associated with a temple or deity, or from a reservoir/river near such sacred sites; also a pilgrimage as in Teerth yatra

Tehsil—An administrative division of a city or town

Thaalam—A traditional rhythmic pattern in classical Indian music, usually expressed with percussion instruments

Thulasi jalam—water of the holy basil Thulasi

Tilak—marking on forehead, usually with a fragrant paste, such as of sandalwood or kumkum

Tirumaduram—a sweet dish offered to the deity and then eaten as blessed food

Tiruvannamalai—Please refer to Arunachala

Travancore—Present day Trivandrum, used to be a kingdom until 1949.

Trayodashi—Thirteenth day of waxing or waning moon phase

Tryakshari mantra—Mantra of three letters

Tyaaga—Sacrifice

Ugadi—Telugu New Yeas Day celebrated in Andhra Pradesh

Upaasya—worthy of worship

Upadesha—Instruction, spiritual guidance

Upanishads—Collection of texts containing central philosophical concepts of Hinduism, concerning the nature of ultimate reality and describing the path to human salvation

Upavas—Timed fasting as part of religious observance

Utsavam—annual religious festival

Uttarkashi—Hindu pilgrim town in the state of Uttarakand, Northern India

Vaastu sastra—Science of Architecture describing principles for design, layout, space arrangements etc.

Vaidika pandit—Vedic Priest

Vaidya—treatment

Vairagya—Dispassion or detachment

Vaishnav—Worshipper of Vishnu

Vaishya—Person from business/merchant community

Vaishya—Refer to Varna

Varanasi—Also known as Kashi or Benaras is a city on the banks of the Ganges in Uttar Pradesh, North India. An ancient city and the spiritual capital of India, it draws millions of pilgrims throughout the year

Varna—Bhagavad-Gita Chap 4.13—states that there are four orders of classes namely Brahmana (Priestly), Kshatriya (Warrior), Vaishya (Merchant) and Shudra (service provider) were created by the Creator/Creation (maya) according to the quality of the individual (guna) and work to be carried out in the society (karma).

Vastram—Clothing

Veda/s—philosophy based on the doctrine of the Upanishads, especially in its monistic form. **Vedanti** n.

Vedi—Altar
Vibhageeya Chinta—Considering oneself different from others
Vibhuthi/Vibhoothi—sacred ash
Vidya—knowledge
Vihara—Buddhist monastery
Vijaya Dashami—see Dashami
Virakta—tuned away from attachment, detached
Virakti—detachment
Viveka—ability to discriminate; true wisdom
Vrata—Religious vow
Vrithy—Physical cleanliness; virtue
Vyaavaaara—removal of doubts
Yagya/Yaaga—elaborate ceremony around a fire, with oblations offered as worship to the accompaniment of sacred chants/ mantras
Yaksha—A broad class of nature-spirits. Feminine form is Yakshini.
Yama—A Hindu unit of time; one-fourth of a day + night is a yama
Yantra—mystical diagram, especially from the tantric traditions
Yatra—procession
Yatri—Traveler
Yoga bhrashtatha—the break in a spiritual aspirant's practice leading to deflecting from higher purpose
Yogini Brahmani—A brahmin women yogi
Zamindari—The Zamindari system introduced by the British in India allowed land owners, Lorships or Barons to collect tax and have workers. This system was abolished in 1951 after India became independent.

Walking Tall in Stature

Gratitude to the Feet that move Hearts

The fire within, the fire without

Beings in Beingness

Guruji with Mohanji and Sulakhe Maharaj

Liberating Uniqueness

I see what you cannot

Guruji with Mila Mohan

Releasing the Guru Parampara picture

Personified Innocence

To know is to be

The Flow of Tradition

Walking in Shirdi streets with Mohanji

Transfering the Tradition

Walking Alone